Douchebag Wisdom
Dealing with Donald Trump

by
Lima Bravo

**To the
Douchebags in our lives
and all we learn from them**

To Cheryl~
Keep spreading the
love, light, and laughter.
And keep doing Yoga!
Simm Bravo !

**Warning: Graphic Language
#sorrymom**

I gratefully acknowledge all of the authors and journalists that I've quoted in this book. I've tried to represent your work accurately and within the context of how it was delivered. If proper credit was not given, I apologize and will make corrections if notified. Thank you for the work you've done. You made this book possible.

Thank you Bitmoji for helping me discover the essence of Lima Bravo by letting me create my own personal emoji. You helped me find my voice.

Thank you to Z.T.Droc for bringing this book to life.

Contact us at:
LB and Company
PO Box 2068
Monument, CO 80132

719 749-6101
limabravo@douchebagwisdom.com

DouchebagWisdom.com
@DouchebagWisdom (twitter)
facebook.com/Douchebagwisdom
@douchebag.wisdom (Instagram)
First EditionSBN

ISBN-13: 978-1979273589
ISBN-10: 1979273588

Table of Contents

* Holy Crap! Or Should I Say, Gee Whiz?!

Donald Trump has bullied and bought his way into the White House and I am appalled. It was clearly a hostile takeover of the Republican party *and* the nation, "hostile" being the operative word. His vile, vicious, divisive and demoralizing campaign strategy makes him the biggest Douchebag in the country. But to see Trump's ignorance on display now against the people of other nations? Shoving aside fellow leaders, attacking others while they deal with terrorism and natural disasters? That makes Trump the biggest Douchebag on the planet.

Trump doesn't pull punches so neither will I. I don't like Donald Trump. Just seeing him on tv with his smug mug and stilted gestures makes me ill. When he opens his mouth and speaks, my spirit goes into a full-body cringe. I want to shake him off like an animal shaking off stink. Mere mention of his name brings on stress-induced Tourettes: douche bag, dickhead, f----wad, ass-clown. Excuse me, pardon my language. See what I mean?! (Tourettes people, don't get all crazy. I'm not joking! Trump's name induces impulsive, uncontrollable outbursts including swearing. I hereby bequeath my brain to science to study this phenomenon.) I'm not the only one driven to foul language though. That's the Trump Effect.

I don't like him, but I never underestimated him, and I give him credit for "winning" the White House. But, just as he ragged on President Obama about a birth certificate, we'll rag on him about being legit. Trump did, after all, lose the popular vote by three million votes. But that alone doesn't make Trump a douche. Insisting there was rampant voter fraud *does*.

We all have friends that annoy us occasionally, but that doesn't make them Douchebags. There are distinctions when it comes to that derogatory phrase. "Douchebags" are arrogant, obnoxious, and despicable human beings for sure. They aren't just mildly annoying—they are majorly annoying. They get under your skin and make you feel *bad*!

We all know people like this, and in truth, they help make us better people. Haven't you learned a lesson or two from the Douchebags in your life? Well, Trump makes people feel and think—in extremes! That's the Trump Effect, which we'll be exploring in this book along with Trump Paradoxes, Trump Truths, and Trumpisms.

The Trump Effect

Love him or hate him, Donald Trump releases something carnal in each of us. I know perfectly respectable people who have turned into complete Douchebags when discussing this election and president--I am one of them!!

You read that right. At times I've turned into a complete Douchebag when discussing him. I'm still sorry for talking so hard at my Mom about Trump.

This President brings out the worst in me. I'm betting you, too. That's why you've bought this book--or someone has given it to you! I wonder how many friendships and relationships have been lost because of Donald Trump? Trump will be a historic president all right, but at what and who's expense?!

I predict Trump will be the president remembered for dividing and defining a nation. If you persecute and hate others, Trump is your leader. If you OPPOSE persecution and hatred toward others—Trump's still your leader. And it's our right to resist. But it is NOT our right to become physically violent or verbally abusive.

Trump-lovers, did your blood pressure shoot through the roof? How dare I infer that you persecute and hate others? Of course, not all Trump supporters persecute and hate others; you support a man who does. In my world, if you don't stand for the oppressed, *you* become the oppressor with your silent consent. The buzz word is complicit, thanks to *Saturday Night Live*.

Trump-haters, are you feeling some righteous indignation? Good! Me, too. I'm not just mildly annoyed, I am outrageously annoyed with Trump and his clown posse. If you're not, you need to read Matt Taibbi's book, *Insane Clown President.*

But this book is not *just* about Donald Trump.

This Book is about *Your Reaction* to Donald Trump!

Trump is the personification and amplification of everything both good and bad about America, and specifically "capitalism."

I don't begrudge Trump his money. So, what if his self-worth is tied to his bank account. He's a 70-year-old man who has yet to learn one of life's most basic lessons--money doesn't equate to happiness. And Trump's money hasn't bought

2

him happiness, class or respect. My problem, however, is **how** he has made his money. He demeans anything and anyone who questions him or gets in his way. He takes money from investors then stiffs his workers and contractors. He uses his immense fortune to hire lawyers to keep from paying what he rightfully owes.

Remember the Peter Principle? You rise to your level of incompetence. When you're good at your job you get promoted and moved into a position you aren't qualified to do. That's the Peter Principle. But, with the proper attitude and training, you can learn new skills and you can become good at the new job.

It doesn't bother me that Trump has no experience. I, too, see that as positive. But what Trump hasn't shown is a willingness to learn, grow, adapt and move beyond his mean-spirited personal attacks that insult and demean others. He has risen to a position he's unqualified for and his pride, ego and defensive posture are keeping him ignorant.

Donald Trump chooses to be this man, intentionally, without apology and with no remorse. He's a bully with a fat wallet and prides himself on it. "I'm really, really rich." Yes, Donald we all know that. Now, please, would you buy some manners? And a conscience and soul while you're at it?

A "Douchebag" is a matter of one's perspective. I'm not asking you to hang this label on Trump or anyone else. What I'm asking you to do is look in the mirror. Are *you* a walking, talking, living, breathing definition of your own truths? Do you know what and who you stand for?

Have you put yourself in the shoes of a Trump-lover? Are you listening for differences or are you listening for commonalities? Have you been respectful? Or have you at times, like me, become the Douchebag?

I'm not suggesting you keep quiet and let others puke their pro-Trump rhetoric on you. I'm suggesting it's up to us to have a respectful exchange of opinions without name-calling and bullying and/or violence. Because we're clearly in this together whether we like it or not.

The Trump Paradox

I can already hear the Trumpets/Trumpettes saying I'm the one being disrespectful!! Yes, I understand that and that is a Trump Paradox: how do I be respectful to someone who doesn't respect others? It's a pretzel that I twist myself into day-after-day as Trump attacks anyone who he thinks has slighted him.

Holy Crap!

That's just one of the Trump Paradoxes we'll look into. And to those I haven't been respectful to, I apologize. But I won't apologize to Donald Trump for calling him a Douchebag. His words and actions speak for themselves.

Please understand: I want to like Donald Trump. I've tried to like Donald Trump. Life would be so much easier and less stressful if I could support Donald Trump. But every time that man opens his mouth, he reminds me why I can't.

This is a book about gratitude, believe it or not, and yes even gratitude towards President Trump!

Thank you, Donald Trump, for:

- Showing me exactly who I do _not_ want to be.
- Revealing some of my own prejudices.
- Helping me find my voice.

This book is my journey from astonishment to empowerment--told with the help of Hollywood movie villains throughout the years. I've grown up around the Hollywood stars; not literally, I grew up in Iowa— before "Build it and they will come." But they were there, with me, Hollywood films and Hollywood stars, telling me stories. They were my get-away from rural life and a peak into another dimension.

I grew up with Star Trek and Star Wars; Godzilla, King Kong, and the Grinch; Batman, Back to the Future; A Christmas Story and A Christmas Carol; Young Frankenstein. I continue to use movies as my retreat from everyday madness into a different story in my head. I choose movies to help me through rough times and the storylines and characters carry me through. I take comfort in a familiar movie when I'm away from home. Movie characters, and ultimately, the actors who play them, are my friends.

It is with the deepest pride and joy I see Hollywood at the center of this #resistance. Trump can continue to threaten journalists and attempt to gag the Free Press, he can flood the market with his made-up "alternative facts," but he and his cronies cannot stop Hollywood from telling the real story.

Holy Crap!

Douchebag Wisdom

God bless Alec Baldwin and--my absolute fave Kate McKinnon! --for helping us all find the humor in the horror. Thank you *Saturday Night Live*! Author's note: I cried the Saturday after election day when Kate McKinnon sang Hallelujah as the show opener. The world did.

While Hollywood continues their role, I will continue mine. I refuse to live my life in fear for the next four years. I choose to stand-up and do something to help others. And right now, we, as a bloody, beat-up nation, need to rise-up. It is time to define your role in the cast of this crazy reality show that is Donald Trump.

I'm hoping these pages will take you from frustration to fascination, worry to wonder, and fear to hope. It'll take a bit of twisty logic and maybe eating a shit-sandwich or two, but I've found hope in a Donald Trump presidency, and I'm *hoping* you will too.

If you're one of the 62,979,879 voters that helped Donald Trump win the electoral vote, turn straight to the back, Chapter 10, entitled the Grinch. Please know, I'm giving Trump a chance. But, I'm not waiting for Trump to have a Grinch moment, although I'm hoping he will. Instead, I'm having my own Grinch moment and opening my heart—not to him, or what he stands for, but for common decency and respect for others everywhere, and that includes you, Trump-lover!

If you're one of the 65,844,954 voters that helped Hillary Clinton win the popular vote, then keep reading. I'm hoping a healing is headed your way. If not a healing, then at least a new perspective that helps you define your mission and unleash your power and help the very people Trump and his followers are persecuting. I'm hoping a few belly laughs will lighten your heart along the way.

If you're one of the 92 million who didn't vote, I'm hoping this book informs you of the policies being changed under our very noses, and I hope this book inspires you to vote. But I hope you'll also seek to understand our current problems and speak up and be part of the solution. Whatever your cause; there are many ways to get involved.

Rob Crilly, a British journalist living in New York, says it is our duty to mock Trump. All right, that was a paraphrase. Here's what he said so eloquently in his CNN article Dec 26, 2016, entitled: It is our Duty to Laugh at Donald Trump. "Humor—of the generous, belly-rumbling sort—is something to unite around as a symbol of resistance. It is not a sign you've given up, that you are complacent or one of the winners. When you remember that all Trump craves is to be taken seriously, it turns out that laughing is your duty."

Holy Crap!

J.K. Rowling chirped in "when a pleasure becomes a duty." She was responding to @TechnicallyRon's tweet asking famous people to keep Donald Trump busy firing insults on twitter which would keep him from killing us all.

Thank you, fellow authors, so on with my civic duty! With pleasure!! Or as mighty Michael Moore suggests, "join the army of comedy" and use humor and satire to push back against this douche. Ok, I added the douche part, but I'm thinking Michael Moore would agree. Check out Michael Moore's 10 Point Action Plan to "Make Trump Toast."

Straight from Michael Moore's website: Points 4 and 5 are Join and March.

4. JOIN! JOIN! JOIN!: We all know it's time for all of us to be part of a greater whole, so let's actually physically sign up online and **JOIN** some of our great national groups. I've joined Planned Parenthood, ACLU, Black Lives Matter, Democratic Socialists of America, and ERA Action. Some charge money to join, so if you don't have much, pick the lowest amount ($5 for ACLU for example) — or join groups that don't charge anything (but if you can help them financially, please do). They will keep you informed of national actions and fight for us in court.

5. THE WOMEN'S MARCH NEVER ENDS: The historical, record-breaking January 21st Women's March on Washington — and the hundreds of other Marches that day across the US and the world, with over **4 million** in attendance! — brought massive numbers of people out who had never protested in their lives. It inspired millions of others and ignited so many local movements we still can't count them all. The day after the Women's March, another two dozen protests took place. The day after that, 2,000 Utahans jammed into their state capitol in Salt Lake City. Then, on the following Saturday, tens of thousands of Americans occupied their local airports to oppose Trump's Muslim ban. And on and on and on. Every day — *still!* — dozens of actions continue to take place as if the Women's March never ended. It hasn't. Join it!

Moore suggests ResistanceCalendar.org for a list of activities to join. I'm all in on points 9 and 10, Be the Media and Join the Army of Comedy. And check-out Moore's one-man Broadway show, *The Terms of My Surrender*. It's getting rave reviews.

Douchebag Wisdom isn't the kindest of titles, some will think it's funny, others won't. #SorryMom That's not the point. This book is a reference tool we can all use by sharing our examples of what Donald Trump's presidency means to us. I've used the movie villains I've grown up with to help define the many issues we all must face.

There are plenty more Donald Trump comparisons to be made; you see them daily, depending which tv/movies you watch: i.e. Game of Thrones and the Walking Dead. We are all struggling with ways to process what is happening in this "restructuring" of our government and lives.

Douchebag Wisdom

Because whether you agree or not, a Donald Trump presidency is affecting every one of us, even those that can't bear to look or choose not to believe it. But we must open our eyes and start talking. Maybe these movie references will help.

I learn so much from them—Douchebags—and I know you can, too.

I have friends who are distraught and terrified by what Donald Trump is doing. He is already having a direct, negative impact on our lives. Often I'll read a disturbing headline and find myself thinking about it hours later. I'm caught in a vortex of swirling energy. I'm outraged by his first months in office, signing executive order after executive order rolling back women's rights with a gag order and closing our borders to refugees.

I can't work and live in an enraged state, so I'm changing my focus. I'm going to turn my fear into self-directed action that will help lift the planet—starting with me—and you!

I admit, after the initial election-night shock wore off, I was angry. I'd see an older white man or older white woman, assume they were Trump supporters and instantly wonder what was wrong with them?! I wanted to blame them for the shit-show that will continue to unfold over the next four years. Not eight. Four.

But do you understand THAT's what's wrong with ME?! That thinking makes ME the Douchebag. That's one of my own prejudices that's been revealed by this election outcome. See? Something positive can come out of this Trump fiasco.

Every person has a story to tell. Every Clinton supporter has reasons why they supported Hillary, and every Trump supporter has reasons why they supported the Donald. Many people have financially been left behind as both corporate greed and government obstructionism have run amok. Many of us have been forced to find new work given the natural evolution of technology and globalization. There are many people and many industries that have been forced to evolve or perish--not just the coal industry!

I've been left behind, too! I'm doing the same job I did one year ago making $400 less a month--with no health insurance! Yes, I'm one of the 20+ million people who have benefited from Obamacare. I understand financial hardship! I'm living it! I wake up regularly at 2 a.m. tossing, turning, and wondering how the hell I'm going to pay my bills and share a little cash with my four millennial kids who all have jobs and are struggling to make ends meet.

Yes, I want a better economy and more money in my pocket, who doesn't? But NOT at the expense of others--and that's what Trump is proposing!

7

Holy Crap!

"How people treat you is their karma; how you react is yours." -- Wayne Dyer

I admit, part of me is wary of Trump's retaliation. We'll talk about Trump's thin skin in Chapter 6, Trumpenstein. Will he threaten me? Will he sue me?

Suing people is Trump's go-to move. That is a Trumpism: Trump's normal modus operandi against anyone who says anything unflattering about him is to sue them. On inauguration day Trump had 75 pending lawsuits with over 4000 lawsuits filed by him or against him over the course of his business career.

Let's break that down. Trump took over his Mom and Pop's company in 1971, 46 years ago, let's call it 50. So 4000 lawsuits divided by 50 is 80 lawsuits a year divided by 12 months is 6.6 lawsuits a month. That's one lawsuit each week of his entire business career. Great negotiator? Great cheater? Dragging people and businesses through the court system is normal for Trump.

Will Trump seek to publicly humiliate me and get revenge like he did with one of his Miss Universe pageant winners of 2004? "Get even with people." Trump said as he addressed the National Achievers Conference in Australia in 2011. "If they screw with you, screw them over ten times as hard, and I'll give you an example: Jennifer Hawkins." He then brought his former Miss Universe up on stage, embarrassed and shamed her because he thought she had slighted him by not introducing him and because she "owed him for her success." Seeking revenge is doucheful! Yes, that's now a word.

Maybe Trump will try and humiliate me on twitter like he did *Vanity Fair Magazine* after food critic Tina Nguyen wrote a scathing review about the food at Trump Tower:

Donald J Trump
Has anyone looked at the really poor numbers of @VanityFair Magazine. Way down, big trouble, dead! Graydon Carter, no talent, will be out!
8:05 PM - Dec 15 2016

Or maybe I'll disappear, locked in one of those "for profit" prisons where Trump and his supporters want to send Hillary—even though there is no evidence that Hillary Clinton committed a crime!! Or maybe he'll send me to Gitmo and water-board me—or worse—pursue my family!! "The other thing with the terrorists," Trump said referring to the use of waterboarding terrorists in order to

Holy Crap!

gain information, "is you have to take out their families, when you get these terrorists, you have to take out their families."

Seems that standing up to The Donald is crime enough in his world. Who's to say he won't brand me a "terrorist" and go after my family because he feels slighted or attacked because I call him a Douchebag?

He's sued Bill Maher for offering to donate $5 million to the "Hair Club for Men" or the "Institute for Incorrigible Douchebaggery" on his behalf. Of course there's much more to that story including a birth certificate, a sex joke and a your-momma joke with a photo of The Donald pictured alongside an orangutan. Google it: Bill Maher, Trump, Douchebaggery. It's funny. And typical Trump.

Or maybe I'll turn-up like Marilyn Monroe: dead. Note to family and the rest of the free world: I am NOT suicidal! If I turn up dead, suspect foul play. And I'm definitely, definitely an excellent driver, so suspect foul play if I'm in a car accident as well.

Or, maybe Trump will simply trample my First Amendment guaranteed right to free speech and use his power and influence with the publisher to shut this book down. Chapter 2, Trumpzilla, discusses Trump's history of trampling on First Amendment rights and especially with targeting the Press.

I can't control Trump's reaction, but I can control mine. What reaction am I having? What is the intent behind this book?

Morally, Legally and Karmically Right

Yes, it is my legal right to say whatever I want, but what about the moral right—my karmic right--and the consequences?! Just because I can say something, doesn't mean I should say something. You'd think even Donald Trump knows that, although it doesn't stop him. "I probably shouldn't say this..." he often says and then says something stupid and mean anyway.

Oh, I know I'll be threatened and harassed by the Trumpeters on Twitter. For all those mean-spirited boys who bullied me in high school, I thank you now, sincerely, because you toughened me up; I know I can take it. The need to write this book and bring some clarity and comic relief is my driving force.

I do fear for my closest relationships though: my sweetheart is a quiet man and won't appreciate the exposure; I have friends and family that voted for Trump who might not appreciate my sense of humor or my perspective, but I refuse to let anger or near-sightedness—theirs or mine—ruin our bond.

These are the risks I'm willing to take because remaining silent is not an option.

"All that is necessary for the triumph of evil is that good men do nothing." -- Edmond Burke

Am I saying Donald Trump is evil? Read Chapter 3, DarthTrump, for the answer to that. Spoiler alert: the answer is "I'm not sure." But without some new perspectives, he's leading us down the path where evil resides. Hate crimes have risen 35% across the country this year. The New York Police Department reported on December 5th a 115% increase in hate crimes since the election of Donald Trump.

Co-inki-dink? Don't you believe it. Donald Trump's vicious rhetoric is inspiring people to take outrageous, violent action. But let me put some spin on it, Kellyanne Conway style. Let me see if I can unravel some of those cerebral knots and help you deal with a Donald Trump presidency. Here is some pretzel-logic and a few mind tricks I'm playing to help me deal with the reality of Trump.

Frustration to Fascination

Trump doesn't just frustrate me, he infuriates me. Again, the Trump Effect. I don't just feel it a little, I feel it a lot. I awake every day wondering what nasty nonsense Trump has tweeted out in the early morning hours. Who has Trump attacked and belittled today? Just the fact that I wake up thinking about Trump is troubling to me. He truly is a nightmare. He's certainly got the nation's attention and he's looking for validation. This is the most absurd reality show ever and the entire world is still waiting to see--are we winners or losers? Although with each day of his presidency he's proving we're all f*@%ed!

There's only one way I can deal with Donald Trump and that's to intentionally step out of frustration and step into fascination. What do I mean?

Holy Crap!

Anyone paying attention to the election and politics is emotionally involved. Like I said, you either love him or hate him. But the Trump-haters have been beat up and bullied by a belligerent entertainer who thinks he's the best business man on earth. I'm telling you now, at 70+ years old, this man is not going to change. Yes, I wish he'd change, I hope he'll change, see Chapter 10, the Grinch, but I'm not holding my breath because Donald Trump is not open to other people's opinions or perspectives, see Chapter 2, Trumpzilla, which means he's not open to change.

To me it's clear, I've got to change myself!

Change Your Reaction to Trump

I don't want to live my life in the negative emotions of frustration, worry, and fear. It's not that those emotions aren't good for you—they are!! A favorite author of mine, Karla McLaren, wrote the book *Emotional Genius*. Reading it gave words to my emotions and I was able to embrace a different part of my heart and my intuitive ability to understand what I was feeling and thinking. Anger is not bad! Frustration and worry are not necessarily bad! They are indicators that something is not right in what's happening around you. Trump has us worried for legitimate reasons, and many of us feel it as a growing sense of unease and dread. Some of us are downright fearful.

I'm going to learn from my emotional state—explore why I'm feeling such intense anger and fear. I'm going to learn why I feel that way, intellectually process it, acknowledge it, and decide what to do with it—that energy—and then step out of it.

If you are absolutely frustrated with the social injustices happening right now, here's a suggestion: stand up, and imagine yourself taking off that emotion of frustration or angst, just like you'd peel yourself out of a wetsuit. Physically do this exercise. Put your hands on the top of your head and slide them all the way down your body and all the way to your feet. Now step out of that emotion like you're stepping out of clothing.

Now turn and look at what's at the ground at your feet: your frustration and angst. Don't feel it—observe it!! Look at that emotion, analyze it, be fascinated by it, but don't let that emotion consume you. Use the energy of that frustration to do something positive, in your world, the world of a friend, the world of a neighbor or that of a stranger.

Take what you observe and have learned about what Trump is doing. Change frustration to fascination and get a new perspective.

"Be the change that you wish to see in the world." -- *Mahatma Ghandi*

Hopefully observing your feelings toward Trump will help with the frustration and anger, but what about the full-tilt worry that's consuming you? I understand; I'm feeling the same way. So let's twist this one around.

Worry to Wonder

There are 62 million people who voted for Trump. Not only are they not worried, they are quite hopeful and optimistic. Me? Not so much. I'm flat-out worried. And I'm not alone.

The American Psychological Association reports in a "Stress in America" analysis, two-thirds of all Americans feel anxiety over the future of the country. A full fifty percent of the country said politics is either somewhat or a significant source of that frustration. Democrats are feeling it more than Republicans. I sure am.

I'm mentally anxious and physically on alert since Trump's been elected and that's increased with his presidency and the policies he's currently implementing. This man is grossly incompetent—he's in way over his head. With each new tweet he reveals just how stupid he is although he thinks the opposite, "I'm, like, a really smart person," he's said. Insert an eye roll here. He's not even a "smart person," he's "like" a smart person. He's clearly not.

He's either stupid, not knowing that he's insulting when he speaks or, if he's really smart, like he claims, then he's intentionally mean-spirited and spiteful. Which one is worse? He's a loose cannon with his finger on the nuclear button. The 65 million people who voted for Hillary are losing their minds with worry! And rightly so. "I'd bomb the shit out of them" Trump said in one of his campaign rallies referring to ISIS. His need to be "unpredictable" and to "leave all options on the table" makes him a very dangerous man! He's using twitter to poke North Korea. Nothing like a "triple-dog-dare" you. See Chapter 7, Scut Trump.

Donald J Trump
I told Rex Tillerson, our wonderful Secretary of State, that he is wasting his time trying to negotiate with Little Rocket Man...
9:30 AM - Oct 1 2017

Donald J Trump
...Save your energy Rex, we'll do what has to be done!
9:31 AM - Oct 1 2017

No Wonder We're Not Sleeping

So, here's how I combat worry, that gnawing dread that eats away at my brain even when I'm trying not to think about it. First, start by breaking it down. What is worry, really? Worry is the question of what's going to happen in the future; it's the question of the unknown. We don't know what's going to happen, but we assume it is going to be bad.

Do you know that to be true? No, really, seriously, is Donald Trump going to be bad for the nation and you? Can you know that to be true? The truth is, we really don't know yet. If he does everything he said he'd do during his campaign, we certainly have reason to worry. His first one hundred days in office have knocked the Statue of Liberty right off her perch and into New York Bay without so much as a hand-up. Women? Forget 'em! They don't need contraception. Immigrants? Forget 'em, keep 'em out! This is 'Merica! I cringe as I write this.

Bottom-line, we don't know what the future holds yet. We might make assumptions, we might think we know, but until the worst happens, worry is our projection of what we think will go wrong. See Chapter 1 for the parable of Schrodinger's Kitten, and read Byron Katie's *Loving What Is* for an in-depth look at what she calls "the Work," a neutral way of questioning the assumptions that are causing you pain. Seriously, run to the store and buy this book. Use it to question all your assumptions. It'll help bring you peace of mind. And power.

13

Find Yours

So, the next time you're worrying about Trump, I want you to change your language. Change the word "worry" to the word "wonder." Not, I'm worried what Trump is going to do, but I wonder what Trump is going to do. Stop. Pay attention! Notice how you feel when you're not worried.

Can you breathe a bit easier? Is there room for your positive emotions to surface? Can you see the light? Can you see your light? Remember, this is about *your* reaction to Donald Trump. When you move out of the negative emotion of worry, you'll be able to open to new possibilities.

Worry and wonder both anticipate the future. Worry is the question of what's going to happen in the future but with negative emotions; wonder is the question of what's going to happen in the future but with positive emotions. You're not sure what's going to happen, but you know it'll be good. Wonder solicits optimism.

I'm stronger and healthier when I'm not immersed in worry, so I choose to wonder: I wonder what I can do to stop Trump and empower those he's persecuting. I wonder where we will be, as a society, on this planet. And I wonder where I will be? Still struggling to pay the bills? Or all kinds of money to give to charity. #feedthechildren #savetheanimals

Fear to Hope

"The only thing stronger than fear is hope," said President Snow, the ultimate villain in the movie *The Hunger Games*. President Snow understood the hope that the Mockingjay represented was what endangered his presidency which he had built on fear. Watch the movie; read the books, *The Hunger Games* trilogy by Suzanne Collins. Hope can start a revolution. If you're an Obama or a Bernie fan, you've already figured that out.

I cannot live my life in a slow-grade worrisome fear where I have to think about everything Trump says or does. He used the words "World War 3" in one of his early-morning twitter rants! I believe our words create our reality. If so, Trump's words are talking war. That terrifies me.

Hang On People Everywhere

In my first book, *Barf Bag Wisdom: When What's Inside Must Come Out*, I wrote "HOPE stands for Hang On People Everywhere" meaning if you just wait it

14

out, things will change for the better. But wait it out four years?! And now Trump's talking eight?! And he's even trademarked his 2020 campaign slogan: Keep America Great! Trump actually "repurposed" this slogan from a zombie movie that spoofed his campaign. Irony?! If so, it escapes Trump, which makes me doubt his superior intellect. He doesn't understand irony. It just might take a zombie apocalypse to pry him out of the White House. He and his family are firmly entrenched. Or maybe I'm the one who doesn't understand: Trump in the White House IS the zombie apocalypse.

No, I've got to find hope internally and you've got to find hope internally. It's not coming from Trump's policies! His policies may inspire hope for Republicans and the rich, but Democrats and the poor know Trump will be syphoning off money from the poorest among us.

When I googled the word "hope" I found these acronyms:

Hang On, Pain Ends

Have Only Positive Expectations

Help Open People's Eyes

Heart Open; Please Enter (dreamtime.com website Ivaylo Sarayski)

I love these versions of HOPE, but the two that really have inspired me are "Heart Open; Please Enter" and "Help Open People's Eyes." I was unable to track the origins of all the acronyms above.

"Heart Open; Please Enter" speaks to me because I know I cannot deal with Trump's negativity when my own heart and head are filled with negative thoughts. Yes, I'm a Democrat. I love people. I'm a student of Deepak Chopra, Wayne Dyer, Marianne Williamson, Neale Donald Walsch, Doreen Virtue, Sonia Choquette, Sandra Anne Taylor and so many others. I'm a life-long learner.

I send "the light" to people, pray for them, give them pep talks, help them to heal. I am a fundamentally kind, compassionate person.

A Quandary and a Paradox

So, I must find a way to deal with this president with compassion and kindness—even when he shows none! THAT's a Trump Paradox that we're all now facing. How to show kindness to people who have been empowered NOT to show kindness to others. Surely Trump would mock us. He's never professed to being kind. He would probably determine it a weakness. But kindness is not what Trump is wired for. It's what I am wired for.

But I will not sit back kindly watching Donald Trump belittle, expel, and suppress genres of people: Hispanics, Native Americans, Muslims, Women, LGBTQ. That I will kindly resist.

Until I'm forced to stand for the persecuted and oppressed, then I will wildly fight for them and their rights--Portland style. #RIPOurPortlandHeros.

I keep asking my angels to help me find the good in this situation, to open my heart and mind so I can find peace-of-mind and confidence in a bright future for us all. And how I'm going to find that peace is by "Helping Open People's Eyes." This book is cathartic for me for that very reason. This is not just about me spewing angry words on a page. This book is about reshaping my thinking and helping others to do the same. And I'd like to start with Donald John Trump.

Even though the man is almost old enough to be my father (gross thought), he's the child in this relationship. He's the petulant toddler that screams in the store and throws a fit when he doesn't get his way.

Finally, after non-stop Trump tantrum after Trump tantrum, Bob Corker, the Republican Senator from Arizona, called Trump's White House out for what it is: an #adultdaycarecenter. Trump is the biggest baby of them all, whining and filling his diaper regularly. He's surrounded himself with "yes" men and women who will only tell him what a good boy he is. The King has no clothes, no morals, and no balls despite his giant size, see Chapter 9, King Dong.

But I don't fear calling him out. This book is my attempt to help Donald Trump see the people he so easily insults and dismisses, to help him understand the effect his words have on others, and to learn there is a better, more respectful way of getting business done. If you're so darned smart, then act like it. Behave like a normal, well-mannered, respectful human being!

CEO to Leader: Can It Be Done?!

I see huge potential in this president—if he can just get his crap together and start caring more about the people than he does his own image. I think one of the reasons Christians like him so much is they think they can "save" him. I'm hoping so. I hope he finds Jesus and sees the light! See Chapter 11, Scrooge Trump, for my hopes on a better, more empathetic, and giving Trump.

Holy Crap!

In the meantime, please Donald Trump, stop behaving like such a douche!!

If you are still angry thinking about the many people Trump has trounced, good for you! Bring it on! An English Dominican friar and Catholic priest said the world needs more anger.

> *"The world needs more anger. The world often continues to allow evil because it isn't angry enough."*
> *-- Bede Jarrett*

Anger in itself is not a "bad" emotion. Anger means someone has crossed one of your boundaries. They are threatening your way of life, your way of thinking, your truths, what you know to be right or wrong. The question is: what will you do with that anger? What action will you take? Are you part of the problem or the solution?

Cutting Meals On Wheels? Who cares? Let Grandma eat dogfood! Cutting heat assistance? Who cares? Maybe Grandma will freeze to death before she starves. Cutting funding to college students? Who cares? Trump's ramping up the war machine, who needs an education?

Who cares? I care, and millions and millions of others care. Do not give in to apathy. DO NOT TUNE OUT! Tune back in! Anger is better and stronger than apathy. Transmute that emotion into action. Don't bury your head and become despondent, and don't move to Canada. America needs you—the world needs you. We have work to do. Let that anger help define what you stand for, make a choice, and move forward—not in fear but with hope and determination. #Resist #Insist# Persist #Enlist

You Can Do It

The world is such a cold, dark place and there is nothing I can do, but God, in all his/her wisdom said, "Just build a better you."

I saw that quote on a sign in a YMCA in Cedar Falls, Iowa a very, very long time ago. It's stuck with me ever since. In the face of such ugly rhetoric and disappointment in my fellow wo/man, 62 million of them, what can I do?

Well, I am no longer angry. I am enlightened. I am motivated. "I is kind. I is smart. I is important." Kathryn Stockett, *The Help.* And you are, too.

Over five million people around the world assembled January 21st, the day after Inauguration Day, in unity to protest the presidency of Donald Trump. The protests that took place in cities across the country—big and small—prove that Donald Trump does not represent us all. Americans are kind-hearted and generous as a whole; we look out for our fellow wo/man despite what Donald Trump says or does. I proudly stand with the mayors, the governors, the politicians and people who continue to support the Paris Climate Accord. Trump's short-sightedness will not be mine.

We Are Being Called

I am being called. You are being called. Called to be the best person you can possibly be. Called to tell your truth. Called to get out of bed, get off your ass, turn off the television, shut down the news, put down the phone--and do something to affect change in an area that is most troubling you: women's rights, the environment, immigration, prison reform, health care, tax reform. There are many areas to get involved.

I'm not a journalist or an investigative reporter. I'm in the marketing and messaging business. I'm just one of the millions and millions of US citizens living in the United States horrified by what Donald Trump is doing.

At first, I was despondent, then angry, now motivated, empowered, and optimistic. So, what can I do in the face of such blatant, hateful rhetoric? Well, I can write a book.

But the better question is:

What can you do?

And more importantly:

What WILL you do?

Keep reading for helpful suggestions at the end of each movie chapter. I believe in YOU, and I believe in US.

In 1970, the badly damaged Apollo 13 spacecraft was circling the earth with astronauts Jim Lovell, Fred Haise, and Jack Swigert inside. The situation looked dire. NASA was doing everything within their power to save the men,

Holy Crap!

and the NASA Director fretted, "This could be the worst disaster NASA's every experienced."

Flight Director Gene Krantz replied, "With all due respect, sir, I believe this is gonna be our finest hour."

Indeed, it was. With the entire world watching, NASA brought the Apollo 13 crew safely back to earth.

Yes, our challenges are many: human rights, climate change, financial inequality...and the list goes on. But, with all due respect, my friends, if each of us rises to the occasion, I believe this could be our finest hour.

I repeat, what will you do?

Holy Crap!

The world is such a cold,
dark place and there's nothing
I can do.

God/the Universe:
Just build a better YOU!

Holy Crap!

Holy Crap!

Donald Drumpf

1. Donald Drumpf: America, You're F*@%ed!

After 146 years in business, the Ringling Bros. and Barnum & Bailey circus, the "greatest show on earth," has shuttered their tents, and moved into the White House. Donald Trump is head clown, main event, ringmaster, owner *and* the huge shitting elephant in the middle of the Big Top.

"I don't care what people say about me as long as they say something." -- PT Barnum

Donald Trump is "The Show" and the only thing worse than people talking about him is people NOT talking about him. Regarding the Press, Donald Trump said in *The Art of the Deal*, "I'm not saying that they necessarily like me. Sometimes they write positively and sometimes they write negatively. But from a pure business point-of-view, the benefits of being written about far outweigh the drawbacks." That philosophy has served him well: love him or hate him, we're all talking about him.

But here's the bad news. We could all turn off and tune out his television reality show, *The Apprentice*, where his money bought him the right to hire, fire, and be a colossal douche; but if we turn off and tune out this current "presidential" reality show, then we risk telling the world that Donald Trump's perspectives represent America's perspectives--and they don't!

Donald Trump does not speak for me! And he does not speak for all Americans! Remember, 65 million people voted for Hillary Clinton, 3 million more than voted for Donald Trump! And over 92 million didn't vote at all!

News for you, Donald Drumpf: I will never unite with you to throw people out of our country. I will never support building a wall. I will never back a Muslim registry. I will never deny climate change in the search of the almighty dollar. I will never support tax breaks for corporations who take advantage of their workers and give huge bonuses to execs. I will never support tax cuts for the richest people in the country because trickle-down economics does not work. I will never support your gag on workers who could help women with family planning issues, and I will never support your attacks on the Free Press.

I will not be disheartened. I will not be silenced. I will stand for common decency and I will unite with others to foster respect, compassion, understanding and helping my fellow wo/man, no matter their gender, the color of their skin, their economic status, who they love or what they believe.

"If you fight with monsters too long, you become a monster." Billy Bob Thornton to Sandra Bullock in Our Brand is Crisis. How do we stand up to a bully without becoming one ourselves?

The Trump Paradox

How dare I call the president of the United States a Douchebag?! Exactly! That's a Trump Paradox in action. I want to be respectful, I was raised to be respectful, but how can I respect a man who doesn't respect others? It's a paradox, a conundrum, it doesn't make sense. HE doesn't make sense. His victory doesn't make sense.

Are there really 62 million Americans out there who think the same way Donald Trump does? Are there that many people who condone his words and actions? How could so many people vote for a bully and a victimizer? And why can't they wear labels on their foreheads, because I want nothing to do with Donald Trump, his nasty divisive politics or the people that voted him into office.

I want to crawl into a hole and come out in four years with a new president, one that I can respect and follow. But I won't. Many of my friends aren't paying attention now. They can't take it--the policies--or him--the liar-in-chief. They want to throw-up their hands in disgust, but I won't let them--and they know they can't. These are dangerous times and we must be diligent to make sure we watch Trump behind the scenes as he distracts us yet again with an absurd statement on Twitter while Bannon, Kushner and toadies are deconstructing our government.

I do know people who really don't care. They don't feel Trump will affect their life dramatically or at all. I've read that 80% of Republicans think they'll be much better off this time next year. Only 18% of Democrats feel the same way. I hope the Republicans are right—but it can't just be about money!! It doesn't matter how rich you are if we're all living in a bunker Kimmy Schmidt, mole-rat style because Trump has started a world war.

PT Barnum was a self-professed showman. In addition to his entertaining hoaxes and the creation of the circus, Barnum wrote a book called *The Art of Getting Money.* Sound familiar? Is there anyone who doesn't know Trump wrote *The Art of the Deal*? Actually, Tony Schwartz wrote the book, but more about that in Chapter 6, Trumpenstein.

Barnum's book is also referred to as "The Golden Rules for Making Money." And this is where the differences between show men shows up. PT Barnum respected his audience. Trump respects no one except for the "yes" men and women with which he's surrounded himself. And even that respect is questionable. I don't think he respects anyone.

"Be polite and kind to your customers," wrote Barnum. "Politeness and civility are the best capital ever invested in business." Can you imagine the kind of impact Donald Trump could have all over the world if he just adopted PT Barnum's outlook on people and the Golden Rule?!

The Golden Rule...Karma's a Bitch

For eight years President Barack Obama had to listen to a non-stop assault from Donald J Trump. "He's not legitimate," Trump cried. "Birth certificate, birth certificate, birth certificate." He even got on tv and lied about sending his people out to Hawaii to investigate. "I have people that have been studying it and they cannot believe what they're finding." They "couldn't believe it" because they found nothing wrong! No fraud, no lies, no conspiracy; just a certificate of Live Birth issued by the State of Hawaii Department of Health to one Barack Hussein Obama, II. Maybe if Trump had practiced the Golden Rule he wouldn't be under such scrutiny now.

John Lewis, the US Representative for Georgia, a civil rights activist, leader, and author, has every right to question Trump's legitimacy to be president now. So do i; so do you. The CIA and FBI have both found ties from Trump's campaign advisors to Russia. There is clear evidence that Vladimir Putin and his associates interfered in our election. The FBI says so. The CIA says so. The NSA says so. Our national allies say so. We certainly know Russia flooded the internet with damaging stories about Hillary Clinton.

Both my personal website and company website were spammed by pro-Trump Russia spammers. How do I know? Because my Google Analytics reported increased traffic from many Russian IP addresses in September and October and because one of the links said specifically "pro-Trump Russian spammer. Vote Trump!" That's how I know, and that's why I believe—along with 65 million other people--that Donald Trump won the election with Russia's help.

Trump himself claimed the system was rigged. He was right, but it was rigged in his favor. Trump can huff and puff all he wants. He can stand atop the White House and declare it—but no denial in the world will convince me that he won this election "fair and square."

Trump courted Putin throughout his entire campaign. In truth, he's been courting Putin for years. It's like Trump never grew up:

Donald J Trump

Do you think Putin will be going to The Miss Universe Pageant in November in Moscow - if so, will he become my new best friend?

10:17 PM - Jun 18 2013

The Rise of a Bully

Every person who doesn't support Trump talks about his spiteful, hurtful, slandering rhetoric to anyone who opposes him. Trump is notorious for name-calling and used the tactic mercilessly against every one of his opponents: Low-Energy Jeb, Lyin' Ted Cruz, Lil' Marco Rubio, Crooked Hillary. It's a Trumpism, one of Trump's go-to tactics. Ironically, Trump has turned out to be one of the lowest energy presidents we've had so far. The old man needs cookies and nap and a golf cart to drive him around the White House.

But his name-calling is not new; it's who he is as a "successful" businessman. And it's *this* choice, to intentionally be mean that makes him a Douchebag!

Name-calling, BULLYING, is a Douchebag move!!! Period! I didn't learn it from Trump. I learned it when I was in Kindergarten, but as I grew and matured, I left name-calling behind. Most of us do. And when I was in high school and being bullied mercilessly by my classmates, I made it a personal vow to never label or intimidate others. I work at being open, loving, and accepting of others. Dammit! Most decent human beings do!

We are taught that principle while still young—respect others. Do unto them as you'd have them do unto you. It's in the Bible, it's a Golden Rule, it's the Law of Karma for goodness sakes!!! Did Donald Trump miss that day in kindergarten? Did his Momma not share that with him through bedtime stories and slight reprimands and redirects while he was growing up? Is no one going to step-up and demand Trump learn some manners?

How is it that a man who calls himself a "successful businessman" can have so little respect for others? And how do we deal with this Trump Paradox and defend ourselves from a bully except by walking away or standing up? That's a Trump Paradox in action.

My training and life experience leads me to believe he's unable to see others. He's in-the-box and old-fashioned. He sees people as a means to an end and that end is money. He doesn't see individuals. He's tapped into groups for the applause, but he doesn't see individuals. He's not wired for that.

Walking away is not an option here. Even though Justin Trudeau is putting together an experienced, qualified cabinet with progressive policies that serve all mankind, including the refugees and the planet. I'm not moving to Canada. I'm proud to be an Iowa farm girl now living in the Colorado Rockies. I've traveled to every major city in every one of our fifty United States and I choose to stay and defend my country from all threats foreign and domestic! And right now, Donald Trump is the biggest domestic threat, and to him, I'm standing up.

Hillary Clinton's momma, God rest her soul, taught her to stand-up. And she did--for all of us! She stood up to the foul-mouthed, hatred-spewing Donald Trump, because Hillary Clinton—and all of her supporters—believe in a different truth: we are stronger together. Trump belittled and knocked her down at every turn, and Hillary Clinton kept getting up because she believes in the goodness of people--all people, not just some people. And so do I.

That's why I've got to look deeper into the politics of Donald Trump and more importantly the philosophies of Donald Trump, because if we're ever going to help him become "presidential," we'll need common talk to help him see the other side. Because no matter how smart he declares himself, he doesn't seem to grasp that the world is NOT full of winners or losers! And he's pledged to help the middle-class and poor, so let's see him do it.

We'll use movies because we know Trump quotes them. I swear he lifted parts of his freaky "carnage" inauguration day speech from Bain, the supervillain in *The Dark Knight Rises*. So much for positive, uplifting and uniting; Trump slandered and vilified many of the people who occupied the stage with him. Trump fancies himself a celebrity above the laws of common decency. And yet we're stuck with him, so we might as well get to know ourselves through this tainted lens—through Trump's crap-colored glasses where only Americans, especially white Christian, can enter and pursue the American Dream.

We'll explore Trump's actions through: paradoxes, fallacies, truths, and Trumpisms. If we can use these observations as talking points then we just might move closer to saving the world from annihilation. Unfortunately, I'm not joking. These talking points might ease your burden when defending "why" you think Trump is so bad for the nation and the world. Don't be an over-emotional douche. Use some logic and facts to support your theories. And call out when others try to use "alternative facts" because agreeing on things that can be measured and proved or disproved is the basis for getting to understanding.

No one knows yet how this story will turn out. It's still being written and you've got a part to play.

Trump Paradoxes

1. Respect: how do you respect a man that doesn't respect others?
2. Bullying: how do we have respectful discourse when we call each other names?
3. Freedom of Speech: how do we preserve the right to free speech when people who speak-out are gagged or attacked?
4. Winner/Loser mentality: how does everyone win with Capitalism? Currently, only a few win at the expense of others.

A paradox is a seemingly absurd or self-contradictory statement or proposition that when investigated or explained may prove to be well founded or true. Or not. It's a mystery, a puzzle, a fucking conundrum—as in "how the heck can a scam artist with no respect for others get elected to the highest office in the land?"

Bully-in-Chief

Am I being a bit of a bully myself? Even though my intentions are good, and I want to help others come to terms with this man, are my thoughts and intentions honorable? Do I really care about helping Donald Trump?

The short answer is "yes!" I want to help him become a better man and president, so he can help others around the world, not just here in America. The long answer is: *No! Not if he continues with his hateful, biased, racist agenda that includes targeting and intentionally hurting others!*

If I use Trump's tactics to get ahead, am I condoning his behavior, or am I just taking advantage of the opportunity, and is there a difference? Who's the bully? Who's being hurt if I publish this book? Trump supporters probably won't see the humor but what if it helps them recommit to Trump ideals as well. It'll help them define themselves and that's what I want, for all readers, not just Trump-haters.

How can I blame every Republican that's jumped on board? I think many of them really want to believe in Donald Trump. How long have they talked about a major "pivot." They, too, are still hoping this man acts more like a grown-up and that he grows into the office. But Republicans must quit thinking they are in control because they can't control Trump. The monster is loose and in charge. But much to their delight, he's come into the office as a conservative. There had been much speculation, but Trump's decided to play the role of a hard, Christian conservative.

Laughable. He doesn't live by any Christian standards I know, and I grew up Catholic. But he's got such potential. I can see it! I understand why people like him. Genuinely like him, like I liked and loved—and still do, always will—President Barack Obama, the man who restored my hope and faith in a leader and the people.

Trump looks presidential, but he doesn't act presidential because he doesn't respect others. He's not open to other people's opinions, which is quite ironic considering he's open to other people's money.

Why can't Trump be more respectful? Is his bluster simply his ignorance and fear showing? Why can't he speak to people respectfully, honor what they know and what they've learned?

And how do I not become a douche bag myself in the maze of his morphing words and lies? How do I embrace the man and disavow the douche in him?

Trump Fallacy

A fallacy is an error in reasoning which causes a false belief. A fallacy is created from arguments, explanations, and definitions and Donald Trump is the master at alternative arguments, explanations, and definitions ... or exaggerations, intentional misdirection, and downright lies.

My own fallacy lies in thinking I need to support this man. I want to support the president, but I believe the opposite of what he's doing. He's not taking these executive actions with love in his heart; he's acting on fear, hate and exclusivity. He's going against everything America stands for—freedom from persecution, no matter what your religious beliefs. He's turned his platform into a "say-anything, do-anything" side show with the intent of getting the whole world to notice.

The simple fact is: our President is a pessimist and fear-monger.

He thrives on stinkin' thinkin'.

"I believe in the power of negative thinking." --
Donald Trump, Art of the Deal

A Campaign of Hate and Fear

I believe Donald Trump's run for the White House was revenge motivated. His anger and disdain for "anything government" was blatantly and proudly on display as he systematically tackled and dismantled every obstacle in his way. Using language and strategy that appealed to the worst parts of us, he attacked his opponents, the Press, people at his rallies, anyone who questioned him in any fashion. He bullied and belittled his opponents, attacked their looks, their accomplishments, their families, their commitment to the country, and their integrity. He incited violence at his rallies, even flippantly suggesting supporters exercise their Second Amendment rights to take care of his opponent. He crafted a message based on fear and blaming and played to the worst fears of his supporters.

Freedom of Speech

Trump made one wild, outrageous, and egregious assertion after another, each lie and story growing in the telling and retelling. Facts simply didn't matter. And his supporters simply didn't care. They needed someone to blame, and Donald Trump, Master of the Steal, pointed, screamed, and raged as he singled out Washington, the Republicans, the Democrats, the President, and most especially the Press.

"No one knows the system better than me," he said at the Republican National convention in Cleveland, "which is why I alone can fix it." He set himself up as a Washington outsider and a corporate savior, and his supporters-turned-raving-fans, desperate for *anything* different, worshipped him, and voted for him.

Adam Gopnik, writer for The New Yorker, noted the similarities between the politics of Donald Trump and the politics of Huckleberry Finn's drunken father. "Call this a govment! Just look at it and see what it's like . . .. A man can't get his rights in a govment like this."

No one can argue that the government doesn't have its problems. The last eight years of Republican obstructionism has cost many middle-class and poor Americans their jobs and their homes. But we're about to find out that capitalism trumps them all. Donald Trump bought himself the presidency—with a little help from his friends--foreign and domestic.

Yes, Donald Trump put on a one-man show, playing to the passion of his angry crowds. He dominated most every news cycle, kept dancing, spinning, directing, misdirecting, and performing for the crowd. And he won.

The nation was shocked. The world was repulsed. America had succumbed to fear mongering and hatred. And Donald Trump was not surprised. He reminded us again January 2 via twitter: "Various media outlets and pundits say that I thought I was going to lose the election. Wrong, it all came together in the last week.... He continued in a second tweet: "I thought and felt I would win big, easily over the fabled 270 (306). When they cancelled fireworks, they knew and so did I." Trump was referring to the Electoral College win which he squeaked out with Russia's help.

Classic Trump, classic Trumpism, a method he uses to discredit his opponents while lifting himself up. He's proved to be a masterful magician, a con artist, a silver-tongued linguist, and a "great, tremendous businessman" if you don't mind treading on a few million souls.

Donald Trump has tapped into deep-seated hatred; he's pitting one group of people against another. We're now all working for the Trump Organization whether we like it or not. Trump has no intention of divesting himself from his businesses. He's trying hard to tie them and the government all together. And don't be looking for a raise. Trump believes American wages are too high already. Thanks to Trump, Republican-led states are already rolling back increases to the minimum wage.

Pessimist or Optimist, You Decide

"Both the optimist and pessimist contribute to society. The optimist invents the airplane, the pessimist the parachute." -- George B Shaw

Let's be clear. You do not ever need to support Donald Trump. As hard as I'm trying to find a silver lining for each storm cloud, that's not something that YOU need to do.

Donald Drumpf

If you are happy with Trump, and you see his actions as positive, then you're working on Trump's airplane. If you don't believe the world is a better place because of Trump, you're still working, only against him, and there's nothing wrong with that. We all need the reassurance of a parachute.

What I am saying is both Trump supporters and haters are necessary to address the big world issues we now all face, and those issues are getting bigger with Trump's big-mouth attitude and tweets.

Using Twitter to Incite Violence

Donald Trump uses his Twitter feed and his words to incite violence, and that's another Douchebag move. When protestors at one of Trump's campaign rallies in St. Louis, Missouri were loud and verbal, interrupting the rally for a full fourteen minutes, Trump had them "escorted out" by his Security detail. He then said, "You know, part of the problem and part of the reason it takes so long is nobody wants to hurt each other anymore, right?"

Really? That's the problem with the world? Not enough violence?

This is the man with his finger on the nuclear button; a man who has bragged that he loves war. At a gathering at Iowa Central Community College on November 12, 2015 he said, "I'm good at war. I've had lots of wars of my own. I'm really good at war. I love war, in a certain way, but only when we win."

Words create realities. Motivational speakers know this, they use affirmations. Wiccans know this, they use spells. Magicians know this, they use the word "abracadabra," an Aramaic word from Jesus's time meaning "I will create as I speak." Christians know this, they pray!!! Words matter.

"Words are, of course, the most powerful drug used by mankind." -- Rudyard Kipling

Trump may not drink or smoke, but he uses words like an addict. He spends his evening swilling down words, crafting ad slogans and catchphrases, chewing them up then tweeting them out from the summit of Trump Tower at 4 a.m. like a drunkard texting an ex. No one can stop him.

"I know words, I have the best words," Trump says. Well, okay, "smart guy," use your words to say something positive. Use your words to lift others up!

And there's the lesson—do you see? Mine--and yours. Yes, this is about the words Trump uses, but more importantly it's about the words YOU use, day-in-day-out. Are your words an accurate reflection of you? Do they heal or hurt? Have you said hurtful things to the Trump supporters in your life? Have you tried to use your words to discover why they so passionately believe in him?

Winners and Losers

There are winners and losers according to Donald Trump. That's another Paradox. How can we all now be winners after Donald Trump so decisively laid out the path of winners and losers: if you're with him, you're a winner. If you are against him, you are a loser. Simple.

And the first few days and weeks after the election, I almost believed I was a loser, that the nation as a whole had "lost" the election, but I've already grown past that—and you must too! That's what we're being called to do: regroup, reevaluate, and redefine who we are as individuals and the policies we'll pursue as a nation.

We must move headlong into the policies that Trump is implementing. We must stare them in the face and challenge Donald Trump's truths. Here they are as I know them, based on his words and actions:

Trump Truths

1. Government is bad: #DrainTheSwamp
2. The Press is bad: they are "the opposition," "the enemy," "bad people"
3. Everyone is for sale so everything can be negotiated
4. Build a wall, no matter how stupid or divisive
5. Kick out the illegal immigrants and the DREAMERS
6. Register the Muslims
7. Repeal Obamacare
8. Tear up foreign treaties and trade agreements
9. Deny climate change
10. Take the oil

How does Trump go about executing his agenda above? Through Trumpism, tactics, modes of operation (MOs). Here are just a few:

Trumpisms

1. Life is a reality show: tune in next week. Leave 'em guessing—he thinks everything is a cliff hanger to be used for ratings.

2. Get revenge, get even. Trump attacks others as he spews and shrugs: maybe Hillary's cheating on Bill, I don't know. Maybe Trump has a small dick, who knows?

3. Sues others when slighted; shuts down their voice. Throw money at it until it goes away.

4. People are saying... I'm hearing... I've got sources... I know things.

5. Mentioning it by not mentioning it and never mentioning a source.

6. Exaggerates, lies, and makes up his own reality.

7. Rewrites history: "I never mocked that disabled reporter"; video clearly shows he did.

8. Brags and boasts taking credit where credit is not due. Takes credit for jobs that were already slated to come back to the US.

9. Blames others. Eight years of Birther movement, then he says, "Hillary started it." And he had the gall to say the "Generals lost Ryan." I'm shaking my head.

10. Actions don't match his words. Holds himself and his businesses to a different standard.

How can people support this man and this agenda?! Here are the things I've told myself about Trump supporters. Some of these assumptions are causing me pain. Perhaps it's time to check my own prejudices at the door.

Truths I've Told Myself About Trump Supporters

All Trump supporters are idiots. Now you see? There's a paradox right there. I know that is absolutely false. I know Trump supporters. They're not idiots!!! They might think a bit differently than I do, but they're not idiots, and I'd be the idiot for thinking so.

This falls into "winners and losers" mentality. There are NO winners. There are NO losers. There are NO idiots. Well, I've gone too far on that. There are always exceptions and we clearly have an idiot in charge. But in general, and in theory, there are only different people with different backgrounds, experiences, and

Donald Drumpf

perspectives. It is my job to respect them all—even when others won't. Even the idiots.

It is my job to realize all my stinkin' thinkin' when it comes to a fellow human being. This is the garbage in my head I've had to let go when dealing with Trump supporters:

1. They are stupid, uninformed, and unable to process logic.

2. They lack compassion, are selfish and out to "get theirs" at others' expense.

3. They are racists, suffer from white privilege, or just straight-out hate Obama.

As Byron Katie would say to each of these statements: Is that true? Can you absolutely, with all certainty know it to be true? No, of course not, almost all of the truths I've told myself about Trump supporters are my own made-up reality. It is impossible to lump all of Donald Trump's supporters into one of these three categories, yet we do it, because their thinking, their support of Donald Trump doesn't make sense--to us! You must know it makes perfect sense to them!

Again, in the book *Loving What Is*, I have to ask myself: How do you feel when you think that thought, that thought that all Trump supporters are ignorant or racists, that thought that you can't really know to be true? What do you think? How do you feel? How does it affect your feelings, thoughts and actions? This thing that you believe, that you really can't know to be true?

See? See how I'm twisting myself in knots trying to give Trump supporters the benefit of the doubt. Then again, I'm assuming everyone was born and raised to be kind. I guess that's the number one assumption I truly want to explore. Not everyone was born to be kind. I fear for our youth because Donald Trump has taught a whole generation what it's like to win by being mean and taking whatever you want.

Spring-breakers in Mexico chanting "build the wall" to the Mexican people are pure proof Donald Trump is a decisive douche, and he's empowered a generation of Douchebags.

There really is evil in the world, and as Dr. Smith said on Lost In Space, "Evil knows evil." It's up to each one of us to determine where evil lies.

Donald Drumpf

The Truths I've Told Myself About Trump

Here are the other "truths" I've told myself about Trump that are keeping me up at night:

1. He's going to "kick people off the island"
2. His greed is classic capitalism-run-amok
3. His tax plan helps the rich, but I'll end up paying for it
4. He's taking away my healthcare
5. He'll take away a woman's right to choose
6. He'll take away LGBT rights
7. He's scammed thousands of people to pay for his lavish lifestyle
8. He's disrespected our Vets and our country
9. He incites and condones violence
10. He's mentally unstable
11. He's bad for me and the country
12. He's going to blow up the world
13. He's a Douchebag

My Truths

The only way I can combat the fear and hatred this man and his administration have brought on is to return to some of my most basic truths.

Truth 1:

If you can't believe in Trump, then believe in yourself!

Truth 2:

"Some things fall apart so better things can fall together."
-- Marilyn Monroe

Truth 3:

"Pour yourself a drink, put on some lipstick, and pull yourself together."
-- Liz Taylor

Hold him accountable to his promises to: women and other minorities.

37

Donald Drumpf

Truth 4:

What Susie says of Sally says more of Susie than of Sally.

So, don't be a douchebag and speak kindly of Sally! Truth 5:

It'll all be okay in the end. If it's not okay, it's not the end.

Truth 6:

Relax and let karma finish it.

Schrodinger's Kitten

Here's the bottom line and the purpose to this book: I wants to beliefs. Like this kitten flying through the air, I want to believe I'll land in something good. I want to believe that Donald Trump will use his unmatched power and wealth to do good—for us all!

While the kitten is still in the air, he's fine and the dream is fine. The potential for Donald Trump to do good does exist. Maybe this kitten is about to pounce on a pile of cash or a dish of fancy feast. He's winning! While the kitten is still in the air, we can be optimistic, hopeful that the kitten is going to land safely. You're not quite sure where or on what, but it'll be good. The great possibilities are endless.

I WANTS TO BELIEFS
SRSLY

If you're afraid that little kitten could be hurling over a cliff or landing in a pile of crap, you're probably scared and worried. You don't know where that little cat will land, but it's going to be bad. You don't know what Donald Trump will choose to do, but you know it'll be bad. Better be making that parachute and fast!

It is Schrodinger's kitten: until the kitten lands, both possibilities exist— Trump could have a very successful presidency, a positive outcome where he's able to help many people--a good landing. Or Trump could trash the economy and create many negative outcomes for many people, a bad landing for the kitten.

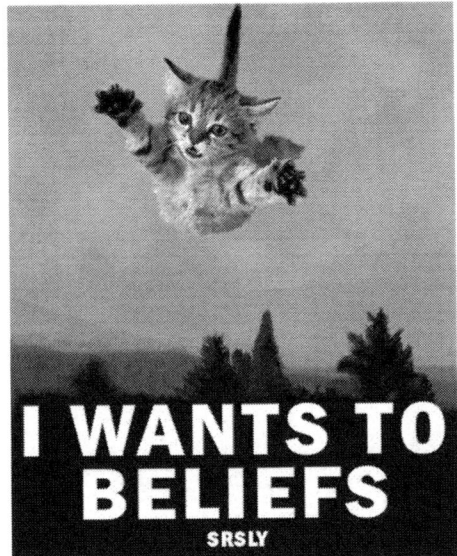

We don't know yet. We're still early in the Trump presidency. My best friend tells me not to worry, Trump can't do that much damage in four years. That's not reassuring. We can't know what will happen. All we can do is hope and pray for the best, then contact our Congressmen and women and let them know what we really think. But for now, the kitten is in the air. Tune in tomorrow.

Tune In Tomorrow

Donald Trump made himself a household brand. He's cultivated a successful, playboy image to some, and others see through to the dark, selfish soul he is. It doesn't really matter if you like him or not. You see, we are all now looking at our own problems through the lens we call Donald Trump. Good or bad, you decide. It doesn't matter—as long as we're talking about Donald Trump.

And now Donald Trump has grabbed both Statue of Liberty and Mother Earth by the--you know what. He's got our attention. Now, what will he do next?

The answer? Schrodinger's Kitten. We don't know.

Will he hold Mother Earth in his hands? Will he protect her, the parks, the animals, the wilderness? Or will he oil her up slowly and frack her when she's crying "no." With executive orders to green light the pipelines and with the "deconstruction" of the Environmental Protection Agency, it's not looking good.

I know. I'm scared, too. That's why I'm writing this book. I don't want to be fracked.

I want to give Trump the benefit of the doubt; I want to believe that some of his most hateful rhetoric is just that, talk. But at the end of his first week in office, it doesn't look good for women, Hispanics, or immigrants. Time will tell.

For now, my kitten is in the air. I wants to beliefs.

Donald, don't be a douche. Don't let the entire world down. Catch that kitten!! And catch a few refugee children to show you really do give a crap about people after all. Think of the press! Be a hero--not a douche.

Each one of us is being challenged to define our own truths. We need to look clearly at the language and actions of Donald Trump and his associates. We

Donald Drumpf

can't look away for one moment or soon we'll find we're the ones being oppressed.

We need to take Donald Trump at his word and believe he really does want to make America great. We have to help him understand what "great" looks like: freedom for all, equality for all. We can't just let him roll America back to the early 1900s before civil rights and human rights questioned the status quo. That was NOT a great time in American history.

"Those who do not learn from history are doomed to repeat it." -- George Santayana

Let's help Donald Trump see it our way. If he really does want to unite the country, he'll work with the 65 million people who didn't vote for him, the 62 million that did AND the 92 million people who didn't vote! There are commonalities! There is room for compromise, if, IF, Trump can get out of that either/or thinking. That right/wrong, winner/loser mindset that doesn't serve us all.

We have a voice, too, and Trump said he would represent us all. I plan to hold him to that. So let me explain to you what I see as the biggest obstacles for supporting Trump. Let's go to the movies.

I've attempted to support my Hollywood assumptions with as many factual details as possible. Like I said, I'm not a journalist or an investigative reporter but I have relied on the research and news articles of many. When I spew facts, I reference my sources. But again, this book is not about my conclusions. This book is about your conclusions. And, like everyone else on the planet, you will draw your own.

Donald J Trump, are you listening?! Keep reading, but only if you're serious about uniting a nation, because as you said in The Art of the Deal,

"You can't con people, at least not for long. You can create excitement, you can do wonderful promotion and get all kinds of press, and you can throw in a little hyperbole. But if you don't deliver the goods, people will eventually catch on." -- Donald Trump

Donald Drumpf

"Words are, of course, the most powerful drug used by mankind." -- Rudyard Kipling

Donald Drumpf

Donald Drumpf

Trumpzilla

2. Trumpzilla: Oh No, There Goes the Status Quo!

He may have tiny little hands, and a micro-conscience, but it is Donald Trump's ego that exceeds even Godzilla in size. Trumpzilla is a triple threat: to Democracy, the Environment, and the avoidance of nuclear war.

Godzilla, King of Monsters, is known for the devastation he causes. Godzilla, created by a film director in Japan in 1954, is a by-product of the nuclear devastation wrought by bombs dropped on Hiroshima and Nagasaki. With all of Trump's talk of nuclear war since taking office, he, Trumpzilla, is the biggest nuclear threat to the world.

Trumpzilla is a by-product of the explosion of capitalism and money into politics. Even though Trump appears to have business cred, he clearly lacks the insight, intellect and temperament to be President of the United States. Trump's stomp and brag mentality combined with exaggeration, lies, and bravado are proof that he respects no one and no thing. He has no understanding of the Constitution or democracy. He's never had to lead; he's achieved his stature in life through buying, bullying, and bullshitting his way to the top. Trump's words convey again and again he respects only those that agree with him. He rails against anyone who has a differing opinion.

Trump chooses blatantly disrespectful language to intimidate anyone he doesn't agree with or any policy he doesn't understand, and that makes him, Trumpzilla, the King of the Monsters—and a monster of a douche.

Kiss Your Ass Good-bye

Trump's reckless use of language has led The Bulletin of Atomic Scientists to push up the Doomsday Clock 30 seconds closer to midnight--that symbolic moment in time when humanity annihilates itself. The planet is now 2.5 minutes before midnight. The scientists made that decision after hearing Trump's casual talk about nuclear war and his total disregard for climate change. I haven't heard updated predictions since Trump shot the missiles at Syria or continues to shoot his mouth off at North Korea. We're "sending an armada" to the North Korean Peninsula. "Submarines, beautiful submarines," he said.

Since then Trump has escalated the tension with North Korea promising calling Kim Jong-un "Little Rocket Man," promising "fire and fury like the world has never seen." Tick. Tock. Tick. Tock. He's backing out of the Iranian nuclear deal. Tick. Tock.

Trump on the campaign trail promoted war: "I would bomb the shit out of them," Trump said to a group of campaign rally-goers in Fort Dodge, Iowa, about ISIS, "I'd just bomb those suckers. I'd blow up the pipes, I'd blow up the refineries, I'd blow up every single inch—there would be nothing left."

When asked about the nuclear triad in the December debate, Trump gave an unintelligible answer that included: "I think, for me, nuclear is just the power, **the devastation is very important to me**."

Reversing three decades of disarmament, President-elect Trump tweeted:

Donald J Trump
The United States must greatly strengthen and expand its nuclear capability until such time as the world comes to its senses regarding nukes.
11:50 AM - Dec 22 2016

Trump also said, "No one is going to touch us, because I'm so unpredictable."

Unpredictable and stupid. It's no wonder the Doomsday Clock has been reset. Trumpzilla and his reptilian-sized brain represent a clear and present threat, not just for Americans but for people all over the world. Trump's first few months in office have been an assault on women, immigrants, Native Americans, all Americans, the Republicans, the Democrats, the Courts, the Constitution, and the very earth we're all inhabiting, as well as taunting North Korea.

A Total Lack of Respect

Obama led with diplomacy; Trump leads with fear and a big stick. He has to because no one respects him for the person he is, only what he has: money, and now, nukes.

The complexities of National Security elude Trump. His ego puts us all at risk. His lack of respect for the Central Intelligence Agency, the Federal Bureau of Investigations, the Department of Justice, and the Intelligence Community in general is staggering. Of course, he's calling ex-FBI director James Comey a liar and a "nut job." It's Trumpzilla's only defense--attack! Comey knows the truth and the facts will come out. But Trump's not capable of understanding because he doesn't take the time to get the facts.

In the first two weeks of his presidency he authorized a covert operation with too little information and got one of our Navy Seal team killed. In addition, there were a dozen civilian causalities including the 8-year old daughter of a dead terrorist. If Trumpzilla had stopped and listened to his intelligence professionals, there might have been a different outcome. But Trump doesn't believe in facts. He gets his military advice from "the shows."

Trump doesn't take regular security briefings because "I'm, like, a smart guy," this he said in an interview with Fox News Chris Wallace, Dec 2016. And Trumpzilla has no understanding of 20th century technology!

When asked about the Russians hacking the election, here was his reply,

"I think we ought to get on with our lives. I think that computers have complicated lives very greatly. The whole age of computer has made it where nobody knows exactly what is going on." Trump has no understanding of a digital footprint but it's there, and it will either exonerate him or convict him.

The fact that Trump doesn't use a computer is another reason I don't believe he's smart or savvy or a great business man – and proves he has a tiny little Godzilla brain. Personal computers have been around for forty years! Forty! I've been using a personal computer for thirty years! The modern internet began in the early 1980s, and most of us have been "online" since the early 1990s. Social media, which revolutionized how people around the world communicated and collaborated with each other, has been used on a global scale for ten years!! But the only thing Trump knows how to do is tweet, but he misses the most important part of Twitter—the feedback. He blocks those he disagrees with, including legion Stephen King.

Stephen King
Trump thinks hitting a woman with a golf ball and knocking her down is funny. Myself, I think it indicates a severely fucked-up mind.
1:30 PM – Sep 17 2017

Most of the world agrees.

"I have a very good brain, and I've said a lot of things."
-- Donald Trump

Trumpzilla recognizes and respects no one or thing—other than the people/places/things he deems worthy. Then those people are praised lavishly, even if the praise comes after a bitter verbal fight with Trump himself using lies and slander to belittle his opponent. Trump employs this same tactic on his peers often telling them publically not to cross them, i.e. Chris Christie and Paul Ryan and Tom Price.

Trump said of Paul Ryan, our current Speaker of the House, at a December rally in West Allis, Wisconsin, (Ryan's)"like a fine wine. Every day that goes by I get to appreciate his genius more and more." Trump then added, "If he ever goes against me I'm not going to say that."

Heads-up, Paul Ryan, Trump has no respect for you or those you serve. You are a means to an end; you're dispensable and you're stompable!

The Trump Effect

Everything about Trump is grandiose. No matter what Trump does, he does it BIG. He tromped across the nation, took swipes at companies, government agencies, opponents. He even disrespectfully told a young college woman in his audience that she was a plant for another campaign and dismissed her question regarding where he stood on women's rights.

Trumpzilla held press conferences and rallies on the tarmac in front of his huge-ass, fuel-guzzling plane with gold bathroom fixtures, and told people "I alone can fix it."

In his Godzilla pea-sized brain he still—after 70 years—doesn't understand that his success comes from others. And in Trump's case, financial success came at the expense of others.

Power by Intimidation

Don't believe me? Need proof? Do your own research. Google "93 year old woman bullied by Trump" and learn how Trump shut off a local Scottish woman's water for years because she refused to sell her property to his $1.5 billion golf course. Trump spitefully built a wall blocking the view of the residents that refused to sell their property to him. He then sent them the bill.

Trump often shows complete contempt for those others hold in high regard, i.e. John McCain, who Trumps said was "not a war hero" because he "likes people who weren't captured."

Trump's disdain for people in general is obvious. He spends his time mocking others and inciting violence. His Twitter feed is a testament to himself. He's drunk on attention and adoration. He keeps the insults coming and coming. It's the story of David versus Trumpzilla, where the little man gets stomped on and then given an ultimatum: get on the Trumpzilla train or get stomped again!

I want to respect Donald Trump, I wish I could respect Donald Trump, but I can't. It's the Trump Paradox: how do you respect someone who has no respect for you or others?

Merriam-Webster says "respect" is:

1. a relation or reference to a particular thing or situation

2. an act of giving particular attention

3. a: high or special regard, b: the quality or state of being

No room for anyone's opinions but his own, he moves to a 3rd grader mentality. "If you don't think so then you're stupid or a fool," says Donald Trump.

Case and Point

In a series of tweets in January 2017 Trump said, "Having a good relationship with Russia is a good thing, not a bad thing. Only 'stupid' people, or fools, would think that it is bad! We have enough problems around the world without yet another one. When I am President, Russia will respect us far more than they do now and both countries will, perhaps, work together to solve some of the many great and pressing problems and issues of the WORLD!"

How can you respect a man who infers you are "stupid" or a "fool" if you don't agree with him? How can you respect a man who sees himself the savior of the world when he can't see the very people he's stomping and crapping on?

No organization is sacred to Trump. He thinks the United Nations is "just a club for people to get together, talk and have a good time. So sad!" And then Trump issued his standard warning: "As to the U.N., things will be different after Jan. 20th." Of course we all know what that means. He's going to Trumpzilla the shit out of them--and he did when he trumped into the G7 Summit and crapped all over NATO, telling them they were treating the US unfairly and they needed to pay up.

Trump's aggressive, mean-spirited business practices prove he's unworthy of my respect. It doesn't matter how much money he says he has, he can't buy respect from the 65 million Americans and countless millions of Trump-haters worldwide who know he only won this election with a little help from his rich friends and future BFF, Putin.

Gators in the Swamp

Trumpzilla's in the swamp. And he's drained it of government gators all right. He's replaced them with nuclear powered capitalists--millionaires and billionaires who have NO understanding of what it's like to work a fulltime job for less than millions of dollars a year. You insert your own number. They can't relate!!! These people wipe their rears on what most of us make in a year.

Trump thinks he is beyond scrutiny. "The President can have no conflicts," we keep hearing from his staff. But, it doesn't matter how many times he and his staff say it, misinterpreting the language to say Trump has no conflicts because he is the President is the exact opposite of what the law means: no one who has a conflict can hold the office of president. But Trump has made it quite clear he has no plans to diversify and leave his businesses. This "law and order" president is above the law of the land.

Trump proved this point when he fired Acting Attorney General Sally Yates when she questioned one of his Executive Orders on immigration that a Federal Judge had ruled as unconstitutional. He proved he thinks he's above the law when he fired Preet Bharara former U.S. Attorney for Manhattan who was investigating questionable practices by associates of Trump. And Trump proved he thinks he's above the law when he fired FBI Director James Comey.

Trumpzilla surrounds himself with "yes" men and a couple of very wily "yes" women. He knows he can overpower anyone with aggression and money. No one is beyond his reproach. Trumpzilla even attacked Pope Francis when the Pope had mentioned that true Christians build bridges not walls. Trump called Pope Francis "disgraceful" and then attacked President Obama--again.

Donald J Trump. Weak-minded. Simple. Thin-skinned. Need more proof?

Trumpzilla VS the DOJ

We know Trump has a history of suing and being sued. He attacks both people and institutions.

Trump launched a series of attacks on a federal judge, Gonzalo Curiel, saying it was "common sense" that the judge, who was born in Indiana, would be biased because of his "Mexican heritage" given the fact Trump wants to build a wall between the US and Mexico border.

There are so many things wrong with that thought: 1. Trump's disrespect of a federal judge, 2. Trump's racist assumption about the heritage of the judge based on his last name, 3. Trump's assumption the judge would be prejudice, 4. The friggin' wall! 5. The lawsuit was against Trump University for defrauding its students.

Personally attacking federal judges is common practice for Trump.

Donald J Trump
The opinion of this so-called judge, which essentially takes law-enforcement away from our country, is ridiculous and will be overturned!
8:12 AM - Feb 4 2017

But Trump has moved to an all-out assault on rule of law with the pardon of ex Phoenix sheriff, Joe Arpaio. Arpaio, accused of barbaric treatment of inmates in his "concentration camp" prison, stood in contempt of the Court and the Constitution intentionally targeting and incarcerating Hispanic people. Trump, tossing out ordinary pardoning protocol, is attempting to circumvent the Department of Justice and the law. That's an example of Trump's authoritarian attempt to thwart the Department of Justice, one of our pillars of democracy. Another pillar? The Free Press. We'll get to that in just a moment.

Trumpzilla, Monster Liar

I'm floored when people say that Trump tells it like it is. No, Trump tells it like he thinks it is. He rewrites history daily with his steady stream of lies. What does Trump lie about? Everything. He's a serial liar. He doesn't know where one lie stops and another one begins. He tosses them out like little trumptations-- snacked-sized lies to engage and enrage his audience. That's because he's not an intelligent man; he doesn't believe in quantifiable data, facts, numbers, statistics.

He believes what he wants to believe and then throws "truths" around like we can't prove they are false and that he's just making crap up.

Using the debates as a scorecard, PolitiFact found 69% of the time that Trump was speaking, what he said was mostly false, false, or down right lies. When Politico attempted to measure how many lies Trump told over the course of 4.6 hours of speeches, they found that he lied, on average, once every five minutes. Trump was even awarded PolitiFact's 2015 Lie of the Year, not for one lie in particular but because Trump is one non-stop walking, talking lie.

The PolitiFact Scorecard

True	4%
Mostly True	11%
Half True	15%
Mostly False	18%
False	33%
Pants of Fire	18%

Politifact.com

Every word out of his mouth is buttered, floured and deep-fat fried in exaggeration. TheStar.com, however, doesn't flour-coat it. According to their website, Trump "has now made 514 false claims over 203 days as president--an average of 2.5 false claims per day."

The Illusory Truth Effect

Why is this important? Because lies repeated again and again are believed. The Journal of Experimental Psychology calls it The Illusory Truth Effect. Even when people know the truth, lies presented as factual information, if repeated often enough, are believed. Even the crazy crap that Trumpzilla says!!

"There are lies, damned lies, and statistics." -- Mark Twain

Or if you're Kellyanne Conway, "alternative facts." That's right, Trumpzilla and his surrogates make up their own facts. They are attempting to rewrite history by simply denying what they don't want to acknowledge and asserting alternative facts when they have no credible facts.

Dictionary.com says facts are:

➢ Things that exist; reality; truth.
➢ Things known to exist or to have happened.
➢ Truths known by actual experience or observation; things known to be true.

Here are some big Trumpzilla lies since Inauguration Day easily proven false:

Trump False Fact

1. 3-5 million people voted illegally for Hillary Clinton, therefore Trump believes he also won the popular vote. There is absolutely no evidence that hundreds of people committed voter fraud, let alone thousands or millions. This is the lie Trump must tell himself every day to justify his acts of disregard.

Trump False Fact

2. More people watched this inauguration than any other in history. The photo evidence is clear; he had a quarter of the people that Barack Obama had in attendance in 2009. Subway fares from that day also indicate low attendance. The Women's March the next day clearly had more in attendance than his Inauguration, but Trump keeps telling people it looked like a million and a half.

Trump False Fact

3. Russia did not interfere with the election. The FBI, the CIA, and NSA have proof that Russia did interfere, and they were tipping the scale in Trump's favor. He barely squeaked out an Electoral College win, even with the help from his Russian friends.

When he didn't like the Intelligence Agency's finding on Russia hacking the election and helping him, he misdirected the activity by "asking the chairs of the House and Senate committees to investigate top secret intelligence shared with NBC prior to me seeing it."

He put out an official statement saying, "there was no effect on the election." He'll say it again and again, trying to rewrite the facts that he chooses not to believe. And yes, there will be many who believe him. But whoever is paying attention knows—and Trumpzilla knows—we will not believe this lie, no matter how often he repeats it or how he's trying to rewrite history, he's in the White House because Russia meddled in our election.

Donald J Trump
Intelligence stated very strongly there was absolutely no evidence that hacking affected the election results. Voting machines not touched!
6:56 AM - Jan 7 2017

That is a Bold-Faced Lie

The Intelligence Agencies state quite clearly Russia interfered. Nine months later we are just discovering the extent of the Russian hack uncovering evidence they tampered with voter information in 39 states.

"We assess Russian President Vladimir Putin ordered an influence campaign in 2016 aimed at the US presidential election. Russia's goals were to undermine public faith in the US democratic process, denigrate Secretary Clinton, and harm her electability and potential presidency. We further assess Putin and the Russian Government developed a clear preference for President-elect Trump," says the report *Assessing Russian Activity and Intentions in Recent US Election.* Read if for yourself at https://www.fbi.gov/news/testimony/assessing-russian-activities-and-intentions-in-recent-elections.

Even though Trump received a formal briefing from the Director of National Intelligence, the CIA and the FBI stating Russia had influenced the election, Trump continues to deny it. Any fact that Trump doesn't want to believe, he simply disregards.

Block the Vote

That leads us to one of the most important areas where we must be vigilant. Voting rights.

Not only does Trump not believe he lost the popular vote, he's put together a voter fraud task force headed by Mike Pence and Kris Kobach, the Kansas Secretary of State known for his strict stance on immigration and voter identification. Kobach is also a paid columnist at Breitbart News. Kobach is searching for those three million "illegal" voters although there is no proof they exist.

Kobach has requested detailed voter information from every state. Some states are complying, others aren't. In the meantime, Republicans are attempting to defund the Election Assistance Commission, the only federal agency dedicated to assuming a secure voting process. And Red State Republicans are making it harder for people to vote by shutting down election sights in areas dominated by non-white populations. Excessive voter i.d. laws are also being implemented.

TIME reported in a California primary some voters were prevented from voting because their registrations had been altered. Russia was suspected of the hack.

Amy Siskind writes a weekly list warning us of authoritarian rule and detailing the activity of the Trump administration. It is truly bone-chilling and a must read. Go to medium.com/@amy_siskind or Google: Amy Siskind, *The List*. Prepare to be amazed and sickened at the actions the Trump "regime" is taking. And thank you, Amy, for breaking it down so succinctly.

According to the List, Hillary's "losing margins in Michigan, Wisconsin, and Pennsylvania were less that a percentage point--a total of about 78,000 votes in all three. Had she won those states, she would be president." It was also reported that in Wisconsin, 5,000 of Trump's 27,000 vote lead were proven to be fake.

Gerrymandering by the Republicans will also help keep Trump in power. Gerrymandering is a redrawing of local district lines based on race or politics with the intent on influencing the vote. Either way, Republicans have been redrawing district lines in their favor in recent years. North Carolina has a case headed to the Supreme Court. Let's see how our newly-minted Neil Gorsuch votes. The League of Women Voters is already working to ensure a fair 2020 election by monitoring the issue. They are dedicated to "ensuring all eligible voters have the opportunity and the information to exercise their right to vote." Find the LMV info at the end of the chapter.

Voting is one of the most sacred acts in a democracy. And this is absolutely essential information to be sure Russia doesn't interfere with the election in 2018. Trump is doing all he can to stay in power--and that includes ignoring Russia's threat to our democracy. Trump must continue the ruse that Russia didn't help and he'll say anything to dissuade us. Including lying!

Former U.S. Labor Secretary Robert Reich and Director Jacob Kornbluth of Inequality Media, publishers of the documentary *Inequality for All*, put together a video explaining how Trump gets away with all the lies.

Lies--10 Steps

1. Trump lies

2. Experts contradict him saying info is false

3. Trump blasts experts and condemns media as being dishonest

4. Trump repeats lie, tweets and says in speeches saying, "many people think I'm right"

5. Main stream media starts describing lie as "disputed fact"

6. Trump repeats lie in interviews, speeches and tweets and Trump surrogates repeat and right-wing blogosphere echoes it

7. Mainstream media begins describing Trump's lie as a "controversy"

8. Polls show growing number of Americans, including most Republicans, believe Trump's lie to be true

9. Media starts describing a claim that reflects a partisan divide in America and found to be true by many

10. Public is confused and disoriented about what facts are.

"Trump wins." Reich concludes, "Be vigilant, know the truth."

"It's easier to fool people than to convince them that they have been fooled." -- Paraphrased from Mark Twain

Currently, Trump's approval level is at 35%. That means over 60% of Americans are unhappy with his performance, so far. News commentators keep asking: what will it take for people to abandon Trump? As Trump said, "I could stand in the middle of 5th Avenue and shoot somebody, and I wouldn't lose voters." For Trump loyalists, there is virtually nothing he could do to lose their support. They are willing to believe every lie that comes out of his mouth. But thanks to the Free Press, and great reporting, Americans are catching on.

"A lie, is a lie, is a lie." -- Dan Rather

Legend Dan Rather has been after his colleagues to call Trump and his people out on their egregious lies. He says Trump is not telling small, white lies, they are untruths designed to mislead. Some deliberately so and others are just timely lies to keep the attention of the media. Trumpzilla plays that game well.

Dan Rather also said, "News is the information that the powerful don't want you to know." And this is the number one reason why Donald Trump is assaulting the media, a major cornerstone of the very foundation of our democracy!!

The Press exists to run checks and balances on power gone amok. That's Trumpzilla! Trump surrogate, Scottie Nell Hughes, said on *The Diane Rehm Show.* "facts no longer exist."

What kind of world do we now live in that facts don't exist? A world where reason has been tossed out the window. Logic, numbers, statistic—how normal people process information and make informed decisions—no longer matter.

Here's some logic for you:

A = B   Trump spews hate

B = C   You support Trump

A = C   You support hate

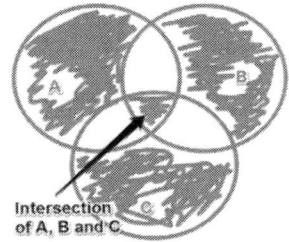

Intersection of A, B and C

This is logic. If you support Trumpzilla, you support the bullshit that comes from him. I don't want to assume this about you, but I do. THAT'S what's wrong with this election. It makes me doubt you, when you support a hater. How do we even have a respectful discourse when the measuring stick of facts is out the window? All logic is gone. I cannot have a logical conversation with a Trump fan because I don't understand their thinking.

One of my college friends and I recently had lunch. We'd spent quite a bit of time together after college: four years as fast-pitch softball wives traveling and hanging with our softball playing hubbies. We had only recently connected after fifteen years apart. We hadn't spoken much about politics and I hadn't seen her since before the election. I suspected she was a Trump fan but didn't know for sure. I was working on this book, coordinating the sketches and final rewrite when she joined me for margaritas. I was so excited, I just laid the whole book out in front of her and threw the whole thing at her before her first drink even arrived. She was a bit stunned and said, "You know I voted for Trump." Then something very logical happened. We had an intense 7-10 minute discussion

56

stating our differing views. The drinks arrived and we continued on. I can't even tell you what either of us said, but it was passionate. When I pressed on a couple of issues, i.e. birth control and climate change, she was quick to say she didn't want to fight about it. I didn't realize we were. Fighting. We were both speaking intently, but I didn't see it as a fight.

But I admit, I might have been turning into a bit of a douchebag. When I mentioned pussy grabbing, she diverted to Bill Clinton—and I was incredulous. When I mentioned Russia, she diverted to Hillary Clinton—and I realized she was a product of Fox News. We agreed we had different sources for information and there probably wasn't much we could agree on. I think we both knew it was time to abandon logic.

We needed a new way of thinking.

"Logic will get you from A to B. Imagination will take you everywhere." -- Albert Einstein

As it turns out, we didn't need imagination in that moment. Imagination usually involves making up something new and we needed an old way of thinking. We needed memories, so we went back to our roots; we talked about our folks, our families, and our farms. My college friend and I were able to reconnect on history. Politics aside.

I did a lot of thinking after our discussion. Two Iowa farm girls, with similar childhoods on the farm, the same college experience at Iowa State, both married with children, divorced and remarried, both business owners. And yet we were on different sides of the Trump issue. Each of us was a product of the news we watched and read. She was Fox News, I was MSNBC. Each of us believed our source but not the other.

With this kind of thinking, logic will never prevail; imagination must lead the way. We need creative, new solutions. And we need a different way to talk about the issues. Maybe it can start with these Trump analogies, but it has to start with something on which we both can agree. How about facts? And accurate news and reporting!! No one knows who to trust. It's hard to separate fact from fiction, but I do trust the numbers. And I trust my sources: Chris and Rachel and Lawrence and Joy and Anderson and Jake. I do not trust the President.

Donald J Trump
Anytime you see a story about me or campaign saying "sources said," DO NOT believe it. There are no sources, they are just made up lies!
2:20 AM - Sep 30 2016

Of course, unless it's the Liar-in-Chief tweeting these whoppers:

Donald J Trump
An 'extremely credible source' has called my office and told me that @BarackObama's birth certificate is a fraud.
3:23 PM - Aug 6 2012

Donald J Trump
Terrible! Just found out that Obama had my "wires tapped" in Trump Tower just before the victory. Nothing found. This is McCarthyism!
3:35 AM - Mar 4 2017

Donald J Trump
How low has President Obama gone to tapp my phones during the very sacred election process. This is Nixon/Watergate. Bad (or sick) guy!
5:02 AM - Mar 4 2017

Our President drops lies like stink bombs in an elevator. And he repeats them again and again. But let's give FDR the last word on this:

"We Americans begin to know the difference between the truth in the one side and the falsehood on the other, no matter how often the falsehood is iterated and reiterated. Repetition does not transform a lie into the truth." -- Franklin Delano Roosevelt

Trumpzilla Destroys the Press

Donald J Trump
Dishonest media says Mexico won't be paying for the wall if they pay a little later so the wall can be built more quickly. Media is fake!
10:05 PM - Jan 8 2017

The way Donald Trump talks to and vilifies the media is down-right scary. The only one he wants to have free speech is himself. He wants to laxen libel laws, so he can sue the Press and put them in jail! Apparently, he discussed this with James Comey before he fired him. But what does he think now?

Steve Bannon, the other belching, shitting T-Rex in the White House who has since rejoined the alt-right hounds at Breitbart News, says the media "is the opposition." He should know, he IS the media and Trump and Bannon used "fake news" as a campaign strategy putting out fake propaganda on Hillary for years. Trumpzilla has declared war on the media calling them "the enemy of the American people," calling them "bad people" and questioning their loyalty to the country.

Donald J Trump
The FAKE NEWS media (failing @nytimes, @NBCNews, @ABC, @CBS, @CNN) is not my enemy, it is the enemy of the American People!
2:48 PM - Feb 17 2017

Of course, Trump hates the Media. They tell the truth. And it's the Media that's keeping the country safe from Trump right now. If the Media wasn't here to report can you imagine the devastation, the "carnage" to use Trump's word, that he would release on the people? But I would be remiss if I didn't discuss "fake news" because there has been a lot of it. As consumers of news we must be diligent.

Gee Whiz

Trump shut CNN out from a White House briefing because he didn't like the coverage of a story leaked (pun intended) by the British Intelligence Agency. The story suggests there are tapes of Trump in Russia with prostitutes peeing, or so the rhetoric goes. Fake news? I don't know. It wasn't that far-fetched that it was totally unbelievable, but it hinted at a twisted part of Trump, and Trump didn't like that.

If you don't know what I'm referring to, let Stephen Colbert explain it to you. In his opening monologue January 11, 2017, he brilliantly cut right through to the heart of the matter—Trump's love affair with Putin—while whizzing off a few zingers. Or should I say zinged off a few whizzers. Google it and watch Stephen Colbert let a little karma loose on Trump.

The pee-tape dossier is getting a lot of press, and Trumpzilla is doing his best to blow that fire in another direction. We're just now finding out what was in the Dossier that MI6, our British ally, put together when he discovered the Trump campaign was talking with Russia.

Instead, Trump suggests we investigate Hillary over what he calls a pay-to-play deal involving Russia, Uranium, and $140 million donated to the Clinton Foundation—seven years ago when she was Secretary of State. All of the fact-checking sites have debunked that lie. The story originated with a book by one of the Brietbart reporters, an online, right-wing, hate spewing site flagged by the Southern Poverty Law Center as cultivating and spreading hate.

And now, Hillary paid for the Dossier. It's all fake news any way. Right?

But Trumpzilla didn't appreciate the news coming out of Russia about him. THAT he denounced while still attributing other fake stories about Hillary as real.

Trump has also banned *The New York Times* and the *Huffington Post* from attending White House briefings. Apparently, they are fake news as well.

Stomp and Brag Mentality

Donald J Trump: January 2017
Wow, the ratings are in and Arnold Schwarzenegger got "swamped" (or destroyed) by comparison to the rating machine, DJT. So much for...
7:34 AM - Jan 6 2017

Donald J Trump
...being a movie star-and that was season 1 compared to season 14. Now compare him to my season 1. But who cares, he supported Kasich & Hillary.
7:42 AM - Jan 6 2017

Trump is trashing the show he's Executive Producing?! He'll continue to trash it and the country because he lives in a garbage scow of his own making. His head is full of trash, stinkin' thinkin'.

I bet the pastors loved Trump at the National Day of Prayer breakfast asking them to pray for better ratings for Celebrity Apprentice. Really Donald? People are dying all over the world, children are starving, and you want us to pray for ratings for your show? Your brain is the size of a pea. And even that eclipses your heart. What a Douchebag.

Donald J Trump
Sorry losers and haters but my I.Q. is one of the highest – and you all know it! Please don't feel so stupid or insecure, it's not your fault.
8:37 PM - May 8 2013

Or this one:

Donald J Trump
Every time I speak of the haters and losers I do so with great love and affection. They cannot help the fact they were born fucked up!
7:21 PM - Sep 28 2014

Trumpzilla Destroys the United States

One of Trump's executive orders signed in his first two weeks says that for every regulation that's added, two regulations have to go. Again, no assessment of why the regulation was there in the first place, just the illogical premise that all regulation is bad for business. Basically, Trump is rolling back everything Obama did, good or bad, it doesn't matter. And one of the areas where Trump is doing his greatest damage is to the environment.

Mother Earth Prepare to Be Fracked

The scariest, most destructive force on the planet is Donald Trump. Like Godzilla loose in New York City, Trump will unleash irrevocable harm on Mother Earth.

Trump calls global warming a "hoax" invented by "the Chinese in order to make U.S. manufacturing non-competitive." It was a sad, dark day for America when Trump pulled out of the Paris Climate Accord. Instead of America leading the Clean Energy/Clean Jobs Initiative, we'll be the ones leading the assault on the natural resources of the planet. Coal mining, oil drilling, fracking; Mother Earth, prepare to be assaulted.

Trump has called the Environmental Protection Agency a "disgrace." After nine months in office, 85% of top science jobs in Trump's executive branch remain open, no nominees in sight. I would much rather have no one in those positions than have Scott Pruitt as the head of the Environmental Protection Agency, the EPA. The *New York Times* reported Pruitt, working with lobbyists, not scientists, has moved to undo, delay, or block 30 environmental rules--more than any other administration in the agency's 47 years in operation.

After thirty years of serving at the EPA, Elizabeth Sutherland left saying this, "The environmental field is suffering from the temporary triumph of myth over truth." What a nice way of saying Trump's policies will destroy the earth.

On day one, the Trump Administration wiped the words "climate change" from the White House website and their vocabulary, as if ignoring it will make it go away. They are also deleting scientific data by government agencies. "A bloodbath" is how one scientist described it. Trump has frozen all EPA grants and forbidden EPA personnel from talking to reporters or engage on social media.

Trump has approved federal lands to be leased to the highest bidder, and green-lighted the pipelines—with total indifference to the Standing Rock Sioux and the people who might be hurt.

Ryan Zinke, Trump's Secretary of the Interior has suggested reducing Bears Ears National Monument in Utah by 88%. The 1.35 million acres preserved under the Antiquities Act is home to more than 100,000 sacred sites belonging to the Navajo, Hopi, Uintah and Ouray Ute, Ute Mountain Ute and Zuni. Trump plans to open it up for logging, grazing, and commercial use. Zinke is currently reviewing 27 national monuments.

Trump is out of touch with the environment and reality. But hey, anything to undo something President Obama put in place.

Donald J Trump
Remember, new "environment friendly" light bulbs can cause cancer. Be careful—the idiots who came up with this stuff don't care.
10:39 AM - Oct 17 2012

Donald J Trump
Wind turbines are not only killing millions of birds, they are killing the finances & environment of many countries and communities.
10:32 AM - Oct 17 2012

Trump wasn't concerned about the birds, he was concerned about a wind farm going in next to his Scotland golf course.

The question in my mind is not "if" Donald Trump is going to destroy the planet, it's "how" Donald Trump is going to destroy the planet. He could do it quickly, with the push of a button (God bless us all) or slowly by letting capitalists rape the land of her natural resources. If Trumpzilla doesn't have a real "people" moment, and realize there are actual people he's trouncing on, then it's just a matter of time. Go ahead, "imagine the horror," I believe is the line Steve Buscemi exclaims in the movie Armageddon as the meteor is hurtling toward earth. I can't remember. I'll have to watch it again. And fantasize Bruce Willis is a Democrat. And speaking of heroes in space...

Protests in Space

The Autonomous Space Agency Network, a Phoenix-based collective of artists, scientists, engineers, students and one "IRL rocket-scientist," launched the first Trump protest in space. They launched a weather balloon to @ 90,000 ft. Aphrodite 1 consisted of a gps sensor, a camera, and a message for Trump on a print-out of a tweet. They launched it 56 years to the day after Russian cosmonaut Yuri Gagarin became the first human in space and the week of Climate Change protests.

ASAN
@realdonaldtrump
LOOK AT THAT, YOU SON OF A BITCH!
2:06 PM - 12 Apr 17

They were quoting Apollo 14 astronaut Edgar Mitchell, the 6th person to walk on the moon. He said about viewing Earth from space:

"You develop an instant global consciousness, a people orientation, an intense dissatisfaction with the state of the world, and a compulsion to do something about it. From out there on the moon, international politics look so petty. You want to grab a politician by the scruff of the neck and drag him a quarter of a

63

million miles out and say, 'Look at that, you son of a bitch.'" -- Edgar Mitchell (1930-2016)

Trump called to congratulate NASA astronaut Peggy Whitson on setting the record for most cumulative days in space: 534 days. He stated his desire to get to Mars and wants to speed up the timeline, "at worst, during my second term." Jesus, Mary and Joseph, just the thought of a second term of Trump turns my bowels to liquid. The earth might not survive eight years of Trump. He signed a bill in March 2017 that increases NASA's budget to $19.5 billion to explicitly get a human-manned flight to Mars. But, he's also gutting the Environmental Protection Agency and planning cuts to Earth Science programs that study solar winds and other climate change issues. He's suggesting complete elimination—absolutely nothing—nada—zero to NASA's education program.

We'd better shoot for Mars since Trump plans on destroying Earth.

Death to Rebirth

Make no mistake, Trumpzilla is destroying sacred institutions, but the American people will not let him destroy Democracy. Trumpzilla is not above the law and he's not above the laws of nature. He may have four years to wreak havoc, but at the end of the movie Godzilla is always defeated.

It'll all be okay in the end. If it's not okay, it's not the end.

According to Japanese movie producer Shogo Tomiyama in reference to his creation, Godzilla, "He totally destroys everything and then there is a rebirth."

I have full confidence; once Trumpzilla is defeated, we the people, will be reborn.

What Can You Do?

1. Watch the movie Godzilla. Matthew Broderick, with the help of our Military and a Frenchman, Jean Reno, topple Godzilla and save New York City
2. Subscribe to your favorite newspapers: *Washington Post, Huffington Post, New York Times*. Put your money where their mouth is
3. Join the *Committee to Protect Journalists* and fight for a free press worldwide
4. Fight for truthful journalism, visit Propublica.org

5. Watch CNN, MSNBC, and even Fox News. Yes, all of them, so you can ferret out the facts for yourself, considering the different political spin

6. Read and donate to *The Guardian*, a neutral place for news, theguardian.com

7. Watch Velshi and Ruhle's segment "For Facts Sake" on MSNBC

8. Read Amy Siskind's, *The List* at medium.com/@amy_siskind

9. Check out the website WhatTheFuckJustHappendToday.com

10. Operation 45 is working to reveal the lies behind Trump, our 45th President

11. Go to TheStar.com for a list of Trump lies

12. Use Politifact.com

13. Support the international environmental organization Green Peace

14. Go to 350.org and join a grassroots climate movement

15. Support the Science Legal Defense Fund. They fight for the rights of scientists to continue research

Trumpzilla

It'll all be ok in the end.
If it's not okay,
It's not the end.

Trumpzilla

Trumpzilla

DarthTrump

3. DarthTrump:The Force Be Damned!

A long time ago in a galaxy far, far away...

A growing band of rebel forces attempt to free Lady Liberty from the clutches of evil DarthTrump and the Orange Empire, a madman and his crew of capitalists bent on destroying Democracy and America.

At stake is the very sovereignty of the United States and its people. Using propaganda, subterfuge and Death Star Twitter technology, DarthTrump and cronies are hiding and distorting truths as they move to an authoritarian regime where the pursuit of money supersedes human rights and the wellbeing of the planet. DarthTrump, with support from the Orange Empire and other galactic foes, uses violent rhetoric against the Press, the Intelligence Agencies, and the Judicial system while they work to deconstruct America's three-branch governing system of democracy.

Individual rights, such as the right to information, peacefully assemble and protest, and to vote--the very core of democracy--are under attack. DarthTrump is waging an all-out assault on immigrants, Muslims, African-Americans, the physically challenged, the LGBTQ community, women, the poor, and anyone DarthTrump labels as a "hater" or "loser."

The rebels, #TheResistance, oppose government restructuring at the expense of human beings and are standing up for Lady Liberty, her people, and those that she beckons yearning to breathe free. There are many, many rebel forces, #LoveArmy, #WomensMarch, and #SisterGiant top a long list. All seek peaceful, non-violent resolution. Their greatest asset is information and they work tirelessly daily to deliver facts to the people.

Using the positive forces of optimism, love, and equality for all, the rebels fight to expose DarthTrump's darkside and lies. Will the light prevail? Or will the Orange Empire, DarthTrump, and dark times of excessive greed and privatization at the expense of the citizens descend on America? The conflict between light and dark wages on.

Star Wars, ahhh, the epic battle of good and evil. Who knew in this century we'd each be called to pick a side?

In a Reality of Duality, You Must Choose

These are strange times. The battle of good versus evil is playing out in front of us, under scrutiny of the Press and the Judicial System, thank goodness. DarthTrump's alternative facts are at the core of his vocal war.

DarthTrump campaigned as the bad guy corporate mogul who could ride in and beat gov'ment--Republicans and Democrats alike. He began by taking on each Republican candidate, then the Republican party until he'd bullied and bought them out. He moved on to Hillary, labeled her evil and, with help from his minions, ploughed right through.

Some people openly cheered and supported Trump. They saw his actions as heroic; they voted to drain the swamp. They like his approach to immigration and climate change. They welcome his divisive rhetoric and don't much care what others think. They'll bend themselves backwards and in knots to justify Trump's actions.

They think I'm evil. Me? I think they are.

These are the two opposing sides of The Force, in plain sight for us to see. Both sides, good and evil, existing for opposite causes.

How do we break through the duplicity, from good to evil, from dark to light or light to dark? How? By looking at them both, together in analysis. Acknowledging how we talk to each other is key to understanding and settling our differences. By assuming we have more in common than we do different and pledge to discover those differences as opposed to extorting the extremes. Yes, there will always be differences in policy, but we cannot become complacent in vocalizing what's different between us--and what's the same!

But to do that, you have to pick a side. "Staying neutral" is doing nothing by default.

Many of us choose not to get involved or tell ourselves we're too busy to get involved. Many of us don't really about government issues until political issues directly affect us: i.e. higher taxes when you've been promised a tax cut. The point is: tet informed and get involved. Or not.

"Do, or do not, there is no try." -- Yoda

This statement is complex and at the heart of what each of us determines is right or wrong.

Here's a challenge for you: Define your life philosophy in a word or a phrase: Live and let live, I did it my way, Hakuna matata.

Just one word or phrase. Seriously, pause and do this.

When asked, most of us have the Wookie in the headlights look. Answering the question is complex enough--putting thoughts and feelings to words; but the answer itself is buried in perceptions of reality and our understanding of it. To each his own. Who determines what's good or bad, good or evil? Each of us does.

Is This Dress Black or White?

Remember the dress meme popular in 2015? Cecilia Bleasdale, Mother of the-Bride-to-be, sent a photo of her wedding-day dress to her daughter. The two couldn't agree on the color of the dress in the photo so one of them posted it to Facebook and their friends weighed-in.

The question itself was simple, but the dichotomy of the replies was clear. Some people saw the horizontal striped pattern as white and gold; others saw blue and black.

The Neuroscientists went crazy with an opportunity to study the effects of perception on color. In layman's terms, it strengthened the hypothesis that we can all look at the same photo but see different things. In this case, a very clear distinction in color.

I've often thought the same of Republicans and Democrats. Some see the dress as black; others see it as white. Some people are Republicans, some are Democrats--and we certainly see things differently, as different as white and gold is to blue and black. Not even close.

We're Looking at the Same Thing!

Who am I to label anyone as good or evil. I'm not a big fan of black or white thinking in general, but Congress is now passing a number of bills that I believe will hurt the people of the U.S. I cannot remain silent.

I see all people who stand-up for those being persecuted as good guys, on the lightside. And it's okay if you look at me and think I'm evil, in cahoots with the darkside, we're both entitled to our opinion. But I will not hide my voice in the dark as Trump deconstructs the government of the people. I will resist. With a little help from my Jedi friends.

"Hard to see the darkside is." -- Yoda

Hard to see the darkside is because it deliberately hides itself. And sometimes it hides itself out in the open. Donald Trump, DarthTrump, has much to hide, taxes and ties to Russia for starters.

DarthTaxEvader

DarthTrump broke with forty years of tradition and refused to release his tax returns. That makes Trump DarthTaxEvader. He's bragged that he pays as little tax as possible, boasted he has worked the system, claimed over a $900 million loss in the one tax document journalists were able to expose, and Trump continues to refuse to release his tax returns. He claims people don't care. That he got elected without releasing them and only the "dishonest media" and "fake news" people are interested.

But he's wrong and he's hiding in the dark, refusing to release the information, as per his strategy: keep people in the dark so they can't see what he's doing. To anyone who challenges him, DarthTrump becomes defiant or he will "deny, distract, distort, deflect" says the Daily Kos. He continues to point his finger at his arch nemesis Barack Obama or his personal tantrum-target Hillary Clinton. It's all deflection.

Trump doesn't dare release his taxes because they'll provide the financial proof that he's in DarthPutin's pocket. That's one more thing he's hiding, his relationship with Putin, but his connection to Russia he's trying to hide in broad daylight!

The Darkside in Broad Daylight

DarthTrump has been clear in his desire to work with Russia and Russian President Vladimir Putin. DarthTrump has never talked smack about Putin. Putin is about the only person Trump has never belittled with his "very best words." DarthTrump has pursued a relationship with Putin prior to his running for president, throughout his entire campaign, and now in the White House. Trump is aligning himself--and the United States--with Russia to the detriment of Americans and our allies around the world.

Trump entertained fellow Russian comrades Foreign Minister Sergei Lavrov and Ambassador to the U.S. Sergey Kislyak in the White House! He swapped a little covert info for God-knows-what as he passed on confidential intel from his own intelligence agencies he's so fond of disparaging.

As information continues to leak about DarthTrump's and DarthTrump Jr.'s ties to Russia during the campaign, Trump and surrogates are jumping right over the term "collusion" and spinning the narrative to *so what, collusion is not a crime.*

The darkside has been hiding in our faces all along. And it has got its hooks deep in this one, DarthTrump Jr.

Trump Jr. is an idiot for sure, bless his heart. He's sliding on the swords edge of what's legal and what's moral. What did he willingly know and do to secure information from the Russian government and use it to influence the election?

There is no distinction between DarthTrump Jr. and Sr.; what one knows the other knows. They've been quite clear on that. As for who's in charge? It's Sr. because he says so.

Donald J. Trump
I call my own shots, largely based on an accumulation of data, and everyone knows it. Some FAKE NEWS media, in order to marginalize, lies!
5:07 AM - Feb 6 2017

DarthTrump knew of DarthPutin and his attempt to help him win the election. So did Jr., so did comrades Kushner, Manaford, Bannon and the list goes on.

Is it a crime that the Kremlin wanted Trump to win? No. Was there money or information that exchanged hands in the desire? If so, yes, DarthTrump needs to be relieved of his post. Winning the election through cheating is not winning, but that's what money will buy you.

Yes, I am skeptical. I've gazed into the abyss of the darkside knowing it'd be easier just to shut up, keep my head low, and keep working "for the man." But in this case the man is Donald J Trump and he seeks to blend his family businesses with government money, like an authoritarian regime.

He's invited Putin to the White House. Gasp! Please tell me you still have anger in you so you can stand up and speak?! Hard to see the darkside is when it's hiding blatantly in your face.

See Something Say Something

We must stand up and point. In this case, the American people have pointed at former FBI Director Robert Swan Mueller III.

"The force is strong in this one." -- DarthVader

I trust Jedi Knight Bob Mueller, former head of the FBI and now Special Counsel on the Russian investigation, to shed light on the dark and uncover the truth about Russia, collusion, and money-laundering. It's been clear to me all along. It was clear Trump answered to Russia and now that DarthTrump Jr has released the email that proves he intended to engage with the Russian government to get dirt on Hillary, it proves it.

In the meantime, we must resist against DarthTrump's direct efforts to hide in the dark. Trump has stopped access to the White House visitor log, and don't bother to call, there's no longer a person answering the White House comment line switchboard. If you were worried about lobbyists and private companies buying government favor before Trump's arrival? Now it's common practice. Lobbyists and big business are now in charge. For more on that, see Chapter 7, Scut Trump.

As reported by Propublica in August 2017, Trump's "administration has installed more than 1,000 people through political appointments at every major federal agency, handing over control of the government's day-to-day operations to industry insiders and loyalists to an unprecedented degree. Among the latest Trump administration appointees is a lobbyist who until March worked for a leading hepatitis C drugmaker that priced its treatment at $1,000 a pill and is now leading a White House working group setting drug pricing policies. The list includes the new head of the government's offshore oil drilling safety and enforcement agency, who previously sat on the board of Sunoco Logistics and who told an industry conference earlier this month that Deepwater drilling should ramp up."

Know that DarthTrump is only motivated by the almighty dollar. DarthTrump's mission is to combine private and government dollars and move America into a more authoritarian state, like that of his mentor and new BFF, DarthPutin. So far the Republican comrades have enlisted to support that cause.

Luke to Yoda: "Is the darkside stronger?"
Yoda to Luke: "No, no, no. Quicker, easier, more seductive."

Currently rumors are flying that Trump wants to privatize the Afghanistan war. What could possibly go wrong? All-out war-for-profit?! Trump has asked more than once why we didn't take the oil while in Iraq. Profit is motive and the motive is strong, seductive, and quick and easy for those with no skin in the game, meaning DarthTrump has no immediate family members that serve in the military.

I fear for what that means for our children. The military should be a peacekeeping, country-building, world-supporting, democracy-sharing battalion of men, women--and transgender people--in service to citizens; NOT young men, women--and those yet to decide--forced into dodging bullets and bombs making minimum wage while capitalists horde income for their investors off the backs, the arms, the legs, the very sanity and lives of our enlisted.

DraftEvader

Do you think DarthTrump's children will be on the front line dodging bullets? Or will they take after good ol' five-time draft dodgin' dad, DraftEvader? Trump is relishing in his role as Commander-in-chief, referring to "his generals" and "his military." That's authoritarian thinking. The military belongs to the people of the United States of America, not to DarthTrump.

In a blatant push to the darkside, DarthTrump is purging information from the White House website and forbidding communication from federal agencies. On the very day Trump was sworn in, all mention of climate change, civil rights, and LGBTQ issues were deleted from the White House website.

DarthTrump, furious with the National Parks Department for tweeting out a photo he didn't like, banned the Department of Interior, of which they are a part, from Twitter. The tweet that made Trump choke showed the small attendance at his inauguration ceremony as opposed to the much larger crowd attending Obama's. DarthTrump is adamant more people attended his event and continues to reimagine a reality that didn't happen. And it's not the first time DarthTrump has reimagined what really happened. He uses this tactic to stoke fear.

"Fear is the path to the darkside. Fear leads to anger. Anger leads to hate. Hate leads to suffering." -- Yoda

To this day Trump claims "thousands and thousands of people" took to the streets of Jersey City, New Jersey to celebrate the day the World Trade Center Towers and our very democracy were attacked. Trump believes he saw Arabs cheering, he's contorted and reimagined what really happened; he's declared it as fact, and continues to state his perception as truth. There is no proof that Arab-Americans, aka Muslims, took to the streets to celebrate, but DarthTrump doesn't need facts, doesn't operate on facts--the darkside doesn't! The darkside uses hate speech and blames and shames others without proof. The darkside labels and sows doubt. If Trump can convince you he saw it, can sell you that he saw it, he's taken your fear and your rage and your pain and pointed it to one group of people--Muslims. He's leading you to the darkside, without any proof other than what he thinks he saw.

Respect to 9/11

We now know, of the 19 hijackers who deliberately and willfully committed the attacks on September 11, 2001: 15 were from Saudi Arabia, 2 from United Arab Emirates, 1 from Egypt, and 1 from Lebanon. That's 15 from Saudi Arabia.

Yet these countries are not the ones targeted by DarthTrump and the Outlandish Empire with their immigrant and refugee travel ban! Why? Because the Orange Empire has financial ties to Saudi Arabia, United Arab Emirates and Egypt! The darkside is fueled by money, by oil.

Everyone keeps talking about Russia, Russia, Russia with good reason; but, the very first place Trump traveled to pay homage was to the Middle East to the King of Saudi Arabia and the President of Egypt.

Of the six countries currently in Trump's travel ban, Iran, Somalia, Sudan, Yemen, Syria and Libya? Trump has no business ties to them. Coinkidink? I think not.

DarthTrump gives preference to those he does business with. Trump is currently facing three emoluments clause lawsuits alleging he's making beaucoup bucks from his presidency. Trump is rumored to operate over 500 businesses in 25 countries. Rebel forces are chasing down the money trail as I write, as you read this.

DarthTrump has documented business in Russia and he hasn't been shy about chasing Putin. DarthTrump is courting money and oil. And it's now come out that Trump had been talking Trump Tower Moscow with the Russians throughout his campaign. No wonder Trump won't say one bad word about Putin. He doesn't want to piss off his business partner.

But it's even darker than that and scarier than that--there are huge world issues that need to be solved. These real-world issues concern people, not just millions but billions of people.

What happens when our fear is turned against each other, neighbor against neighbor, communities targeted and watched by law enforcement, people labeled as good or bad, worthy or not. Trump doesn't trust people in general and he's turned that mistrust into an unhealthy fear of others. The darkside wants you to fear others. And fear the future.

Trump's labeled Muslims as terrorists and he refuses to acknowledge that Islam, like Christianity, preaches peace. Yes, extremists from both Islam and Christianity have taken lives, but Trump has now declared himself a Christian. In Trump's small me-versus-you, us-versus-them mentality, that means Muslims are "bad" and to be feared. Who wins when we look at each other with fear and suspicion? No one. We all lose.

Fear Leads to Anger; Anger Leads to Hate

And hate leads to hate crimes, most recently against Muslims, Jews, and the transgender communities. The Anti-Defamation League reported anti-Semitic incidents in the U.S. rose by 86% in the first three month of 2017, over the same period last year. DarthTrump's White Nationalist rhetoric at work.

Anti-Muslim hate crime incidents rose dramatically in 2015 and then increased a further 44 percent in 2016, going from 180 incidents in 2015 to 260 in 2016, so says researchers at California State University.

White Nationalism is on the rise. DarthTrump made it clear after peaceful protester Heather Heyer was run-down by a White Supremacist in Charlottesville, Virginia that he thought violence on "many sides" was to blame. Trump's failure to call out hate, racism, and violence gives power to the darkside. Heather was a 32 year old paralegal who fought for people's rights. She was at a rally standing up to hatred with a message of peace and justice. As Heather's Mom said, "You didn't shut her up, you just magnified her." #RIPHeatherHeyer

DarthTrump has built his empire on lies and half-truths designed to get you to enlist. His focus is fear mongering, blaming, and the denigration of others. He began his entire political campaign descending from Trump Tower to accuse Mexican immigrants of being rapists and murderers; he blamed them for taking American jobs and "killing our economy." He calls them "bad hombres."

He's promised to build a "great big beautiful wall" on the US-Mexico border. To keep us all safe, Trump says. He has vilified an entire country. He doesn't see the individual people.

DarthTrump's declared himself the "Law-and-Order" president. He and fellow-racist Attorney General Jefferson Beauregard Sessions, Yoda's darkside albino twin, are pushing for private, for-profit prison reform demanding increase in occupant capacity with longer, harsher jail sentences for all! This is literally encouraging companies to make a profit on human suffering!!

Bed space and quotas have been increased. Yes, you read that right, Immigration Customs Enforcement, ICE, has quotas regarding funding--the more bodies the more bucks! That's the darkside. The Orange Empire monetizing human trafficking! For-profit prisons will argue they provide a better, safer experience for inmates; that's not what the data proves. You'd better not do something wrong, or if you do you'd better have enough money to buy your way out of trouble.

A report by Grassroots Leadership states the top two for profit prisons, Corrections Corporation of America (CCA) and GEO Group "have profited handsomely" from government quotas and dollars. Their investors get rich; their inmates go hungry with inadequate care. *The Consumerist* reports that, thanks to DarthTrump and Jeff Sessions, Corrections Corporation of America, now operating as CoreCivic, and GEO stock shares are trading at a five year high.

GEO is being investigated for contributing $225,000 to a DarthTrump supporting Super PAC in violation of federal law. Sometimes the darkside hides in plain sight.

Making money from someone's suffering is wrong. And I rarely use the word wrong, but Trump sees people as profit centers. Fill those beds! ICE's quota is now 50,000 detainees. If that doesn't make you sick, check your humanity meter; it's off.

Go straight to Youtube, watch and listen to Brett Dennen, *Ain't No Reason*.

"Prison walls still standing tall, some things never change at all. Keep on building prisons, gonna fill them all. Keep on building bombs, gonna drop them all." And the answer to all of that is Love.

PEOPLE People!

Trump's both empowered and funded ICE's efforts to deport all 11 million immigrants regardless of their situation for being in the United States. According to Amy Siskind's List, ICE arrests were up 33% in the first 2 months of DarthTrump's reign, including a doubling of non-criminal arrests. Data shows 41,000 arrests in Trump's first 100 days, a 38% increase over the previous years.

ICE's Acting Director Thomas Homan has said, "If you're in this country illegally and you committed a crime by entering this country, you should be uncomfortable. ... You should look over your shoulder, and you need to be worried."

I understand that Acting Director Thomas Homan is "doing his job," but can't he do it with a sense of compassion? He and his 10,000 new agents are coming to destroy lives. Does he have to use fear? And does Trump have to go after the DREAMers?!

Juan Manuel Montes, a 23-year-old living in the U.S. since the age of 9, was the first DREAMer deported by Trump. How much money is being made by the for-profit prisons as Juan is detained before deportation. And where will Juan go? Will he be on his own as he's kicked out of the U.S. and forced to return to a country totally foreign to him? He's the same age as my kids. He needs his Mom! Apparently, she's been detained as well.

In Ossining, New York, ICE agents took 19-year-old Diego Macancela into custody on the day of his Senior prom, just weeks before his graduation. Where in the world is Diego? Is he still in an ICE prison or has he cruelly been sent back to Ecuador?

When Lizandro Claros, a registered DREAMer reported in a courtesy call to ICE that he'd obtained a soccer scholarship for college and he'd be moving in the fall, ICE asked he and his 22-year-old brother to come in and they were detained; they are slated for deportation back to El Salvador.

Who would support that? The Outlandish Empire and members such as Iowa Republican congressman, Steve King, that's who. King celebrated Montes' deportation by tweeting a photo of a frosty beer mug with the words, "First non-valedictorian DREAMer deported. Border Patrol, this one's for you."

Iowa needs to deport Steve King; he certainly doesn't represent the friendly, nurturing Iowa family values I grew up with. My siblings, still living in Iowa, agree. Iowa's farm industry has been strengthened with immigrant labor. DarthTrump, with no understanding of farming and its impact on trade and the economy, is making decisions that impact the state, that impact real people and their livelihood.

Deporting people is evil. And I'm not talking about the criminals. We can all agree, people convicted of crimes should go. I'm talking about the immigrants, the ones Lady Liberty beckoned. The ones who fought to get to America to find a better life; the ones who want to serve, contribute and strengthen people and communities. Why can't they stay? There's plenty of acreage; we have the room and we have the ingenuity to house, clothe, and feed them until they can support themselves. That's good business, but it's only good business for Trump if it puts money in his pockets.

Deporting people--without giving them a path to citizenship is an assault on human rights. Why? Why can there not be a path to citizenship?

Why is DarthTrump deporting our DREAMers? This, to me, is the most evil, cruelest act he's taken. DREAMers refer to the children who were brought to the U.S. by their parents. They've grown up here, gone to school here, have no other country to call home. They are U.S citizens in heart and mind but lack the appropriate "documentation." The DRE   AM Act (Development, Relief, and Education for Alien Minors) was created by President Obama when Congress failed to act on a resolution to address the problem. Paul Ryan wouldn't even put it to a vote.

Trump has just decided DREAMers "must go, they gotta go," he's said. He's given Congress six months to figure it out and if they don't, he'll "revisit" it. What kind of cruel dictator does that to 800,000 kids?! And in the meantime, DREAMers are being deported when they make updates as required, go get marriage licenses, and as they go to school and work and about their daily business.

#DefendDACA

These "Childhood Arrivals" are our classmates, our neighbors, and our friends. It's called Deferred Action for Childhood Arrivals, DACA. Do or do not; either stand with them or don't. There is no "try." But not standing for them is standing against them. We cannot become complicit. Especially since DarthTrump plans to cut immigration in half over the next decade. #Resist #Persist #Insist #Enlist

"The Force can have a strong effect on the weak-minded."
-- Obi-Wan Kenobi

Weak-mindedness and short-sightedness are both part of the darkside, so are meanness and spite. Steve King, Thomas Homan of Immigration and Customs Enforcement, ICE, DarthTrump: heartless capitalists and fear mongers immersed in the darkside. Three intergalactic Douchebags.

And even as I declare these three people intergalactic douches, I have to ask myself, what are their motivations? What do they have to gain? Maybe they're not weak-minded as much as they are close-minded. Maybe they don't understand there's a better way to work with our undocumented immigrants.

Isn't it our job, #TheResistance, to stand up and educate and inform; there's a better way to treat people. Isn't this why this persecution is happening? So we, as a people stand-up and share our opinions? That you, I, me, we start defining what we will or will not tolerate? And eventually, do? Can't we honor our lives and cherish our neighbors, working together for the safety of all of us?

If we remove the label that the darkside is BAD and the lightside is GOOD and look at them more as opposites that reveal some very large rifts in thinking, doesn't that create the space and place for dialogue?

I am not evil because I think differently than you. You are not evil because you think differently than me. Can we come together? Can't we talk this out? DarthTrump says he's the best negotiator, then let's see him negotiate. Trump continually says "all options are on the table" but then closes off dialogue, i.e. North Korea!

Donald J Trump
The U.S. has been talking to North Korea, and paying them extortion money, for 25 years. Talking is not the answer!
6:47 AM - Aug 30 2017

And then there is the terrifying tweet:

Donald J Trump
...Save your energy Rex, we'll do what has to be done!
9:31 AM - Oct 1 2017

When the alternative is NUCLEAR WAR, TALKING IS ALWAYS THE ANSWER! For all DarthTrump's big talk on being a "negotiator," he's missing the prime element: DIALOGUE!

"We all must learn the ways of the Force." -- Obi-Wan Kenobi

"The Force," explains Obi-Wan to Luke Skywalker in Star Wars: A New Hope, "is an energy field created by all living things that surrounds us, penetrates us and binds the Galaxy together." It's how we're all connected. I call that the Universe. Some might interpret that as God.

The Force contains the dichotomies of black and white, right and wrong, good and evil, and all degrees in between. Tapping into The Force allows each of us to exercise our own power, to be one small part in a much bigger whole.

Voting is how we #resist DarthTrump and the Orange Empire. We tap into the energy of something much bigger than just one person, we tap into the universal whole, we cast our vote for what we perceive is either good or evil.

That's how we #resist; that's how we #rediscover America and what it could be when we take the time to define what and who we stand for. And one thing I know for sure is I stand with the DREAMers and stand for a TRUCE with North Korea!

"You must unlearn what you have learned." -- Yoda

Using Twitter Death Star technology, DarthTrump has used violent rhetoric against his opponents and those he thinks have slighted him. Trump's Jedi mind tricks contain lies and half-truths, in 140 characters or less. I'm truly fearful the new 280 character count will help Trump destroy the world. @biz @jack @policy--delete his account!

Twitter is the tool that is doing DarthTrump as much damage as good. It's his direct line to the people and a direct reflection of his psychosis. The majority of us aren't stupid enough or impulsive enough to tweet out our 3 a.m. delusions. DarthTrump is. He's fully immersed, not able to step back and see a bigger picture.

An ABC/Washington Post poll shows 67% of Americans disapprove of Trump using Twitter; 68% say his tweets are inappropriate; 50% said his tweets are dangerous.

He continues to have his own best interests at heart and refuses to listen to the American people he so casually tweets at. He doesn't use Twitter for the Death Star tool it truly is. Trump spends very little time interacting with others preferring to retweet tasteless memes and self-aggrandizing tweets from the Trumpets.

If he truly wanted to use the Twitter tool, he might ask a few questions, ones designed to get feedback on policy and agenda. It's called "crowd sourcing" and one of the most beautiful and powerful things about social media--instant feedback--if you are brave enough to hear it.

If Trump was isolated before in his golden Trump Tower, he is even more so as he jets around on Air Force One, "what a dump," the equivalent of flying coach compared to Trump1, Trump's personal plane. Trump didn't actually call Air Force One "a dump." That's what our shallow, calloused President called our White House.

A Peek Into the Death Star

Let's look at Trump's Death Star technology. We'll start with the numbers for the geeks and nerds.

In Trump's first 50 days as president-elect, Trump tweeted 221 times, that's the average of 4 times a day. Of his 221 tweets, 87% of them were "emotionally charged," that means they were intended to invoke an emotion in his followers. I personally don't follow him because I don't want his bullshit and lies intruding in my life through my Twitter feed. If I want to see what DarthTrump has been tweeting, I go to his twitter account and look. He's always retweeting some sort of Twitter meme. Remember that's one of his strategies; using repetition of lies, lies, lies in his efforts to brainwash readers. Twitter is a perfect format for that, 2-3 short sentences at a time.

Hang with me because this gets interesting. It also speaks directly to Donald Trump's mindset and MO; his modus operandi--something he must unlearn!

So 87% of Trump's tweets are "emotionally-charged." What does that mean? For an in-depth explanation, go to the NerdWriter's YouTube channel and watch the video entitled *What Makes Donald Trump's Tweets So Powerful?* He'll break it down for you in video/graphic format; here's the short explanation.

Donald Trump uses Twitter to speak his mind: he'll make a statement, give a one phrase summation, then add in motion or a command--ending in an exclamation mark to reinforce his assumptions! True or false, right or wrong, the validity of the statement doesn't matter. When Trump tweets his opinion, people take it as true. Example: "I'm really, really smart." That statement is very much up for debate and DarthTrump's actions are proving otherwise but he continues with that story and tweets many versions of self-praise.

Trump talks directly AT us via Twitter. He's not engaging in a two-way dialogue with his followers. He's simply spewing his mind. And what he talks about is fascinating! It's mostly himself! Or things he'd like us to think are true. Even when they're not. It reminds me of a post I saw on Facebook: I hope your life is as good as your Facebook page makes it out to be.

The Washington Post has called Donald Trump's Twitter account "prolific, populist, and self-obsessed, noting its particular utility as a 'real-time message tester' for the candidate, who whips his most liked Twitter barbs into talking points on the trail." And of course, now, the White House.

"Control, control you must learn control." -- Yoda

Let's go back to the beginning of Donald Trump's presidency. Nerdwriter recorded that the Tweeter-in-Chief (shout out to Bernie Sanders who I first heard say the phrase) in his first 50 days as president-elect, sent out 221 tweets.

Of those 134 emotionally-charged treats:

- o 61% or 94 of them were negative
- o 27% or 40 of them were positive
- o 12% or 19 "neutral" in tone

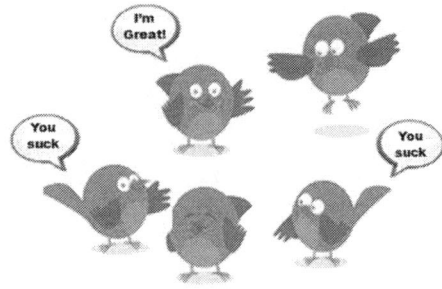

Did you read that?! 61% of what Trump says is negative, 27% of what he says is positive--and those are mostly self congratulations and boasts. "Trump" means "blow your own horn" according to Old English. Perhaps that's why Grandpa Trump changed it from Drumpf to Trump.

Donald J Trump
Mitt Romney called to congratulate me on the win. Very nice!
6:45 AM - Nov 13 2016

Donald J Trump
Appreciate the congrats about being right about radical Islamic terrorism. I don't want congrats, I want toughness and vigilance. We must be smart!
9:43 AM - June 12 2016

Donald J Trump
Thank you @Jake Tapper for giving me credit for My Vision on bombing the oil fields. Should have been done long ago. #Trump 2016
1:35 PM - Nov 13 2015

When he's not tooting his own horn, he's ragging on someone else two-thirds of the time. Remember, he's a master of deny, distract, distort, deflect. CNN Politics reporters Gregory Krieg and Will Mullery analyzed Trump's tweets his first one hundred days in office and found:

- o 165 political comment or argument
- o 142 typical presidential tweet
- o 86 self-plugs
- o 53 complaints about the Press
- o 26 conspiracy theories

- 18 personal attacks

Simple translation. Of Trump's 490 tweets during his first 100 days in office, 183 or 37% were negative to others or self-serving. He's rewriting "his story, history" one tweet at a time. The question is, do you believe him?

In addition to what Trump says, it's how he says it, using phraseology that ends with an emotional plea and powerful punctuation: "Sad!" "NOT!" "I don't think so!" "Big problem!" "Scam!" "Wrong answer!" "They'll never learn."

Amanda Hess, writer for slate.com, wrote an excellent article, *How Trump Wins Twitter*. She refers to Trump's triangulation tactic where he includes Aristotle's modes of persuasion: appeal to logic (logos), the appeal to credibility (ethos), and the appeal to emotion (pathos).

Donald J Trump
A suicide bomber has just killed US troops in Afghanistan. When will our leaders get tough and smart. We are being led to slaughter!
10:08 AM - Dec 20 2015

Can you hear the blame? Can you feel the fear? Can you taste the slaughter? If you can, Trump's done his job. He's calling you over to the darkside. He doesn't care what he says or how he says it, as long as he's getting inside your head.

We must become discriminating consumers of information. Not everything we read on Twitter is true; not everything we read in the newspaper is true; not everything we watch on cable news is true; and not everything we see on social media is true.

Case and point: DarthTrump has launched the pilot of what could become Trump TV. Trump has begun featuring short video clips of his daughter-in-law, Lara Trump, reading what she calls "the real news." It's straight propaganda, a Jedi mind trick, hoping to gain control of you.

As Trump tries to gain control, we, too, must learn control. More specifically what we can control and what we cannot control. We can control what we say to whom and at what time and on what social media platform. There are times to talk politics and times not to. And respectful dialogue is the best way to discuss our similarities and our differences.

First Amendment Rights

Our First Amendment Rights are currently being challenged. The First Amendment says, "Congress shall make no law respecting an establishment of religion, or prohibiting the free exercise thereof; or abridging the freedom of speech, or of the press; or the right of the people peaceably to assemble, and to petition the Government for a redress of grievances."

The Fourteenth Amendment protects this same right, but at the state level. Yet 18 states under Republican lawmakers have proposed bills that would criminalize protesting. If passed, punishments for peaceful protests will include jail time, fines, and/or seizure of property. They even include a clause that would indemnify drivers who hit protesters with their cars! This is just wrong--especially since vehicles are being used more and more by extremists as methods to kill people en masse.

Republicans have said these bills will cut down on paid protesters, but so far, the only people who have been paid to show up are being paid by DarthTrump.

Trump paid actors to show up at Trump Towers the day he announced his candidacy. How do we know? The company who hired the talent agency had to aggressively pursue Trump to get paid. It's also rumored that Trump was advertising for supporters for his Phoenix rally. According to a Craigslist ad, Trump was willing to pay $50 in talent fees and "minorities" were encouraged to attend.

We have the right to come together in peaceful protest. Anyone who says otherwise is siding with evil. It is one of our most basic Constitutional rights. Those states, by the way, adopting legislation to thwart protesters, include: Washington, Oregon, Colorado, Arizona, North Dakota, South Dakota, Minnesota, Iowa, Missouri, Oklahoma, Michigan, Indiana, Tennessee, North Carolina Virginia, Mississippi, Georgia, and Florida.

There are times, when working with others, we cannot control what they say or do. But we can always always control our reaction. And we never use our fists, we use our words and our vote!

That's why it's imperative right now that we monitor and evaluate the voting process. Russia's role in hacking our democracy must be exposed. The only way for this problem to go away is to fully look it in the eye and learn what it knows. But I don't trust DarthTrump's people to do the job. Bob Mueller is as neutral as it gets. If he says Russia did not influence the outcome of the election, I will attempt to believe that Trump won fairly. That's a big assumption for me right now. Everything and everybody points squarely to help from Russia.

And don't dare give voter information to DarthTrump; I fear he'll use it to suppress the vote, like in Wisconsin. As reported by theNation.com:

"According to federal court records, 300,000 registered voters, 9 percent of the electorate, lacked strict forms of voter ID in Wisconsin. A new study by Priorities USA, shared exclusively with *The Nation*, shows that strict voter-ID laws, in Wisconsin and other states, led to a significant reduction in voter turnout in 2016, with a disproportionate impact on African-American and Democratic-leaning voters. Wisconsin's voter-ID law reduced turnout by 200,000 votes, according to the new analysis. Donald Trump won the state by only 22,748 votes."

The fact is, DarthTrump won the Electoral College vote with the help of three critical states: Pennsylvania, Michigan, and Wisconsin. In each state, he won the vote there by less than 1%.

He lost the popular vote by 3 million, a fact Trump still refuses to believe. He's established a voter-fraud task force to search for 5 million illegal voters. He so desperately needs to prove he's legitimately elected, but he and the nation are haunted by doubt.

The number one thing we can do and must do is vote. And then keep resisting, and talking, and marching, and reading, and thinking, and striving to expose the darkside.

We Don't Turn Off the Dark; We Turn On the Light

How do we stand against hate and bigotry? How do we expose the dark without ourselves being consumed? We turn on the light.

"Returning hate for hate multiplies hate, adding deeper darkness to a night already devoid of stars. Darkness cannot drive out darkness; only light can do that. Hate cannot drive out hate, only love can do that." -- Martin Luther King

It's up to us; each one of us. We must turn on our own light and then shine that light on others. Marianne Williamson is my favorite spiritual leader. And wow, can that woman pray! From her September 3rd Facebook post:

"Dear God, Send legions of angels to all the leaders of the world. Heal their minds of thoughts of war and fill their hearts with thoughts of peace. May their emotions be calmed and their higher selves emerge. May wisdom and nobility and spiritual brilliance guide their every move, now and forever. And so it is. Amen." -- Marianne Williamson

See what I mean? But my favorite Marianne Williamson quote comes from her book *A Return to Love*. Take this passage to heart and indeed we'll change the world.

"Our deepest fear is not that we are inadequate. Our deepest fear is that we are powerful beyond measure. It is our light, not our darkness that most frightens us. We ask ourselves, Who am I to be brilliant, gorgeous, talented, and fabulous? Actually, who are you not to be? You are a child of God Your playing small does not serve the world. There is nothing enlightened about shrinking so that other people will not feel insecure around you. We are all meant to shine, as children do. We were born to make manifest the glory of God that is within us. It is not just in some of us; it is in everyone and as we let our own light shine, we unconsciously give others permission to do the same. As we are liberated from our own fear, our presence automatically liberates others."
-- Marianne Williamson

Are you ready? Because it's time to liberate others.

We must keep focused on DarthTrump and we must turn on the light. Most everything Trump is doing--or undoing--with his streak of executive orders I am opposed to.

- o No! It is not ok to persecute immigrants. Give them a path to citizenship.
- o No! It is not ok to deny refugees entry to our country. Vet them and let them in.
- o No! It is not ok to turn back equality for our LGBTQ community. Discrimination is senseless.
- o No! It is not ok to take Medicaid away from the poor. That would be heartless and unhealthy for the economy.
- o No! It is not ok to build a wall. Talk to our neighbors like you're a civilized human being.
- o No! It is not ok to cut funding to Vets. Put our money where your mouth is, help them.
- o No! It is not ok to deny women equal pay for equal work.
- o No! It is not ok to deny women access to birth control and family planning options.
- o No! It is not ok to frack the crap out of the land or pollute our water.
- o No! It is not okay to shit on the Press, to verbally assault them or incite violence at them.
- o No! It is not okay to pick fights with foreign leaders.

And the list keeps going. But this is my list. You must have one of your own. What do you think is good versus evil? Now is the time to ask yourself. And now is the time to stand up and turn on the light!

We must keep searching for and sharing the truth. But how can we break through DarthTrump's onslaught of lies and lies and more lies via Twitter? Don't be fooled by braggery or buffoonery and be willing to call out the Douchebaggery.

Information Exposes the Truth

James Harbach, a hypnotist weighing in on Trump explains how Trump hypnotizes his audience with these simple moves: he's funny, he's confident, he's a bully, he repeats repeats repeats, he invokes an emotion, he declares himself and his followers winners.

Bobby Azarian's article, The Psychology Behind Donald Trump's Unwavering Support, in Psychology Today, September 2016 gave me a new perspective on people seduced to the darkside, they don't know that they don't know. But they want someone to blame and DarthTrump uses that to his advantage.

What can you do, besides be informed? Stay informed and share your information with friends! And when you go to vote—take them with you! Take action!! Go to rallies, call your congressmen and women. And most importantly, don't despair and ...

> *"Don't give in to the hate. It leads to the darkside." –*
> *Obi-Wan Kenobi*

I believe artist Cleo Wadde summed it up beautifully on the Women's March instagram account:

> *"And may the appalling hate of others fuel you to step*
> *more deeply into your work as a warrior of love,*
> *justice, and freedom in the fight against oppression*
> *and bigotry." -- Cleo Wadde*

And...

May The Force be with you.

Okay, I added the last part, but it seemed appropriate. As for me? This little light of mine? I'm going to let it shine. How about you?

Here's What You Can Do to Help:

1. Watch the Star Wars movies, any of them or all of them
2. Dress like Princess Leia or a Jedi Knight and practice mind control on your own bad-ass self
3. Join or give to the American Civil Liberties Union, ACLU. They defend fundamental rights and liberties afforded everyone by the Constitution
4. Support the Anti-Defamation League. They fight anti-semitism and hate
5. Support the NAACP, the National Association for the Advancement of Colored People. Help tamp down the racists Trump's empowered
6. Join the Human Rights Campaign. Advocating for LGBTQ rights

7. Follow: the #womensmarch, #lovearmy, #sistergiant, #pantsuitnation or any of the hundreds of organizations launching grass root action to oppose Trump

8. Vote! Register now for the 2018 election

9. Join SwingLeft and get involved in helping your community vote

10. Join the League of Women Voters who work to ensure everyone the opportunity to vote

11. Check-out Indivisible.org/guide and start your own grass-roots movement

DarthTrump

May
The Force
be with You

General Jan Dodonna
and a Million Others

May The Force be with us all

DarthTrump

Grand Nagus

4. Grand Nagus: Trump's Rules of Acquisition

Red Alert! All Hands On Deck!

There's been a catastrophic event on planet Earth and only the crew of the Enterprise has survived. Returning from an away mission, the Enterprise crew views the devastation from outer space.

Captain Kirk, his mouth agape in disbelief is the first to speak, "What could have caused this? The continents have been leveled."

Spock, lifting an eyebrow replies, "Man, Captain. Only man could have wreaked this total devastation."

Which to Bones replies, "They're dead, Jim. All eight billion of them. Every man, woman, and child."

"Did they go mad?" Chekov asks under his breath.

"I'm unable to access Starfleet communication logs, Captain," says Uhura.

"You don't need the Starfleet logs. I've got all the explanation you need," says Sulu pulling out his communicator. "Let me show you my Twitter feed."

As the bridge crew gathers around Sulu's communicator and begins reading through the tweets of the planet's world leaders, the story becomes perfectly clear. Indeed, man wiped out the planet.

"Laddies," said Scottie, "it's time to break out the Romulan ale."

Well isn't that an interesting episode opener. We can call it "WTF Planet Earth." I immediately want to write myself to the end of the episode where JJ Abrams reveals an alternate universe where the entire planet is still very much intact and plugging along at the spiritual evolution of a slug.

But if there was ever a time to be on Red Alert, it is *now* as Trump and crew ramp up the nuclear threat. It's called nuclear chicken and both madmen--Trump and Kim Jong-un are too stupid to back down.

Turkey and Trek

Donald J Trump
Let us give thanks for all that we have, and let us boldly face the exciting new frontiers that lie ahead. Happy thanksgiving.
9:17 AM – Nov 23 2017

Being an avid Star Trek fan, the tweet caught my attention. Had president-elect Donald Trump caught a little of BBC America's Star Trek marathon over the Thanksgiving holiday weekend? My sister and I had Trekked out ourselves watching the new movie, Star Trek Beyond (her first time, my seventh), and a few episodes of The Original Series, the ones we grew up with. We were ages four and five when Kirk, Spock and the Enterprise crew first materialized in our family room September 18, 1966. Stardate: 1312.4

Could Donald Trump be a Star Trek fan?! Had Trump gobbled up turkey and star trek episodes, too?! The thought struck me as interesting and odd: Could Donald Trump be a good Captain? Maybe he did have the people's best interests at heart. What if he really could lead the crew and the ship? What if his vision for the United States, the planet, and the galaxy include peace and prosperity for all? What if we really could boldly face exciting challenges together?

Further investigation revealed the farce. More than likely Trump's speech writer was a Trekkie because it wasn't just an early morning tweet Trump sent out after an all-night The Next Generation marathon, it was a full minute and a half of bullshit that Trump presented to us via video message, calling for "unity" after a "brutal campaign." Now that he had lied and cheated his way into the Oval Office, he wanted to make nice and unite. It was clearly Trump using someone else's words because if he truly was a Trekkie then he'd understand The Prime Directive—a futuristic live-and-let-live philosophy forbidding Starfleet personnel from interfering with the development of another society's natural evolution--but he doesn't. And Trump would understand his mission to seek out "new life and new civilizations" should be in kindness and with friendship in mind--not to identify them, take their resources and kick them off their own damned planet!

I think Trump should be made to sit through every Star Trek episode ever made, both tv series and big screen movie, to watch the leadership displayed by Captains Kirk, Picard, Sisko, and Janeway. My apologies to Captain Archer; I didn't have cable when Star Trek: Enterprise was on. And, here's a future shout-out to Captain Lorca, Star Trek: Discovery. Can't wait! Trump might learn what respect and collaboration can accomplish. Captains don't lead by bullying or whining or because they are rich, they lead because they've demonstrated the mindset and skillset necessary to lead. They put their crew first. But then, Donald Trump's bone spurs would have kept him out of Starfleet Academy.

Trump should begin by watching The Next Generation and Captain Jean-Luc Picard, and in particular, the movie, Insurrection. When confronted with the illegal "forced relocation" of the Baku people by a rogue Federation captain, Captain Picard declares, "It stops here and it stops now." Ironically, Trump used similar language in his Inauguration Day speech when he declared the American "carnage stops here and stops now," obliviously unaware that he is the "carnage" that must be stopped. "Forced relocation" of a fictional alien species is wrong! The forced relocation of American immigrants is wrong!! Rounding up undocumented people and putting them in detention centers on their way to deportation is wrong!

No one is more aware of this than George Takei, the actor turned activist who played Hikaru Sulu, helmsman of the USS Enterprise in The Original Series who eventually rose through the rank to become Captain of the USS Excelsior. Takei, a U.S. citizen born in Los Angeles to Japanese-American parents, was forced into a U.S. internment camp during World War II at the age of five. He, his family, and another 120,000 people were rounded up and jailed because of their Japanese heritage. They were held in war relocation centers until the conclusion of WW II.

Takei has been quite vocal in his criticism of Trump and particularly on the issue of immigration and forced detainment. Meanwhile Trump's Immigration and Customs Enforcement, ICE, agents have escalated their efforts to deport anyone not fortunate enough to be born an American citizen. Deportations are up 200% over this same time last year.

Takei is also an out-and-proud member of the LGBTQ community which is also under attack by Trump and the current Republican administration. I'm appalled that Trump is the first president ever to address the Values Voter Summit, a proudly anti-LGBTQ and hate group as classified by the Southern Poverty Law Center. And George Takei called our attention to the fact Trump called them "friends."

I've loved Sulu my whole life. John Cho plays the character beautifully in the Star Trek series reboot. The family scene in Star Trek Beyond where Sulu's family meets him at Yorktown Station made me go "aaawww." I thought it a touching tribute to George Takei, the man--who I simply adore! George Takei is the actor that brought Sulu to life in The Original Series. George Takei in his own witty is calling out Trump on his bogus policies and lies. He's speaking up for human rights and does it with kind, positive words. Mostly. It's hard to avoid a dig or two when Trump himself provides the material. Set your phaser to stun. And follow him on Facebook or Twitter, @GeorgeTakei.

Trump could learn quite a bit by watching Star Trek and by following on social media both George Takei and Sir Patrick Stewart. In fact, Trump should follow all The Original Series and The Next Generation cast members on Twitter. Like the Star Trek characters they play, all of them are humanitarians speaking up for alienable rights. Pun intended. Twitter is witness to the comedy and the tragedy.

Who's Your Favorite Captain?

All of them! Why do I have to choose? Especially when all of them will be at Destination Star Trek London in October 2018; October 19-21, Birmingham. Beam me up! I couldn't resist.

The fact is, each Captain brings their own philosophy and style into leading. Trump should at least watch one of the Star Trek Anniversary shows to understand the philosophy behind the series. It's about people! JJ Abrams might have lost sight of that a bit as he's been blowing up planets and crashing starships, but it is.

Patrick Stewart, the English-born actor embodies the upstanding moral Captain Picard. Stewart is also an activist who speaks up for the rights of others. He's lent his voice and talents to stop bullying--and he's applying to be a U.S. citizen to oppose Donald Trump! I loved him before--Captain Picard is my favorite of the captains; I even have life-sized cut-outs of Captains Picard and Janeway, my second--but, this explains to me why Queen Elizabeth II Knighted him. Sir Patrick Stewart is a wise, kind soul with passion, vigor and a thirst for knowledge and justice. Both he and Takei are humanitarians with the conviction and courage to speak up and take action.

Then it dawned on me. Donald Trump is no captain! I'd argue he's not even human. Donald Trump is a Ferengi.

A Ferengi: This Explains Sooo Much

The Ferengi are the greediest, most rapacious, money-hungry capitalists in all the known Universes. Their religion is commerce and their societal status is determined by profit. The Ferengi offer prayers and monetary offerings to a

101

"Blessed Exchequer" in hopes of entering the "Divine Treasury" after death. Sounds like a "so-called Christian" I know of.

To Bigly Go

But Trump is not just any Ferengi. Remember the Trump Effect? Bigly; translation boldly? Trump is Grand Nagus, leader and the most ruthless of all the gold-pressed-latinum-loving Ferengi. Trump, like most Feregni, doesn't just tell small, white lies; Trump will say anything, make up any story, insult and demean anyone and anything to get what he wants. And all he wants is money, and more money, and more money, because that's how Trump measures his self-worth: money. That's how a Ferengi measures his self-worth: money.

As stated in the *Ferengi Rules of Acquisition*

#18 A Ferengi without profit is no Ferengi at all

If you're unfamiliar with the Ferengi, I suggest a weekend binge of Deep Space Nine. You'll learn more about their lust for latinum and lack of character from Ferengi Quark, proprietor and profiteer of Quark's Bar, as he shares life lessons with his son, Nog. The Ferengi also appear in The Next Generation where Captain Picard easily sidesteps their oftentimes comical plans for profiteering.

From Deep Space Nine, episode The Nagus: Part 1, Quark states, "Every Ferengi business transaction is governed by 285 rules of acquisition to ensure a fair and honest deal for all parties concerned... Well most of them anyway."

Trump, like a Ferengi, will have his own back, but not necessarily yours. He and his family will profit bigly from Trump's time in office. I'm betting the "average joe" will be hurt. Not Trump; he'll make out like a bandit. A Ferengi.

Trump is clearly breaking the Emoluments Clause:

> *"No Title of Nobility shall be granted by the United States: And no Person holding any Office of Profit or Trust under them, shall, without the Consent of the Congress, accept of any present, Emolument, Office, or Title, of any kind whatever, from any King, Prince, or foreign State." -- US Constitution, Article I*

Because Trump's business dealings are a sticking point for many, let's explore them through the *Ferengi Rules of Acquisition*: the sacred business aphorisms, proverbs, principles, philosophies, and guidelines of the Ferengi uber-capitalists.

We have neither the time nor space to recap ALL of the rules, but here are the top 20 or so that need revealing. To the drafters of the *Ferengi Rules of Acquisition*, my apologies if I get the numbers wrong.

#28 Morality is Always Defined by Those in Power

The very core of our American belief system is being challenged. Trump is using his power, influence, and money to back policies I'd call un-American, i.e. calling us to worship one God.

Really? Really?! Trump doesn't understand the most basic of our fundamental rights. I can worship a bowl of Chex party mix if I want, or pray to an almighty mouse-God in the dirt if I want. As long as I'm not causing harm to anyone, there's no harm in me believing what I want. That's religious freedom. That's why we have separation of Church and State. But Trump doesn't understand or doesn't care about religious freedom.

That's just one of the moral issues each one of us must define for ourselves. But many Americans are having basic rights withdrawn due to Trump's lack of morals. For example, Trump's border wall. Trump has just revealed the reason he is deporting our DREAMers is, so he can use them as a bargaining chip with Democrats to get funding for "border security," the Republicans are calling it. It's the wall. And the fact that Trump would put 800,000 souls, young kids, their lives on the line shows he has no heart. It doesn't matter how many times Trump says it. You don't deport people you "love." You lay down a path to citizenship. Only a cold-hearted Ferengi would use lives to negotiate. Don't think this affects you? Just wait until Grand Nagus Trump uses you as a pawn.

Donald J Trump
The golden rule of negotiation: He who has the gold makes the rules.
1:53 PM – Feb 6 2015

103

Grand Nagus

> *"The golden rule of negotiating:*
> *he who has the gold makes the rules."*
> *-- Donald Trump*

Donald Trump thinks he's the best negotiator. Ever. He campaigned on it. In his delusional world, he's building a successful presidency on that thought: he's the best negotiator. But he's not. Donald Trump has always had money behind him. He's always done exactly what he's wanted because he's owned the company. No one has held him accountable. Until now.

#10 Greed is Eternal

Trump himself said to a campaign crowd in Iowa that he was a "very greedy person." Then he said he now wants to be "greedy for our country."

"Now, I'll tell you, I'm good at that – so, you know, I've always taken in money. I like money. I'm very greedy. I'm a greedy person. I shouldn't tell you that, I'm a greedy – I've always been greedy. I love money, right? But, you know what?" he continued, "I want to be greedy for our country. I want to be greedy. I want to be so greedy for our country. I want to take back money."

Take back money?! Who do you think Trump is going to "take back" money from?! "I take, I take, I take," he said again in Iowa at a rally, "and now I'm going to start taking for you."

It looks like Trump is set to make good on that promise. Currently he's set his sights on the Mexican people. He's signed an executive order to build the wall between the U.S. and Mexico border—and he fully intends to make Mexico pay for it.

He says he'll negotiate the North American Free Trade Agreement, NAFTA, in order to make that happen. But be assured, Trump intends to build the wall at the expense of the Mexican people and the citizens of the United States. He could care less that money could go into rebuilding Houston and roads, bridges, schools, and housing across the nation. He'd rather take the fence that already exists along 650 miles and pour billions of dollars into it and an additional 1300 miles for a wall that will be deconstructed when anyone with half a head and half a heart will tear down.

I saw a photo of an eight-year-old girl holding a sign. It said, "My generation will tear down your wall." The waste of money for a wall is staggering.

And let's call it what it is, "the great wall of Trump," as Trump himself referred to it in one of his many rallies.

Remember Ronald Reagan said, as he stood next to the Berlin Wall, near Brandenburg Gate, addressing parties from both East and West Berlin:

"We welcome change and openness; for we believe that freedom and security go together, that the advance of human liberty can only strengthen the cause of world peace. There is one sign the Soviets can make that would be unmistakable, that would advance dramatically the cause of freedom and peace. General Secretary Gorbachev, if you seek peace, if you seek prosperity for the Soviet Union and Eastern Europe, if you seek liberalization, come here to this gate. Mr. Gorbachev, open this gate. Mr. Gorbachev, tear down this wall."

Reagan continued, "As I looked out a moment ago from the Reichstag, that embodiment of German unity, I noticed words crudely spray-painted upon the wall, perhaps by a young Berliner, 'This wall will fall. Beliefs become reality.' Yes, across Europe, this wall will fall. For it cannot withstand faith; it cannot withstand truth. The wall cannot withstand freedom."

Trump could work with Mexico on the problem of security and immigration, but Trump prefers to intimidate and demand. Estimated cost of Trump's wall between the United States and Mexico? $25 billion.

Mexico's president Enrique Pena Nieto has quite forcefully said they will NOT be paying for the wall. It is an affront to the Mexican people, it's against their dignity. Does Trump give a crap? No. He fully intends to squeeze that money out of them. He's going to take and take from the Mexican people. That does NOT make America great again. That makes Donald Trump an international bully and Douchebag.

#13 Anything Worth Doing is Worth Doing for Money

In 2002 Trump said, "It's very possible that I could be the first presidential candidate to run and make money on it."

And he did. And he still is. Trump is currently under scrutiny for violating the Emoluments Clause forbidding him from making money off the presidency. Yet he continues to do it, unapologetically.

Grand Nagus Trump will continue to profit off the people but this time not so subtly. Trump has not removed himself from his business ventures, if anything, he's tangled his business with government business: the Secret Service pays $130,000 per month to Trump to rent space in Trump Tower. The RNC will be holding their big holiday party at a Trump property so our tax dollars are directly making their way into Trump's huge bank account.

According to the American Progress Action Fund, Trump spent over $20 million in taxpayer money for trips to his golf resorts--in the first 100 days! To add insult to injury, The Secret Service paid over $65,000 in golf cart rentals to Trump that first 100 days and another $72,000 in these last 150 days. Yes, people are dying in Puerto Rico and the Virgin Islands, and Trump is golfing at his own club and charging the American people to do so.

When @damiranz tweeted Trump in August of 2014, "Pls don't run for president. If you do win, the rest of the world would be screwed." Trump responded, "So true, (except for friends)!" And those friends he's rewarded with cabinet positions. More on that later.

#261 A Wealthy Man Can Afford Everything Except a Conscience

Trump has profited *from* the people and *off* the people, living lavishly as his businesses filed for bankruptcy. He shifted personal financial responsibility to his casinos, taking a personal profit but leaving his defunct businesses to default on contractors, investors, and the community.

Michael Bloomberg, former Mayor of New York said, "I have known Trump for decades. We have traveled in the same business circles. He is known among other millionaires as a con artist and among business owners as a cheat out to stiff everyone."

Trump's done business deals all over the world. He's hooked up with big oil and big gas. Trump's milking millions out of people daily with various ventures across the world and we don't have a clue as to how much because like a Ferengi, he is secretive and unpredictable.

USA Today conducted in-depth research regarding the people using Trump's private properties. "The review shows that, for the first time in U.S. history, wealthy people with interests before the government have a chance for close and confidential access to the president as a result of payments that enrich him personally. It is a view of the president available to few other Americas."

Mar-a-Lago, Trump's "winter White House," doubled their $100,000 initiation fee to $200,000 after Trump became president. Trump National Golf

Club in Bedminster, New Jersey is referred to as the "summer White House." "Trump crashing parties" are part of their marketing campaign.

"This type of naked profiteering off a government office is what I would expect from King Louis XVI or his modern kleptocratic equivalents, not an American president," said Norm Eisen. Norm Eisen is board chair of Citizens for Responsibility and Ethics in Washington. He's also an attorney who previously served as White House Special Counsel for Ethics and Government Reform. Norm would know.

Donald Trump willingly and unashamedly admits to screwing people over to make a buck. Now that he's Grand Nagus of the United States he'll be attempting to screw over every person in the world—except for those few he's deemed worthy, the Wall Street millionaires and the billionaires he's added to his team.

The Ferengi, and especially Grand Nagus Trump, want you to fail. When you fail, he—and his cronies—make more money! In 2006, Trump said he was rooting for the real estate market to collapse, because "people like me would go in and buy" and "you can make a lot of money." Steve Mnuchin, now our Treasury Secretary, thought so, too. As co-owner of OneWestBank, Mnuchin oversaw scrupulous foreclosure standards.

According to National Public Radio: "The bank developed a reputation during the recession for being quick to foreclose on delinquent homeowners, closing on more than 36,000 households under Mnuchin, according to the housing-advocacy group California Reinvestment Coalition. In 2011, protesters went to Mnuchin's Bel Air mansion with a sign that read, "Stop Taking Our Homes." Both Mnuchin and Trump know the Ferengi Rule of Acquisition #162.

#162 Even In the Worst of Times Someone Turns a Profit

Grand Nagus Trump, the self-proclaimed "King of Debt," see Chapter 9, King Dong, isn't worried about capital. "Don't forget," he told CNN host Wolf Blitzer, "I'm the King of debt. I love debt." It's because he uses OPM, other people's money. He also said, "if the economy crashed you could make a deal." Someone is going to be at the end of that deal? Who do you think it'll be? If we have another housing crash and the bank forecloses on you, know it's got the full backing of Grand Nagus Trump and the Treasury Secretary. Don't think that's you? The average American household is only one paycheck away from homelessness, says a study done by the Association for Neighborhood and Housing Development.

Trump is not at all worried about where you sleep. On day one, hours after being sworn in, Grand Nagus Trump signed a resolution essentially raising the cost of buying an average home for first time home buyers and low-income borrowers. Who will be hit hardest? Millennials. But then Trump is counting on Rule #49/

#49 Old Age and Greed Will Always Overcome Youth and Talent

Old age and greed will always overcome youth and talent?! Don't you believe it. Belief, combined with optimism and talent, will help create a prosperous economic plan. Millennials see the world differently. They are more apt to do things differently. They've embraced Albert Einstein and know "we can't solve problems by using the same kind of thinking we used when we created them." They know it'll take belief, optimism, talent and imagination. They are up to the task; we should know; we raised them. I look forward to them taking over the world. They are more diverse and accepting. Millennials, our hope is with you. Can you imagine a better world for us all?

#17 A Contract Is a Contract Is a Contract, but Only Between Ferengi

Trump boasts he's a successful businessman worth $10 billion, but *The New York Times* writes "It is hard to find a project he touched that did not produce allegations of broken promises, latent lies or outright fraud."

Trump is notorious for not paying his bills. As I mentioned previously, Grand Nagus Trump currently is involved in over 4000 legal actions. The *USA Today* has that number at 3500. "Analysis finds 3500 legal actions by and against Trump, fighting everyone from the government to the Vodka makers."

It's Trump's MO to stiff the people that work for him and with him. According to USA Today, "At least 60 lawsuits, along with hundreds of liens, judgments, and other government filings reviewed by the USA TODAY NETWORK, document people who have accused Trump and his businesses of failing to pay them for their work. Among them: a dishwasher in Florida. A glass company in New Jersey. A carpet company. A plumber. Painters. Forty-eight waiters. Dozens of bartenders and other hourly workers at his resorts and clubs, coast to coast. Real estate brokers who sold his properties. And, ironically, several law firms that once represented him in these suits and others."

In a recent ruling, the Florida court of appeals ruled Trump had to pay $300,000 to a paint company for stiffing them on work performed and supplies provided at his Trump National Doral Miami golf resort.

It's common for Trump to stiff the people around him. Take Trump's neighbors in Aberdeenshire where Trump International Golf Links house Trump's operation. Neighbors of the golf course are suing Trump because he built a fence blocking a sea view at the houses of homeowners who refused to sell to him. He then sent them a bill for it. Sound familiar?

And just so you know how great of a business man Trump is, *The Guardian* reported Trump hasn't paid UK taxes on his golf courses in Aberdeenshire and Turnberry in Ayrshire because he has lost nearly $31 million on his Scottish golf empire on an investment of some $123 million.

To hear Trump talk money to Puerto Rico in the wake of the huge humanitarian crisis after hurricane Maria is galling and damned right criminal. Trump walked away from his Trump-branded and managed golf course in Puerto Rico leaving fellow U.S. citizens with a $32 million-dollar loss.

And now, to be talking money, when people have no water or electricity proves what he values--the almighty dollar. I don't have words enough to describe how sickening this is.

Trump has proven again and again he takes advantage of people. He'd probably take advantage of his own mother.

#33 Never Make Fun of a Ferengi's Mother; Insult Something They Care About Instead

Not much is written about Donald Trump's mother but we all know she didn't teach him manners. I've got four kids, all Millennials. If any of them had grown-up to treat people the way Trump treats people, I'd be mortified. I could care less how much money they make. That's a small percentage on my "success" scale. Did they leave the world a better place? Did they serve people? Did they live and love zestfully? That's a worthy measuring stick. Do they respect and value others? If so, I've done my job. Make all the "your momma" jokes you want. When I see how my kids treat others, I know I did something right.

#211 Employees Are the Rungs on the Ladder of Success, Don't Hesitate to Step on Them

Trump settled a lawsuit with his Las Vegas hotel housekeeping and service staff allowing them the right of Union representation. Note: Grand Nagus Trump was not settling a direct dispute against any of his business practices. He was trying to shut down the voice of the people and he paid a firm half million dollars to fight them before he finally lost allowing them Union representation.

Asked if he was sympathetic to the protesters demanding a $15-an-hour minimum wage, Trump said: "I can't be." He went on to say, "Taxes too high, wages too high, we're not going to be able to compete against the world. I hate to say it, but we have to leave [the minimum wage] the way it is. People have to go out, they have to work really hard and have to get into that upper stratum. But we cannot do this if we are going to compete with the rest of the world. We just can't do it."

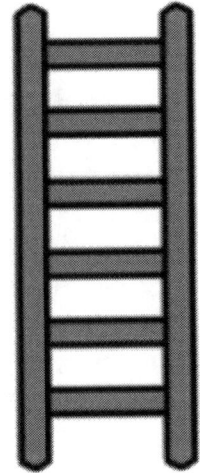

Donald Trump started his business on Daddy's dime, 140 million of them. That's $14 million! But Grand Nagus Trump thinks *you* need to work harder. That's it, just hard work will get you into the "upper stratum."

Let's do the math on a 40-hour work week making $10 an hour:

$10/hr x 40 hrs/wk = $400/wk

$400/wk x 52 wks/yr = $20800/yr

Let's say you double that--forego sleeping, eating and exercise and put in a 80 hr work week.

$20800/yr x 2 = $41600/yr (gross)

Subtract one third for taxes because you're a not a millionaire or billionaire that pays only %15 of your income for taxes. That gives you $28,000 to live on. I live in 600 sq ft, have a clunker of a car with no car payment. I spend @$2500/mo to live. By the time I'm done paying bills and flipping a little cash to the kids, I have nothing to save or invest.

Grand Nagus Trump has no idea what it's like to work for minimum wage and neither do his Douchebag kids, but tell me again that hard work will get me into the upper stratum. It's the great American dream after all: with enough pluck and determination, you can beat the system and get rich. Not everyone wants to be rich; some of us just want enough to live comfortably in a small house in the mountains. But that's not happening on $10/hr. But hey, who needs money when you have friends who have money. Grand Nagus Trump has lots of friends with lots of money.

#121 Everything Is For Sale--Even Friendship

Trump is silent about Russia; the GOP is silent about Trump. I say follow the money and you'll explain the silence. Could be a few comrades in the fold. There have been rumors that both McConnell and Ryan received Russian funds as well.

This is one of Trump's biggest issues and speaks to his lack of conscience. He believes everything and everyone is for sale. He ran his campaign on Make America Great Again but what he meant was Make America Rich. The rest is irrelevant. And the people who donated to Trump are the wealthiest of the wealthiest--and they are being rewarded with cabinet positions that they are grossly unqualified to do.

Eric Trump's wedding planner will now oversee the Department of Housing and Urban Development in NYC. She has no experience in the housing industry but will be handling billions of dollars that touch millions of lives. Well, that might not be the best example of the rich leading the rich. I'm assuming the wedding planner did a great job so Trump rewarded her, but I can't imagine she is a multi-millionaire. That's just straight "friendsies," she's a friend.

Other friends Trump has rewarded handsomely, include:

Betsy DeVos, heir to the Amway Fortune, our Secretary of Education. Betsy and her family donated $1.8 million to Trump's campaign. She continues to grease Trump's pockets by paying to stay at his DC hotel as she does her job selling out our children's futures to whoever can privatize education and make the biggest buck.

Linda McMahon, co-founder of World Wrestling Entertainment, WWE, gave $7.5 million. She now runs the Small Business Administration. But, there is a difference. McMahon co-founded the WWE, and it took work to build that business into a multi-billion-dollar industry. She is deserving of her position. Betsy DeVos, however, had barely stepped foot in a public school before she was confirmed. She's not qualified. I'm not saying Betsy is not qualified to do a job, just not this job.

Trump ran his campaign on #drainthneswamp, but make no mistake, Trump is bought and paid for by people in the corporate world as opposed to political world. Self-funded? Grand Nagus Trump has swampland to sell you, but know he's the biggest gator of them all.

Know Your Enemy But Do Business With Them Anyway

Trump is redefining who our "enemies" are. Trump's first overseas trip was to the Middle East. After paying homage to the kings and Sheiks and rubbing the magic orb, Trump arrived at the G7 Summit and delivered a defiant speech to NATO telling them they needed to "pay-up." He then hand-deliver a fake invoice to Germany's Angela Merkel for £300 billion, a number he calculated based on Germany's GDP for the last decade, plus interest. He then went on to stroke Putin's ego completely throwing into question just where our allegiance lies.

Perhaps our enemies have something on him which is helping him embrace them? Gee whiz.... what could it be? Now, let's take a minute and look at Russia. Russia, who renewed six unused Trump trademarks in 2016, four of those six were officially registered on November 8, Election Day, 2016.

A little congratulations gift from Putin maybe, or maybe a small reminder of all the money they could make together?

I wonder if that was before or after the Trump Organization renewed more than 1000 web domains, many having to do with Russia including, for example, TrumpTowerMoscow.com. No wonder Russia interfered with the election. A little Russian tit-for-tat. Here are your trademarks, now lift those Obama Russian sanctions! And even though the Congress approved more sanctions on Russia after this election, Trump has yet to put them into effect. The collusion is right in front of our faces! Our intelligence communities have proof.

Sorry, Grand Nagus, you didn't win fair and square. As the evidence is being released it's becoming quite clear why you were saying the election was rigged if you didn't win--because you were helping to rig it. And, you did win.

I keep reminding myself more people disapprove of Trump than approve him. But, he couldn't have won at all if he hadn't had a crap-ton of votes. So I, you, me, we have to embrace a man who thinks I'm his enemy. That goes back to respect, Paradox 1. How do we respect a man who doesn't respect us? He values money. Worships money. And adoration. He can't get enough of that either.

Grand Nagus Trump is a very simple, stupid man only capable of seeing the world in black and white, friend or enemy. "I have some very very good friends and I guess I have some very good enemies. And I like it that way, somehow and I really believe in trashing your enemies."

Too bad there's not a rule about doing business with your neighbors without slandering them and building a wall between. I stand with President

Enrique Pena Neito, former-President Vicente Fox, and the people of Mexico. Trump's wall is an affront to the Mexican people and the American people--and proof positive that Trump is a Douchebag!

How do I say "Trump is a Douchebag" in Spanish?!

My Bing translator says: Trump es un idiota. (Bing doesn't get it.)

Google translate says: Trump es un desastre. (Neither does Google.)

#76 Every Once In a While, Declare Peace. It Confuses the Hell Out of Your Enemies

Donald J Trump
Happy New Year to all, including my many enemies and those who have fought me and lost so badly they just don't know what to do. Love!
8:17 AM - Dec 31 2016

Love? Yes, I'm confused. Trump built his campaign and now presidency on hatred and loathing of others. He says he loves the DREAMers but just moved to kick them out of the country. He said during his campaign that he was a friend to the LGBTQ community and now he's kicked transgender service wo/men out of the military. And at a time that he's going to need them! Because Trump believes...

#34 War Is Good for Business

"I'm really good at war." "I love war, in a certain way," Trump has said. God help us all. Trump's cavalier attitude towards war should have us all on Red Alert! And it does!! Two-thirds of us lose sleep over this very issue! Trump is ramping up the war machine and putting money into new nukes. After decades of disarmament, Trump, with one tweet, started up the arms race.

Donald J Trump
The United States must greatly strengthen and expand its nuclear capability until such time as the world comes to its senses regarding nukes
11:50 AM - Dec 22 2016

Since that time, Trump has escalated verbal attacks on North Korea, taunting them with threats of "fire and fury" and hinting at a first-strike.

Let's hope it's just in a show of strength and he'll never use them!! But so far, he's launched missiles at Syria and dropped the "mother of all bombs" on Afghanistan. He sold $18 billion in weapons to Qatar after saying they were the biggest terrorist threat to the Middle East. Trump knows that.

#25 Fear Makes a Good Business Partner

Is Trump escalating the odds of war just to sell weapons to our allies?

Donald J Trump
I am allowing Japan & South Korea to buy a substantially increased amount of highly sophisticated military equipment from the United States.
7:36 AM - Sep 5 17

Is this why Trump is deliberately poking Kim Jong-un? Trump is also trying to sell military equipment to Finland. F-35 fighter jets. At a White House press conference with Finland's President Sauli Niinisto, Trump was attempting a hard-close sales technique without the buyer's consent.

"One of the things that is happening," said Trump, "is you're purchasing large amounts of great F-18 aircraft from Boeing, and it's one of the great planes, one of the great fighter jets, and you're purchasing lots of other military equipment, and, I think, purchasing very wisely. I know all of the military equipment and I actually agree with everything you purchased."

Not so fast, Grand Nagus Trump. Niinisto refuted your claim via Twitter:

Sauli Niinisto
The news of the purchase of F-18 fighter planes is a duck.
3:29 PM - Aug 28 17

In other words, Trump lied.

#35 Peace Is Good For Business

Grand Nagus Trump thrives on chaos, but the world is about to pay the price. Trump needs to stop, look around, and tune in. We want peace and we want Trump to start working toward that as opposed to stirring up controversy. Peace is good for business! It'll take our economy in a whole different direction. We do not need war to create jobs. And we don't need revenge politics and philosophies putting us all at risk.

#83 Revenge Is Profitless

Donald J Trump
Revenge is sweet and not fattening.
4:53 PM - Dec 15 2014

Trump was quoting Alfred Hitchcock. He's spoken again and again about his need to get even. He'll do anything or say anything if he feels he's slighted. He threatened to throw Hillary and her lawyers in jail. What kind of man threatens to throw his opponent in jail? A dictator, not someone who understands democracy. Someone who has always played by his own rules: he who has the gold makes the rules. Money has indeed bought Trump the country.

But those sitting in white houses shouldn't throw stones. Karma is already coming Trump's way.

#164 Never Spend Your Own Money When You Can Spend Someone Else's

Trump claims he self-funded his campaign. He shouted it from the stump and tweeted it from his Tower. "I'm self-funding, I'm self-funding," Trump said again and again throughout his primary campaign without "donors, special interests or lobbyists" is how he put it.

And he did. Self-fund, at first. It was the only way Trump could join the campaign. If Trump had been poor, he wouldn't be in the White House now. No one would have listened to his vile rhetoric if he'd been some poor old fat man in the street. He'd likely have been tossed in an institution by now--oh, but those no longer exist due to funding cuts. Old fat man Trump would be living in a machine shed on a golf course somewhere. But he paid his own way.

And he used the media and did it in the most nefarious way. Remember PT Barnum? Trump doesn't care what people are saying about him as long as they say something, and he dominates the news cycle. The crazier the better. No such thing as bad press. And, oh hey, I'm self-funding. Yeah, right.

Plain and simple, Donnie, we're not buying that. That goes against your core business principles as you explained at one of your campaign rallies in North Carolina. *Bloomberg View* reports when asked about his strategy billing other countries for U.S. Military Support, Trump said, "It's called OPM. I do it all the time in business; it is called other people's money. There's nothing like doing things with other people's money because it takes the risk. You get a good chunk out of it and it takes the risk."

Trump used OPM to finance his campaign, and once he won the Republican primary he started directing Republican campaign funds to his own coffers. The Republican Party essentially paid Trump for the hostile takeover. As I just mentioned, he increased the rent for his campaign offices in his own Trump Tower and the Secret Service, in addition to paying money to follow Trump's lazy cart-drivin' ass around the golf course, is also paying money to follow his family. His older children are enthusiastically using Daddy's status to further their international business dealings and using taxpayer money for fodder. Can you say family ski vacation in Aspen? Anybody?

The entire Trump family is violating the Emoluments Clause which forbids them or Trump from making money off the presidency, which they are all doing, unapologetically and enthusiastically. Wonder what I'm talking about? Follow the money trail. You can begin with 666 5th Avenue in Manhattan.

#144 There's Nothing Wrong with Charity as Long as It Winds Up In Your Pocket

Don't look for any of that money to go to charitable causes. Grand Nagus Trump has a reputation for accepting other people's money, especially through his "charitable foundation," but little is documented on who received the money. Except we do know some money went to Pam Bondi, Attorney General of Florida, shortly after Bondi chose not to investigate allegations of fraud against Trump University.

Trump's foundation is also under scrutiny for his Vietnam Vet scam. Trump said he'd personally give a million dollars to Veterans. He didn't do it--give it away--until the Press questioned him: where did it go? Who received the funds?

Currently the Trump Foundation is shut down by the New York Attorney General for violating state law by soliciting donations without proper authorization.

Trump has pledged $1 million to #HurricaneHarvey for disaster relief. Without Trump's foundation to tap, many believe he won't follow through. I am hopeful--but wouldn't bet on it. And, of course, in racist fashion, he pledged none to Puerto Rico.

And the apple falls right next to the tree. Eric Trump's charity is also under scrutiny by the NYC attorney for paying his Dad's business $1.5 million from charity donations. Thank goodness we have people inquisitive enough to investigate the matter.

#79 Beware the Vulcan Greed for Knowledge

I wouldn't use the word "greed" when referencing Vulcans. "Thirst" would be a better word. "Greed" implies "need" with an emotional attachment; obviously a Ferengi wrote the rules. But Vulcans are dogmatic in their search for the truth. Leonard Nimoy, #RIPLeonardNimoy, perfectly brought the character Spock to life. The story line of Spock working hard to control his emotions generated much talk around emotions and logic between the main characters, in particular Kirk, Spock, and Bones.

The Ferengi are fearful of Vulcans because the truth will expose them. Grand Nagus Trump is fearful of the Press for the same reason. They will expose him and his questionable dealings.

Trump's side-kick, Bannon, declared the Press "the opposition party." Trump himself has called the Press "fake news" too many times to count, unless you're *The New York Times* and you're keeping track. Google it: *New York Times* List of Trump Lies.

The reason Trump doesn't like the media's reporting is because they hold him accountable. They don't just let him and his surrogates say any old false thing. They call the Grand Nagus out on his bullshit and bullyshit. As MSNBC says, they are connecting the dots. And they are hot on the money trail. Remember, money makes the Ferengi world go 'round.

#180 Never Offer a Confession When a Bribe Will Do

When forced in court to divulge information, Trump ops instead to settle … hundreds of times, most recently the defrauded students of Trump University, and the housekeeping staff of his Las Vegas casino. Keep on saying it to yourself, Grand Nagus, "I don't settle lawsuits." We all know he does. We can see with our own eyes. For those that have been bulldozed by the Trump train, keep fighting. Make Trump honor his word and contracts. #resist!

#98 Every Man Has His Price

I do agree Trump is good for business. Love him? Do something to support him. Hate him? Do something to oppose him. Either way, Trump has lit a fire under our behinds! But before you get too self-righteous, me included, let's stop for a moment and address our own prejudices.

I read an article by Tony Schwartz, the man who "co-authored" Trump's best-selling book *Art of the Deal*, he felt guilty for helping to create the Trump persona. After spending 10 feet within Trump's physical sphere for 18 months, Schwartz developed a working understanding of Trump. Schwartz said he sold out for money. That's okay, Tony, I'm hoping to make money on this book, too. That's the Trump Effect. The question is: can I write about Trump and remain true to myself? Can I remain hopeful? Can I offer a new perspective? And what am I willing to do to heal the planet?

Part of me thinks it'd be easier to join the Trump train, but he's destroying the planet with corporate greed, crapping on the poor people who voted for him. Many of Trump's supporters make just minimum wage. Why isn't Trump giving them a raise? What about tax cuts for the middle-class and poor? His current tax plan includes huge cuts for the wealthiest and the middle-class gain will pay more.

#1 Once You Have Their Money, Never Give It Back

The now-defunct Trump University swindled 6,000 of their students out of millions of dollars in tuition money. Trump promised to make them rich with his real estate secrets and methods. Students poured their life savings into Trump programs that didn't pay off. Trump settled to the tune of $25 million. He bought his way out of the lawsuit. That's a Trumpism: throw money at it until it's yours or your opposition is silent. Or until they've been persuaded to see it your way.

#125 A Lie Isn't a Lie Until Someone Else Knows the Truth

This is the theme song of Trump's Administration. Trump lies and lies and lies and is indignant when the truth comes out. When it does, Trump labels it as "fake news." Any story Grand Nagus Trump doesn't like he calls "fake." People opposing him? Fake news. People in the streets protesting? Fake news. Over 60% of people disapprove of him? Fake news. Anything Trump doesn't want to believe, he denies and labels fake news. In addition, he tells people what they want, even though it's what *he* wants.

Donald J Trump
Any negative polls are fake news, just like the CNN, ABC, NBC polls in the election.
Sorry, people want border security and extreme vetting.
7:01 AM - Feb 6 17

And even as he's crying the stories are fake news, he launches a full-scale investigation of the leaks. "The leaks are real, but the story is fake." If it's not a real story, then it's not a real leak.

Besides, Trump does most damage to himself. He was labeled Leaker-in-Chief after inviting the Russian Foreign Minister Sergei Lavrov and Ambassador to the U.S. Sergey Kislyak into the Oval Office. Apparently at Putin's request. If you haven't seen the picture, you need to take a look. Trump and comrades are really yuckin' it up.

The American Press was not invited, but the Russians released a picture of the jolly trio on their RT news network. It also came out that Trump shared classified info with them. Can you say collusion?

But to draw attention from his own leaks, Trump is pursuing whistleblower Reality Winner. Reality Winner is a 25-year-old NSA contractor who released classified info on Russian interference in our election. It's a shame she is in jail awaiting trial. The documents were proof that NSA was investigating hacks by Russians on 122 electoral officers prior to the election. I thank Reality Winner for that piece of information. Like the Ferengi said, "a lie isn't a lie until someone knows the truth." And now we know the truth.

#94 Females and Finances Don't Mix

Trump said, "I think that putting a wife to work is a very dangerous thing. If you're in business for yourself, I really think it's a bad idea to put your wife working for you. I think it's a really bad idea. I think that was the single greatest cause of what happened to my marriage with Ivana."

Douchebag Wisdom

I'm betting it was because Trump had his big ears and small...hands on someone else's booty. Trump's first divorce cost him $110 million. I don't care enough about the second to even research it. Grand Nagus Trump has expanded his thinking on this. Trump's not beyond using the women in his life to continue his quest for money and world domination.

Melania, so I've heard is suing a newspaper because she thought one of their stories kept her from a "once-in-a-lifetime" money-making opportunity of being First Lady. How shallow. I see why POTUS and FLOTUS are a couple. And what's with the "blue steel" face? Seriously? Okay, that was a Douchebag thing to say, but does every photo op have to be so...crafted? Jesus, Mary and Joseph, this is not the new fall line-up: The Trumps Take the White House--and I don't give a crap who's wearing what. People are dying in Puerto Rico and California!

It doesn't really matter what I think of Melania. She doesn't have much of a role as far as I can tell. Trump's kept her in her place. Maybe she's the desperate mob-wife blinking twice to let us know she's become a hostage, or maybe she's seriously perfecting her blank model face keeping her thoughts as blank as her expression. I don't know. She might be a genuinely nice woman trapped in a putrid marriage or she could be Cruella De Vil, in cahoots with him. Seems to me she has no influence over this grand douche.

And it's a family affair! Daughter Ivanka has been granted three more trademarks from China even while the women in the factories who make her clothes, earning crap wages, can't even afford to live with their families.

Grand Nagus Trump is an equal opportunity capitalist. We all bleed green as far as Trump is concerned, and he'll take your money whether you are a man or a woman. But when it comes to paying his female employees, Trump is behind the times.

The Washington Post reports the White House gender pay gap has more than tripled under Trump. Female staffers now earn an average 63% of what their male counterparts make. It's the biggest White House gender pay gap in decades.

Then again, anything they pay to Kellyanne Conway and Sarah Huckaboo is too much. And that doesn't make me a Ferengi, it makes me a liberal woman who can't believe the lies that come out of these ladies' mouths. I know little about Ferengi women but Conway and Huckaboo pledge allegiance is to their Grand Nagus, Trump.

#3 Always Exaggerate Your Estimates

"I'm really, really rich." Sure Donald, we know you're rich, but no one believes you're worth $10 billion. He exaggerates everything, including his dick size which he brought up in the first debate. "Believe me there's no problem," he said after Marco Rubio had accused him of having small hands. Gross. #sorrymom People need to know how disgusting this man is.

Trump exaggerates the value of his properties until tax assessment time when he undervalues them to avoid paying taxes. He greatly over estimates the revenue his properties generate or will lose. In a reverse of fortune, thanks to the Oval Office, Trump's expected $2.1 million loss on his Trump Hotel DC, turned a $2 million profit the first four months of 2017. Of course, there is that little problem of the $5 million lien brought against Trump Hotel DC by three vendors. But at this high revenue rate, Trump just might have to pay some taxes.

Don't bet on it. Trump and cronies are rewriting and rigging the tax system now. The rich will get richer; the poor poorer. No exaggeration there. But that's okay as long as you...

#209 Tell Them What They Want to Hear

Grand Nagus Trump campaigned on a dozen contrived slogans: make America great again, build the wall, lock her up, drain the swamp. Trump continues to tell people what he wants them to hear and what they want to hear: promises kept, winning, and other nonsense. Trump is his own brand. He's crafted this presidency to be a big game show we don't dare turn off or the Ferengi capitalist next door will figure out some way to relieve you of your money.

#102 Nature Decays, But Latinum Lasts Forever

Donald Trump doesn't respect people and he doesn't respect things and he certainly doesn't respect our planet. He's an avid climate change denier, even calling it a "hoax" created by China. He sees the land and water as mere opportunity for plunder. He immediately green-lighted the keystone pipeline and the Dakota pipeline. Standing Rock Sioux? What protests? Native Americans.... Native what?

"As you know I approved two pipelines that were stuck in limbo forever. I don't even think it was controversial. You know, I approved them, and I haven't even heard one call from anybody saying, 'oh, that was a terrible thing you did,'" he told members of the media.

How do you deal with a man who is oblivious to the obvious? His head is so far up his own profit-driven rump that he refuses to see what and who is around him? Of course, the Grand Nagus sold his stake in the Dakota pipeline in December, a month before signing his executive order, or so I read. I'm sure his friends partied all the way to the bank.

Kelsey Warren CEO of Energy Transfer Partners, the company leading the assault on the Indians and tribal lands, gave $100,000 to Trump's presidential campaign. In case you're wondering, this is a perfect example of the "pay-to-play" politics Trump accused Hillary of. Laughable, since Trump's entire campaign was "pay-to-play" --and now his entire administration is--don't believe me? See chapter 9 King Dong.

#214 Never Begin a Business Negotiation On an Empty Stomach

Or you might end up cavalierly greenlighting unsuccessful military raids or shooting off missiles over "the most beautiful piece of chocolate cake."

#103 Sleep can interfere with....

Tweeting!

Donald J Trump
Despite the constant negative press covfefe
11:06 PM – May 30 2017

For covfefe's sakes, Donald, put down your unsecure phone and get some sleep! The above tweet was sent at 11 p.m. ... and then nothing. No explanation. No follow-up. I think Trump fell asleep, and God knows he needs it. Arianna Huffington is right. Everyone's life will be better if he'd just get some sleep. Maybe he'd be less Trumpy, and we all need that break! But when he woke up, he was right back at it, trying to save face.

Donald J Trump
Who can figure out the true meaning of "covfefe"??? Enjoy!
5:09 AM – May 31 2017

Press Secretary Sean Spicer didn't elaborate at that day's White House briefing when asked about it. Spicer said, "The president and a small group of people know exactly what he meant."

Hillary Clinton had a theory, "I thought it was a hidden message to the Russians." Ha! Hillary nailed it!

The Unwritten Rule: When No Rule Applies, Make One Up!

Warning! If a Ferengi can't figure out a way to get your money, don't be surprised if he throws in an Unwritten Rule. Ferengi are notorious cheaters and apparently Grand Nagus Trump is known for it on the golf course. Grand Nagus Trump might call it a mulligan, but it's still cheating.

He applies that same principle to business. Grand Nagus Trump has admitted to working the system to his advantage again and again declaring, "I alone can fix it." Oh, he's fixing it alright. He's fixing it in his own favor. And he's making it up as he goes and taking a do-over whenever he can.

#267 If You Believe It, They Believe It

Grand Nagus Trump is a master of deception but even Trump is not able to pull this off. We don't care how many times he says it or how much he believes it, he did not win the popular vote, the sun did not shine on his Inauguration Day, he did not have a larger inauguration crowd than President Obama, and the legitimacy of his presidency will always be in question.

Trump clearly believes he's the greatest business man ever put on the planet. He thinks he's the best at everything. It's like his brain never developed past third or fourth grade. He lives in a reality of his own making where he can solve the entire world's problems in one episode, or at least a season. But now that Grand Nagus Trump is getting a taste of power that only money can buy, he realizes it might take more than one season; it might take a second. Heaven forbid!! I fear for the planet if this man continues to sell everything to the highest bidder. We just might be forced into space.

And speaking of...no Star Trek chapter would be complete without it so, for the newbies, and for the log...

Space, the final frontier. These are the voyages of the Starship Enterprise. Its continuing mission: to explore strange new worlds, to seek out new life and new civilizations, to boldly go where no one has gone before.

Where will you boldly go?

What will you boldly do?

Here's Are a Few Suggestions

1. Binge watch one of the Star Trek series, or check out the three movies in the "reboot" that stars Chris Pine as Captain Kirk

2. Live by your own Prime Directive: do no harm, work for the betterment of yourself and all humanity

3. Take a die-hard look at Trump's budget and then pledge to support the causes and people he's abandoning. i.e. Meals on Wheels where Trump and the GOP plan to cut $76 million and will impact 6 million senior citizens

4. Boycott Trump: hit him where it hurts, his pocketbook. Download the Boycott Trump app and only frequent companies that don't support his divisive politics. Yes, that means Ivanka, too

5. Follow @GeorgeTakei, @SirPatStew and the entire crew on Twitter

6. Get yourself a tribble. Don a Star Trek uniform. Drink some Romulan Ale

7. Get a Picard/Riker for President/VP 2020 t-shirt

8. Watch Star Trek: Discovery. Martin-Green, an African-American woman playing the role of #1 to the Captain, said to the Twitter trolls online: "I would encourage them to key into the essence and spirit of 'Star Trek' that has made it the legacy it is--and that's looking across the way to the person sitting in front of you and realizing you are the same, that they are not separate from you, and we are all one." #sisterpreach

9. Join the Captains--all 5--at Destination Star Trek London, Oct 19-21, 2018

10. Give the Vulcan "peace sign" and use the phrase "live long and prosper," yes, even when speaking to Trump fan

11. Think like a Vulcan. Turn the page

Infinite Diversity in Infinite Combinations

Vulcan Proverb

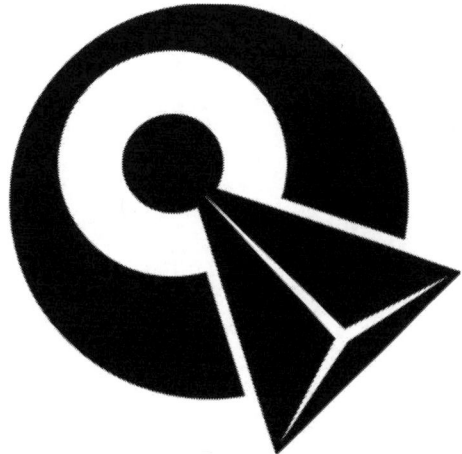

Grand Nagus

Grand Nagus

TrumpFace

5. TrumpFace: In Your Face, Behind Your Back

Harvey Dent: The only way to get by in this place is to get ourselves some respect.

(switches personalities)

Two-Face: Fear! That's how we get respect! Show them all how we do things!

Batman: Arkham City (2011)

Fear

Donald trump built his candidacy on fear. "Fear the Hispanics, they are murderers and rapists. Fear the Muslims, they are terrorists. Fear the government, they are corrupt and can't be trusted. Fear each other, it's a cold, harsh world out there. Fear your neighbor and here's a phone number to call and report them."

He blamed government greed and international treaties as the reasons why people were losing jobs. He got on Twitter and bashed other nations--China and North Korea especially. Everyone, except for Russia. He criticized NATO and NAFTA without understanding what they were and who they represented. Instead he chose to burn down partnerships between the U.S., Mexico and Canada. He blames the immigrants again and again, and he's still promising every U.S. citizen their life will be better, and they will be safer with a wall on the Mexico border.

Fear North Korea, fear ISIS, fear for your lives--but "I will keep you safe," says Donald Trump. "Trust me." "Believe me." "I alone can fix it." And there you have the two faces of Donald Trump, TrumpFace. Fear for your lives and believe in me.

The American Carnage Speech

On a gloomy, raining Inauguration Day, TrumpFace let his gloom-and-doom side show. No positive spin from an optimist speech writer, hell no, Trump wrote it himself. This speech focused on the great wrongs that had been done unto the people. Trump must have been watching The Dark Knight Rises when he wrote it. *Deadspin's* Timothy Burke does a great side-by-side comparison of Trump's speech to the villain, Bane, after his take-over of Gotham City. But make no mistake, the words below belong to our President, Donald Trump:

"For too long, a small group in our nation's Capital has reaped the rewards of government while the people have borne the cost. Washington flourished – but the people did not share in its wealth. Politicians prospered – but the jobs left, and the factories closed. The establishment protected itself, but not the citizens of our country. Their victories have not been your victories; their triumphs have not been your triumphs; and while they celebrated in our nation's Capital, there was little to celebrate for struggling families all across our land."

"That all changes – starting right here, and right now," Trump continued, *"because this moment is your moment: it belongs to you. It belongs to everyone gathered here today and everyone watching all across America. This is your day. This is your celebration."*

Insert some other bat-shit crazy Trump words here, and then...

"From this day forward, a new vision will govern our land. From this moment on, it's going to be America First. Every decision on trade, on taxes, on immigration, on foreign affairs, will be made to benefit American workers and American families.

We must protect our borders from the ravages of other countries making our products, stealing our companies, and destroying our jobs. Protection will lead to great prosperity and strength.

I will fight for you with every breath in my body – and I will never, ever let you down. America will start winning again, winning like never before. We will bring back our jobs. We will bring back our borders. We will bring back our wealth. And we will bring back our dreams. We will build new roads, and highways, and bridges, and airports, and tunnels, and railways all across our wonderful nation. We will get our people off of welfare and back to work – rebuilding our country with American hands and American labor. We will follow two simple rules: Buy American and Hire American."

Oblivious to the Obvious

I interrupt this speech of gloom and doom to point out the hypocrisy of Donald TwoFace Trump. Even while imploring, incenting, and shaming other businesses to hire American and buy American, he has a different standard for himself and his family.

TrumpFace loses all credibility--if he had any! Donald TrumpFace needs to put his money where his mouth is and bring his own businesses--and those of Ivanka--back to America! Buy American and Hire American?! What a joke.

Most of Trump's cheap-ass clothing is made in other countries. The Washington Post reports that Trump is currently or has previously manufactured apparel, home items, hotel items, and beverages in at least 12 countries, including: China, the Netherlands, Mexico, India, Turkey, Slovenia, Honduras, Germany, Bangladesh, Indonesia, Vietnam and South Korea. The only products Trump manufactures in the U.S. are his red/white/blue/and every-other-color-under-the-sun including camouflage! -- #MAGA hats and now the white 45 hat he'll use to suck cash from people's pockets.

"China, China, China is a currency manipulator" he screamed throughout his campaign. He flipped the moment President Xi and his wife showed up at Mar-a-Lago. Then China granted Ivanka three trademarks and Trump got a couple of his own.

Then, with the audacity of someone who believes he's above his own decree, Trump declares July 17-23 "Made in America" week while his Mar-a-Lago Club applied for H-2B visas to hire foreign workers as cooks, housekeepers, and servers. Google the word "hypocrite" and you'll find Trump.

Good Guy > Bad Hombre

Harvey Dent, also known as the villain Two-Face, first appeared in the Batman comic series in the 1940s.

Harvey Dent, Gotham's amiable, courteous district attorney becomes a schizoid criminal mastermind. If you are a Dark Knight Rises fan, you'll attribute this evil transformation to the Joker who killed Dent's girlfriend, Rachel, in the same incident that horribly disfigured Dent. The disfiguration on one half of his face leads Dent to see two distinct personalities in himself.

Dent is aware of his duality, but he's unable to control it. This could be due to Harvey Dent's childhood.

Harvey Dent had an abusive, mentally ill father that caused Dent to develop bipolar, schizophrenia at a young age. Dent's dad played a perverse nightly game with a two-headed coin. No matter how young Harvey called it-- heads or tails--it always led to a beating. That led to Harvey's inability to deal with free choice and free will and his eventual inability to make choices on his own. Instead Dent relied on a coin to make his decisions.

I won't speculate here on the relationship between Trump and his Dad, but former Mexico president Vicente Fox has. In a video telling Trump Mexico will not be paying for the wall, Fox showed a picture of 5-6 yr. old Trump. He suggests Trump build a bridge across time and go back to tell his younger self that--even though his daddy didn't love him--he, Donald Trump, could still build a better world.

In his most recent trolling video, Fox suggests he'll be running for President of the United States. Fox says he would have more support than Donald Trump. I agree.

Harvey Dent is obsessed with the number two--duality, and more specifically "good versus evil." Dent makes all decisions by flipping a lucky two-headed coin which was damaged by acid at the same time Dent's face was. In Dent's everyday reality, he pretends he has a choice, but he really doesn't. He knowingly chooses the direction he wants to take, sets up the question, flips a coin and confirms it.

Some people say (recognized the Trumpism? Translation: no source and here comes some bullshit) he's got two personalities, and the real Donald Trump is warm and personable, and this tough-guy act is just that--a part he's playing for ratings. We certainly saw him play to ratings throughout his campaign and at every rally. He continues visiting cities in states that he won. He doesn't acknowledge the rest of the people, the majority of Americans according to the latest polls. Trump's approval rating is down to 33%, except with Republicans who still think they can trust him to push through their extreme agenda.

Republicans witnessed first-hand the two faces of Trump. Without a fight and with little discussion, Trump impulsively accepted the Democrats offer to raise the debt ceiling, extend our current budget, and approve money for hurricane relief.

Republicans were salivating at the chance to cut what they call "entitlements," but Trump took that option off the table. I'm not complaining about that one deal but I don't trust Trump. What does he expect in return?

Trump is good at putting on an act. But seriously, which side of him do you believe is the act? Donald Trump is a self-professed mean, spiteful human being. He boasts of revenge and teaches it as a life lesson. Look no further than Twitter for the @realDonaldTrump.

@realDonaldTrump

Is it a coincidence that his handle is "real" Donald Trump? You might think it's just a word to replace "official" so people understand it is indeed The Donald in real life. But it's more than that.

The "real" Donald Trump is not just the man playing to the camera in the White House, creating photo opportunities, filming self-serving propaganda ads, signing executive orders, and exploiting others, he's a man who thinks he's doing the best thing for the people, the country and the world!

And here I'm trying to give Trump the benefit of the doubt. I do think he thinks he's helping. He believes he's creating jobs and has single-handedly set Wall Street on fire. He thinks he's good guy Harvey Dent.

But then this sinister, mean-spirited Trump comes out--kicking transgender people out of the Service, going after DREAMers for deportation, rolling back regulations to protect LGBTQ citizens and our planet from corporate abuses denying contraception for millions of women. Now we're looking at Trump's other side.

The other side of Trump, the Trump behind the Twitter account, the real Donald Trump doesn't sleep. We know what keeps him up at night. He telegraphs it to the world; he tweets it! Trump's tweets are a different level of knowing and understanding Trump.

Trump says people don't know him, but we do. Twitter is an insight to his dark, putrid soul. His 3, 4, and 5 a.m. tweets run the gambit of scary to preposterous, from downright dangerous to absurd, from self-congratulatory to celebratory. His Podesta tweets the morning of the G2 Summit were bat-crap crazy.

Donald J Trump
Everyone here is talking about why John Podesta refused to give the DNC server to the FBI and the CIA. Disgraceful!
1:40 AM - Jul 7 2017

What world is Trump living in? His own DC comic book?! Or maybe he was dreaming ... zzz ... covfefe anyone?

I think Trump spends a great deal of time in that "real dump" of a White House thinking about what we, the common folk, think of him. He needs to be respected. He needs for you to think he's a successful businessman. Trump needs to read Byron Katie's *Loving What Is* and learn her perspective: What you think of me is none of my business. Then maybe, just maybe, Trump could do his job.

Trump will do anything and say anything to keep a "successful" facade going. But the truth is, he's made his money off of other people's hardships. He's taken advantage of business loop-holes and he's made money off the American people, in practices both legal and questionable. Contractors having to sue to get paid the final portion of a contract? Yeah, that's questionable.

> ***"You either die a hero or live long enough to see***
> ***yourself become the villain."***
> ***-- Harvey Dent***

TrumpFace has shown us "many sides" of his "so-called "successful businessman persona, but these two stand out: he can be charming and engaging, or he can be vengeful, mean-spirited and hateful.

Trump threatens anyone who opposes him using fear and intimidation. He's pitting Democrats against Republicans; Americans against each other.

According to a Pew Research Center report on fear, anger, and frustration between the two political parties, 49% of all Republicans fear the Democrats; 55% of all Democrats fear the Republicans. And Trump likes it that way. This was the message of Trump's campaign and now his presidency. Fear.

Trump Wins: America Loses

Donald J Trump
If the Senate Democrats ever got the chance, they would switch to a 51 majority vote in first minute. They are laughing at R's. MAKE CHANGE!
4:47 PM - Jul 29 2017

No, Democrats would not make that change because Democrats believe in Democracy. Trump does not own the government. It might have been a hostile take-over, but we will resist. And I'm hoping and praying Republicans will too. I voted Republican half of my voting life but not lately. I want to believe

Republicans will not change the Rule of Law or our Constitution. That would give Trump authoritarian control. That's not Democracy and that's not America. But watching Trump dismantle the government now--with the help of Republicans--makes me ill. They've sold our country out to be in control. They may work for him, but I do not.

None of us do--except by choice or abdication. Trump associates willingly choose to support him. So many others have simply tuned out. I am one of the few I know who is tuned into politics, but I understand how and why people are tuning out. This shit-show is just too bloody to watch.

While Trump is letting off stink bombs everywhere, keep your eyes on Jeff Sessions. He's got more private prison beds waiting for someone. Not you? Are you sure? Sessions is just itching to put someone in jail. Undocumented citizens, legal marijuana users, journalists, a woman who laughed during his congressional hearing! One judge already threw out Desiree Fairooz's conviction, but Session's DOJ is coming for her. Frightened yet? If not, you're not paying attention. Session's DOJ wants to take your property. It's called "legal forfeiture." What it really means is your property and assets can be seized with the mere suggestion of wrongdoing. No conviction--or charge--needed!

The Charm Offensive for All to See

Didn't Donald Trump look distinguished on his first address to Congress? I wasn't fooled, and neither were you. (*That*, by the way is a Trumpism: "I wasn't fooled, and neither were you." Trump has often said "I don't believe that and neither do you." It's like he's hypnotizing us.)

That night he toned down his rhetoric, stepped up his "heart-felt" commitment and put on a "presidential" demeanor. The brash buffoon, in dress-for-success fashion donned a dark suit with blue-and-white striped tie. Tweedledum and Tweedledee, Pence and Ryan, wore dark suits also with colluding blue ties. Did I say colluding? I certainly did. Pence and Ryan are willing accomplices to the act.

Was it Samantha Bee or Bill Maher that compared Trump, Pence, and Ryan to The Three Stooges? More like the three Scrooge's if you ask me! For more on that, read Chapter 12, Scrooge Trump.

Donald TwoFace Trump, used his "best words" when promising what he'd do if he were president.

"I am your voice," he said as he bashed Republicans and Democrats saying anything to get elected. No one knows where he stands on the issues. He's for sale. He's allowed more lobbyists in the door of the White House in the last few months than Obama did in eight years and he's hidden that fact by not releasing the visitors' log.

Trump used to be pro-choice, now he's pro-life. He used to be for gay rights but now he's rolling back protections. He did and said anything to get elected; he talked out of both sides of his face never focusing on the details. Oh healthcare, it'll be great and so easy. He spent hours talking at rallies saying nothing but a few trite repeatable slogans he fed to his crowd. He was the ultimate diplomat with a super-villain twist. He doesn't really care about health care. He simply wants a "win" and has proven he'll side with anyone who agrees with him.

"To say nothing, especially when speaking, is half the art of diplomacy."
-- Will Durant

Like Dent, Trump is obsessed with polarity, by flipping on many issues. He talks both side of the issues, intentionally, out of both sides of his face. But it's not an "either/or." It's both sides of the issue in the same sentence. When questioned on his position on Syria, TrumpFace said, "I don't have to have one specific way, and if the world changes, I go the same way, I don't change," he said. "Well, I do change and I am flexible, and I'm proud of that flexibility."

What the hell did he just say?! Donald TrumpFace is the biggest double-talking Douchebag on the planet. Part of Trump's communication strategy is to say anything and nothing at the same time. He talks with the intention of appealing to everyone, so he throws a bunch of contradictory statements together hoping each of us will hear what it is we want to hear.

It's rare to get a straight answer from Trump, so monitor his words but don't mind them. Trump often says one thing and does another. That's because Trump's entire campaign was about "winning." He has no idea how to run a country, but if he runs it like his business, we're collectively hosed. Filing for bankruptcy is another Trump MO.

You don't have to agree with everything Trump does. As much as I love Obama, I didn't agree with everything he did. But, I trusted him to make the right decision. I respected him and the Office.

TrumpFace I neither trust or respect. He serves the interest of only a few.

Do you have to approve of everything he says or everything he does to respect him? No, but you have to approve of *something* he says or does, so you can respect him.

Can you look away when he does or says something stupid or hurtful to an entire group of people? Or are you more apt to call him out and his two-faced, flipped-flopped erratic approach to governing. Or whatever-the-hell you call this.

Hyperbole to Hypocrite

Early in his presidency TrumpFace signed an executive order banning people from seven Middle Eastern countries from entering the United States--on the same day he honored International Holocaust Remembrance Day.

How can Trump not see the irony? Sure, "together we will make love and tolerance prevalent" just not on U.S. soil because "Donald J Trump," said referring to himself in third person, "is calling for a total and complete shutdown of Muslims entering the United States until our country representatives can figure out what is going on."

Trump surrogate Rudy Giuliani said, "Trump called me to ask how to make it a Muslim ban without calling it a Muslim ban."

Let me help you out here, Donny, let me tell you what "is going on." You are using your words to define a religion, Islam; and your supporters, with their lack of education, are letting your hatred and bigotry play out in Muslim communities, Jewish communities, and African-American communities across the nation. Bomb threats in Mosques and Temples, graveyards desecrated and an 8 yr old bi-racial boy lynched in New Hampshire! Donald Trump is the cause. His words and actions are an example that others are following. Bully pulpits beget bullies.

Muslim hate crimes are up and Trump doesn't speak out; Jewish hate crimes are up and Trump stays quiet; police brutality against black people is on the rise and not only does Trump not speak up, he arms the police with Military equipment. It took a young white woman, a peaceful protester at an anti-hate rally, who was run over and killed by a White Supremacist hater, this time Trump did speak up. He sided with the haters, the white nationalist saying there was violence on "many sides."

Trump says he's not racist, but he doesn't use his words to tamp down the hate, instead using them to incite further violence. That makes Trump a douche; a two-faced one at that.

Trump is directly responsible for the number of hate crimes rising across the nation. He is perpetuating intolerance by blaming immigrants and Muslims for the woes of "real Americans." His executive order tried to ban people from other countries which we all know are predominantly Muslim although there is no proof they are terrorists.

I might have believed Trump--that he was trying to protect the country--if he had also banned Egypt and Saudi Arabia, but he didn't. He didn't want to risk his personal foreign investments being affected by the ban. Can you say "Hypocrite"? Surely, he must know by now that 15 of the 19 terrorists who perpetrated the Twin Tower attacks on 9/11/2001 were from Saudi Arabia, 2 were from the United Arab Emirates, and 1 each from Egypt, and Lebanon.

Trump said his travel ban is good for the United States, but it's good for Trump first and foremost. And he's implementing it in an unAmerican and immoral way. His near-sighted American first policy has us turning our backs on people, and specifically refugees that desperately need help.

Instead, Trump sits in his golden tower, denying human beings the same privilege his granddaddy got so many years ago. Look what he's done, the son of an immigrant--he's bought himself a government and adoring fans. Trump, a little Scotsman / German / Swede, depends what article you read and which story he was pushing at the time, grew up to run the United States of America. He thinks he's the next best president to Abraham Lincoln. He's joking about having his face on Mount Rushmore. He's delusional.

Thank heavens the ninth circuit court denied Trump's first executive order on the Muslim ban and thank heavens for the Hawaii court to kibosh his second attempt at the unlawful Muslim ban. Too bad and how sad for us all as a nation that a partial ban is currently being implemented while the Supreme Court reviews its constitutionality. In the meantime, Trump's fear-based agenda is keeping people out of the country.

"I listen to myself." -- Donald Trump

"I'm, like, a smart person." -- Donald Trump

Donald Trump thinks he's smarter than everyone else.

Donald J Trump
Sorry losers and haters, but my I.Q. is one of the highest-and you know it! Please don't feel stupid or insecure, it's not your fault.
8:37 PM - May 8 2013

My 50+ years of experience tell me smart people don't need to tell others how smart they are. Their words and their actions prove it. Looking and listening to Donald Trump is like listening to a small child except even a child is smart enough to know they don't know everything. As smart as Trump claims to be, he certainly hasn't figured that out yet.

Smart people don't:

1. Continually tell us how smart they are
2. Bully and taunt others
3. Attack people for their looks
4. Think everything and everybody is for sale
5. Call other people losers
6. Blame news that you don't like as being fake
7. Claim you will unite us and then ignore us
8. Get high on adulation

Smart people do:

1. Use facts, numbers, figures and statistics to prove a point and make decisions
2. Treat others with respect
3. Understand hypocrisy and irony
4. Have a sense of humor
5. Seek the truth

TrumpFace believes that he's worthy of our respect. But even if you don't respect him, you'd better fear him. He's showing his warped and depraved side and people are getting hurt.

TrumpFace prides himself on unpredictability. He calls it a "strength." He doesn't realize it's his weakness. He thinks he can out-crazy Kim Jong-un. And he's going to put our children on the front lines to prove it. He already has increased the number of U.S. men and women in Afghanistan by 4000. The very same war he criticized Obama for.

Donald J Trump
It is time to get out of Afghanistan. We are building roads and schools for people that hate us. It is not in our national interests.
1:34 PM - Feb 27 2012

Donald J Trump
A suicide bomber has just killed U.S. troops in Afghanistan. When will our leaders get tough and smart. We are being led to slaughter!
12:08 PM - Dec 21 2015

He says he'll make our world safer but he's putting us and most especially our military people serving overseas in harm's way. We just lost four Green Berets and one Nigerian soldier in Niger. It's the first time U.S. service members have been killed there. And TrumpFace has not tweeted out one word in condolences. And it's not just overseas where Trump is inflicting harm.

Trump's tweet declaring transgender people would no longer be able to serve in the military was an aggressive move no one saw coming. He said he made the decision after consulting "my Generals." He actually didn't consult the Generals before he made the announcement via Twitter. More on this in Chapter 8, Biff Trump.

During his campaign, Trump promised to be a friend to the LGBT community. Now he's saying they are not worthy to serve our country. We've got over 15,000 transgender military personnel whose lives and livelihoods are now threatened. And these aren't the first government employees he's canned.

"I'll be the greatest jobs president there will ever be," he said as he declared government "bad" and then fired thousands and government employees. Trump is clearly the bad hombre of which he speaks.

Government is good! Government jobs employ people, government employees serve people. How can Trump not understand this? Jobs are good, but only private sector jobs? How narrow-minded can he be?! How many positions are still unfilled as he tasks his son-in-law, Jared, to solve all the world's problems? With no help from people who would normally do those jobs? How many government employees has Trump fired as he's hired and appointed a pay-to-play entourage?

"Who knew healthcare could be so complicated?" --Donald Trump

Seriously? What a douche. We all knew! Trump said again and again that everyone has to be covered and the premiums will be lower and pre-existing conditions will be covered. "It'll be so easy," he said. Now that we know Trump thinks healthcare premiums are $12 a year. That explains that. He has zero understanding of the issues involved.

When the House of Representatives passed a bill that will knock 24 million people off healthcare, Trump threw a kegger in the Rose Garden to celebrate. Then he called that very same bill "mean."

That's double-talk out of both sides of his face. Currently health care legislation is stalled. Trump is blaming everyone but himself. His response when the Senate was not able to come up with the votes to pass the crappy bill proposed by the House? "Let Obamacare fail," he said, "I'm not going to own it."

He acts as if he has nothing to do with it, but he sabotaged his own party. That's because Trump has no loyalty to a party. He's independent and out to get all he can.

The American people spoke up demanding that Obamacare not be repealed. So now Trump is setting up Obamacare to fail. He's shortened the enrollment period, then slashed the ad budget by 90% hoping enrollment will be low. He got rid of about half of the workforce of people helping people to get enrolled.

And TrumpFace just signed an executive order eliminating money to the insurance companies providing plans for low-income people. And then he tweeted:

Donald J Trump
Very proud of my Executive Order which will allow greatly expanded access and far lower costs for HealthCare. Millions of people benefit!
4:27 AM - Oct 14 2017

HOW will millions of people benefit? He ignores every expert in the field, every fact that says millions will lose coverage. He says all the right words but he's doing his best to sabotage the current system when he has no plan of his own. Because he truly doesn't understand. He's TrumpFace: say one thing and do another. It doesn't matter if he thinks he's Harvey Dent; he's the villain.

John McCain, America's Hero, Once Again

John McCain became the nation's hero when he cast the final "no" vote on the Senate's Repeal and Replace bill. Without a defined plan in place, John McCain along with two other women Senators, cast the deciding votes. A simple little thumbs-down gesture said it all. Mark Zuckerberg should make a special Facebook thumbs-down button to honor John McCain. Yes, John McCain who wants to go back to working across the aisle. Amen.

Side note: Zuck, we need to talk. We need the numbers and we need the ads. The public needs to know the message Team Trump put out and the Russian trolls put out. We deserve to know when we are getting brainwashed.

But this isn't just about the two faces of Donald Trump, it's about the two faces of politics: the republican and democratic parties. There couldn't be two faces more different when it comes to ideology. And Trump delights in creating chaos and doubt. It's his "management style," he's a "disrupter," his supporters claim. But he can't rise above his limited understanding of his role as President to all. People keep looking for the "pivot," meaning they want to see more Harvey Dent and a lot less Donald Trump.

Trump's running the White House like he would a season of Apprentice-- Armageddon edition. Small mindedness or deliberate strategy, it doesn't matter. Either and both are causing damage to our country. We are terrified and horrified! The whole world is tuning in.

TrumpFace Breaks a Record

Trump's track record of saying one thing and doing another continues to grow. I believe he's broken his own record, although he's the only one clamoring for the title. He said he'd work for the little people, the ones who voted for him, and now he's kicking them off insurance and taking away their food and heat. His budget is an assault on the poor. TrumpFace is deliberately taking food out of the mouth of babes.

And he's doing it! Nine million kids and hundreds of thousands of pregnant women were just knocked off of CHIP, Children's Health Insurance Program. The Republicans just let the deadline for reauthorizing go right on by.

And Trump is not just screwing over children, he's screwing Moms first. TrumpFace has flip-flopped on many women's issues, but the one that angers me most is denying women access to family planning services—birth control!

"I love women. No one has more respect for women than Donald J Trump." Then he repealed a bill assuring women will get equal pay. One of the first things Trump did was cut access for women to get family planning info, contraception and abortion counseling. Then he pledged $50-million of taxpayer money to his daughter Ivanka's fund to help women get started in business. Yeah, we can use that money to set up clinics that provide family planning info, contraception and abortion counseling. Geez, sounds like Planned Parenthood. Which Trump is defunding! Tell me again how TrumpFace is a friend to women.

But who truly knows what Trump believes. He's used the words "I'm pro-choice" and "I'm pro-life" in interviews with various interviewers. This is TrumpFace having it both ways.

TrumpFace Shoots for the Moon

Trump's two-talkin' ways were once again confirmed, this time with the help of daughter Ivanka and Education Secretary, Betsy DeVos. At the National Air and Space Museum event promoting women in the field of STEM--science, technology, engineering and math, Ivanka said Daddy Trump had "expanded NASA's space exploration mission and added Mars as a key objective." Yes, because Trump plans to destroy Earth. But Trump is cutting funding to internships, enrichment programs, camps, and scholarships for young scientists. Sure, tell them they can do anything but then deny them the funding to do so. Just another example from the double-talking douche, TrumpFace.

And Speaking of Destroying the Earth...

Environmental Protection Agency--you're fired!

And America, you're _____!

TrumpFace flat-out lied to Congress and the American people when he said he was going to protect the environment. Researchers said the Trump regime has been deleting scientific data collected by government agencies. One scientist said, "It's a bloodbath."

Trump said in an Earth Day statement that his administration is "committed to keeping our air and water clean, to preserving our forests, lakes and open spaces and to protecting endangered species." And then the Trump Administration denied endangered species status to the walrus. The polar ice caps are shrinking, and the walrus are dying out, but who needs walruses? Or bees for that matter? #fucktheenvironment

Trump has rolled back laws that have prevented big business from dumping sewage into the river. Need to deposit some of that mountaintop you've displaced? Sure, send it downstream. Need to dump some chemicals you want to discard but don't want to pay to dispose of properly? Just dump it down the river. Forget the fish and waterfowl, who gives a crap about the people who work and play on the river? And just try to prove toxic chemicals caused another Flint!

Trump promised the people clean water but then rolled back the regulations to make that happen. Clean air? Who needs it? Trump has ended the Clean Power Plan designed to lower carbon dioxide emitted by power generators.

Are you that naive to think big business will police itself? Or is it that you just don't care? Trump is intentionally putting profits over people. He wants to defund the Environmental Protection Agency. Does he even care that Ivanka's babies won't be able to breathe clean air? Does he not see what's happened in Japan? His disregard for the planet is astounding. Pulling out of the Paris Climate Accord is one of the worst decisions Trump has made.

The United States is incurring the wrath of Mother Nature: #Harvey, #Irma, #Maria, the west coast is on fire!! And our neighbor, Mexico, just experienced a 8.1 magnitude earthquake. But climate change isn't real. The White House doesn't even allow the words "climate change" on its website. Instead of making him look tough, it makes him weak and pathetic and abdicating America's leadership role. This is Trump proving he's a leader. To quote the dude from *The Office*, "Riiiiiighht."

Trump green-lighted the Dakota and XL Pipelines at first acting tough. He said they must use US steel, then he folded. The project is moving forward with Russian steel. Trump sees all business as good business, but he's not being a good steward of the land. But then Trump must have missed that week in bible school where we learned to take care of each other. As I remember, the only Bible passage he remembers when asked is "an eye for an eye."

For TrumpFace, now in the Oval, it's still about revenge, but more on that in the next chapter, Trumpenstein.

Russian Dressing on a Trump Salad

Sean Spicer famously joked, if Trump had Russian dressing on his salad, the Press would make a story out of it. Damn straight!

Wake up people! The news anchors use the term "allegedly" and qualify their phrases such as "Russia tried to hack our election with the effort to help Trump win, but we're not sure if Russia successfully hacked our election."

What can you not see? Trump is in the White House! Russia successfully hacked our election. Trump won, and Russia won. And now Trump is serving up America to Putin on a platter. Putin, the man who jails or kills journalists and political opponents. Putin, one of the richest men in the world, siphoning off funds from the Russian people, even as he expands his empire into the Ukraine.

I know it's been hard to see especially with all the stink bombs Trump drops. Obama tapped Trump Tower? Stink bomb to cover up Russia investigation. Tweetin' smack to North Korea? Stink bomb to cover up Russia investigation. Cut EPA funding by 30%? Stink bomb to cover up Russia investigation. Cut healthcare benefits to 24 million Americans and throw party. Stink bomb to cover up Russia investigation. Personally, persecutes his own Attorney General. Stink bomb to cover up Russia investigation. Toss in foul-mouthed Scaramucci--stink bomb; kick 800,000 undocumented citizens--KIDS no less--out of the country? Stink bomb. Well, I think you get the picture.

Answering questions regarding former National Security Advisor Mike Flynn's dealings with Russia, Trump said, "I didn't direct him, but I would have directed him if he didn't do it." TrumpFace just stated he'd have directed Flynn to have talks with the Russians after saying he didn't tell Flynn to have talks with the Russians.

Okay, so that explains that. More double-douche talk.

"I don't know Putin." -- Donald Trump

"I got to know him well." -- Donald Trump

Okay, which is it? Trump tried to downplay his relationship with Putin declaring relations were "at an all-time low." But then he groveled at his BFF's feet saying, "Things will work out fine between the U.S.A. and Russia. At the right time everyone will come to their senses & there will be lasting peace!"

Trump's supposedly first face-to-face meeting with Putin was at the G20 Summit where he had a two-hour meeting, and another undisclosed hour long meeting after dinner. Maybe they were talking about the six new Russia-Trump trademarks, four of which were approved on Election Day.

Or maybe they were talking about the XL pipeline which Trump promised would be made with American steel. But it turned out 40% is Russian steel. Or maybe they were talking about that back channel Trump-to-Putin direct line set-up. Or Trump Tower Moscow? Or maybe adoptions. Or maybe salad dressing.

I Heart Trump? Are You Bonkers?!

I'm flabbergasted. I spoke with a Trump fan recently. Not just a Trump-liker, a Trump-lover. Like I love Barack Obama, a Trump lover. It was astounding to hear her praise him. She was full-heartedly committed to Trump and his agenda.

Not stopping her, I let her tell me exactly what she loves about Trump. She loves his unapologetic bombast. She loves his hard-line stance on immigration and flat-out refused to believe a woman with a brain tumor, an undocumented patient, was removed from the hospital and taken into a detention center. She flat-out refused to believe the story. She said only the "bad guys" are being affected. She was not open to hearing any stories that conflicted with her view. Now that Trump's kicking out the DREAMers. I wonder if she'll believe me.

She knew and admitted that Donald Trump lies but didn't care. She acknowledged his wild exaggerations as just part of his showmanship and that didn't bother her.

She considers herself an informed woman but would not acknowledge any wrongdoing by Trump; in her mind there was none. She sees Trump as a great humanitarian; I'm astounded. She called him brilliant; I call him an idiot. I don't understand.

Through the Looking Glass

Here's what was true for me: she believed with everything she is that Trump can make a difference. She is hopeful. Now granted, from what I know, she has much. She and her husband are average middle-class, white-collar workers who own their own home and have been able to help their children afford college. Maybe they are multi-millionaires with money in the stock market now making money hand over fist. I don't know them except through a mutual friend. I do know them as being kind, respectful, and intelligent.

She wanted to know if I'd ever listen to Trump or watched him speak. I assured her I had. She is inspired. I am disgusted. She says he speaks the truth. I know he speaks lies.

Still astounded we moved on to the next topic: Democrats. She then went on a full-tilt rant about Democrats trying to impose their thinking on Republicans, and I can't even remember the rest because I was right there with her! Everything she said about Democrats I feel exactly the same way about Republicans! I blame Republicans for the same things she blames Democrats for!

It was like looking in a mirror where we were both experiencing the same reality but from a different side. There was something between us. I even had her raise her hands and I held my hands even with hers with a space at about 2 inches between us. I said, "Everything you just said, Sister, except from the other side. I think the same things about Republicans that you think about Democrats." We were both experiencing the same perception but from the opposite sides of reality.

What's In Between?

What is this, we both wondered. What was this between us? If we're both experiencing the same reality, each of us from our own side of "good versus evil," would we ever be able to agree on the problems we all face? It's as if our philosophies were in the way of the results we both wanted.

In my truth, there's an alternate reality being fed to us by Donald Trump and the White House. Maybe this is what my friend meant when she said he was brilliant. He is brilliantly distracting us from an extremist agenda. Bannon and Trump are "deconstructing" our government and tying private and government funds together. And don't be fooled, Bannon, now back at Breitbart, is bold-facedly challenging anyone who is anti-Trump, including members of the GOP.

This is a new economic reality where Trump believes in merging government and private interests, i.e. private prisons and investors making money off of companies profiteering in imprisoning people. Isn't that human trafficking? That's what Trump is doing--moving people back and forth across the border in search of financial gain. It's happening right now under our very noses, it's happening. Trump is also looking for ways to privatize the Afghanistan war and the Federal Aviation Administration. No conflicts of interest there. Riiiight.

I actually enjoyed my conversation with the Trump fan because I like her. I've known her for years as a dear friend of one of my dear friends. I've been to her house. I hear her speak only well of others. I respect her and I respect that she respects Trump, but that still doesn't make me respect Trump.

I wondered what she thought of Obama, but that was a conversation and topic best left for another time. But just to set the record straight. #Iheartbarackobama #Iheartmichelleobama #44FanGirl #thankyoubrackandmichelle #lovelettertoOinback

The Face in the Mirror

So, is this some sort of existential crisis we are collectively experiencing? A world-wide clarification of our beliefs. Isn't this the best time to evaluate our own thoughts and actions? How do you fit into the whole? How do you want to be remembered? And does this come down to my own, your own two faces in the mirror?

Believe in Yourself

Most spiritual philosophies embrace the dichotomies of good and evil. We know those traits exist in each one of us. An old Indian proverb speaks of two wolves, one that lives off of hate, the other on love. Which wolf wins out depends on which wolf you feed.

I know I can't believe in Donald Trump. He has us all scared to death of each other and of "unpredictable" him. But I refuse to live in fear or in despair. I choose to feed the wolf that needs love. How do I do that? By taking action. How about you? Which wolf will you feed?

What Action Can You Take?

1. Watch The Dark Knight Rises or any of the Batman movies

2. Don a pair of Presidential Flip-Flops highlighting Trump's opposing tweets. PresidentFlipFlops.com, "Going back on your word, one step at a time."

3. Get the Russian story at InvestigateRussia.org, a site championed by Rob Reiner, James Clapper, Charlie Sykes and so many competent others

4. https://www.linkedin.com/pulse/think-you-know-how-deep-trump-russia-goes-again-blow-your-frydenborg/ Just go here and see the crime board

5. Get the facts at FactCheck.org

6. Join Face2Face and help create a local volunteer network

7. Sign-up to received text messages from the Sierra Club Foundation. SCF educates and empowers people to protect and improve the natural and human environment. They also notify you when it's time to call your Congressmen and women

8. Support the Environmental Defense Fund and help companies become better stewards of the land. Focus on climate change, oceans, wildlife and habitats

9. Join MoveOn.org a policy advocacy and political action committee

Face

Everything

And

Rise

Feeling

Excited

And

Ready

TrumpFace

Trumpenstein

6. Trumpenstein: The Monster is Loose

There's a monster in the White House, in my closet, and under my bed. Is this monster a figment of my imagination? Or is he real? According to a NBC/Survey Monkey poll in February 2017, two thirds of the country goes to bed every night worried about Trump starting a war. That number continues to climb as Trump taunts North Korea and sells billions of dollars of weapons to the Middle Eastern countries. That's the monster under the bed.

The monster in the closet is the fear that Trump is coming for our health care, Medicaid, and social security. If the Republicans end up repealing the Affordable Care Act, my worst fear has happened. I am one of the 24 million people who will no longer be eligible for benefits but unable to afford monthly premiums on my own. Being self-employed has its advantages and disadvantages. The monster seems pretty friggin' real to me.

I don't know what I'm more scared of? Trump knowing he's a monster, wreaking havoc on the system, or that he doesn't know he is a monster. He thinks everything he is doing is right!

- Demolish the Department of Education by hiring mega donor Betsy DeVoss to voucherize and privatize the education system (so that all kids get a better education)? Trump does have the best interests of all children in mind, right? Or not. Currently Betsy DeVoss is rolling back regulation that will keep sham for-profit schools, such as Trump University, from profiting off students. There's also a rumor her family is invested in online, for-profit schools. No conflict of interest there. Riiiight.

- Ban middle-eastern immigrants (so Americans are safe from terrorists). That doesn't include countries where Trump is doing business and making a fortune.

- Build a wall on the Mexico border to keep out murderers, rapists, and drug dealers and all Hispanics (so we are safe from crime). Trump is such a racist he doesn't even recognize he's vilified an entire country.

- Sell the National Parks to the highest corporate bidder, remove restrictions on environmental mutilation (so private businesses can create jobs). Trump, who's only outdoor excursions include a trip to one of his golf courses, will probably add 18 holes to each park and raise the park pass entrance fees to $200,000/year. That reference is to the fees to join his Mar-a-Lago club. Before he was elected, the fee was $100,000/year.

After his election, he doubled it to $200,000. Only the rich will be able to afford it.

You might think, no biggie, I'm not in the market for a golf membership and that's just Trump taking money from the wealthy. But that's Trumpenstein just getting started! And here's how it affects you, and me, the common people.

The Trump Administration wants to double the cost of entry fees into the National Parks. Currently, the cost is $35 for one vehicle and all its passengers to enter. Trump wants to push that to $70 per vehicle. That's money right out of the pockets of Americans—and not the richest amongst us. Many families take advantage of the National Parks as cheaper vacation alternatives.

Tell me again how a $1.5 TRILLION tax cut for the wealthy will benefit me?! That money should be going to support our economy—and our Parks. But instead, the result is middle-class/poor people will have to pay more for every day small things, such as park passes. THIS is the type of stick-it-to-the-masses mob mentality that made Trump rich. How can he get the little guy to pay more?

As deplorable as this man is, I might not criticize him if all his outcomes were better systems and a better life for all. But there is a class of people, the townspeople, that Trumpenstein doesn't recognize or even see. He only sees his constituents, the very rich, and the ones that serve him and shield him from the ugly truth: he is indeed a monster. Who pushes for knocking 24-million people off health care insurance for the sake of pushing a deadline and getting legislation passed? A monster. Who pushes for tax cuts for the uber-rich? A monster.

Again, Trump doesn't see himself as a monster; he sees himself as working hard for the American people; he sees himself as a savior. And that's even scarier.

Frankenstein, the History

In Mary Shelley's book, *Frankenstein*, Dr. Victor Frankenstein, the main character, a scientist with a passion for chemistry and alchemy, makes himself a new friend, literally. He reanimates a dead body and creates a new man, Frankenstein. For those who haven't read the book, here's the Cliff Notes version:

Victor creates life, Frankenstein, but the creature is so hideous to look at that Victor is overcome with remorse and guilt. Unsure of how to take care of him, Victor leaves Frankenstein unattended as he wanders the streets figuring out what to do with his creation. Meanwhile, Frankenstein leaves, is ridiculed and frightened by the town's people, hides in the woods and ends up living with a family whose father is blind so unafraid of the horribly disfigured Frankenstein. Frankenstein becomes articulate, educated and well mannered. Frankenstein is a sensitive, soft soul who just wants a companion, someone to be with. The problem? He's ugly and scary.

When Frankenstein is shunned by the local village people, he becomes angry and demands that Victor create him a companion. When Victor fails and gives up, Frankenstein swears revenge on his creator.

Frankenstein's need for revenge becomes his undoing. Frankenstein goes on a killing spree that includes Victor's best friend, his brother, and Victor's own wife on their wedding night. Victor's dad also dies in grief.

Frankenstein runs, Victor chases. Victor dies in pursuit. Frankenstein feels remorseful and alone, vows to kill himself, drifts away on an ice raft at the North Pole.

No wonder I never read the book. To quote the monster in the White House, "Sad!" I much prefer the Mel Brooks movie version, Young Frankenstein. "It's pronounced Fronkensteen." Sorry, couldn't resist.

A Career of Revenge

It's revenge that destroyed Frankenstein. Could revenge be Trumpenstein's undoing as well?

Donald J. Trump
Revenge is sweet and not fattening. - Alfred Hitchcock
4:53 PM - Dec 15 2014

Donald Trump has built his career on revenge. In a 2007 speech as reported by Mother Jones, Trump explained his first rule of business:

"It's called 'Get Even.' Get even. This isn't your typical business speech. Get even. What this is a real business speech. You know in all fairness to Wharton, I love them, but they teach you some stuff that's a lot of bullshit. When you're in business, you get even with people that screw you. And you screw them 15 times harder. And the reason is, the reason is, the reason is, not only, not only, because of the person that you're after, but other people watch what's happening. Other people see you or see you or see and they see how you react."

Donald J Trump
Always get even. When you are in business, you need to get even with people who screw you. - Think Big
9:20 AM - May 3 2013

Ironically, Trump's tweet is quoting his own book, *Think Big,* when just the opposite is true: only the simple and small-minded focus on revenge. This isn't big thinking by a successful businessman; it's the thinking of a monster who thinks he's a God. He is judge, jury, and executioner against anyone he feels has harmed him.

"I have some very, very good friends and I guess I have some very good enemies. And I like it that way, somehow, and I really believe in trashing your enemies," says Trumpenstein. For real. That was a young Donald Trump spewing his nonsense in an interview he no doubt set-up.

This is the thinking of a stupid monster with an "Abby Normal" brain. If only this were the Young Frankenstein movie version; we'd bring in Madeline Kahn to "take care of business." If you don't know what that means, watch the movie! It's clear to all of us, this monster needs a companion and Melania's not taking care of business. But who can blame her? Trump is repulsive.

Man-Made, Self-Made or Russia-Made?

Where did this man come from? Trump has claimed to be born in New Jersey to Swedish parents. New sources, however, report he was born to German and Scottish parents living in the Bronx: Frederick Christ Trump and Mary Anne MacLeod.

Trump comes from the lineage of Friedrich Drumpf who apparently arrived at Ellis Island in 1885. Fred appears to have changed his name from Drumpf to Trump while becoming a naturalized citizen. Apparently, it didn't look good or sound good to be German in America at that time. Perhaps this is why Trump pursued Barack Obama so long and hard about his birth certificate. Having come from a family that changed their name and heritage for their own gain, Trump assumed Barack Obama would do the same.

Trumpenstein, while secretive on most business dealings, is completely transparent as he projects his small thinking onto others. Whatever he accuses someone of doing, he's involved in that activity and diverting attention, so you won't know. Crooked Hillary, Lyin' Ted? We all know who the crooked liar is.

Trumpenstein: Creator and Monster

Whether this is brilliance or stupidity only you can decide. To me, it proves the brainpower of a ten-year-old; or if he truly is as intelligent as he says, a monster--since only a monster treats people how Trumpenstein does.

Trump claims to be self-made although he received lots of financial help from his rich slum-lord daddy. Trump claims to have received a small $1 million loan from his dad to get his first property. Conflicting sources say it was more like $14 million.

Trumpenstein loves blowing his own horn. His surname is after all now Trump, as in trumpet, and man does this douche of a monster blow.

He admits to calling into magazines and newspapers under the pseudonym John Baron where he's shared juicy bits of gossip about himself. *Trump's dating so-and-so and Trump just closed this big deal.* Trump still loves talking about himself in third person. Can't get good press in New York City? Make something up and spoon-feed it to the Press. Trumpenstein has deployed this marketing tactic for decades.

Phoning into "the shows" and doing his own press was critical in his quest for the White House. He continues doing his own press often shooting himself in the foot. Think of his disastrous interview after firing FBI Director James Comey. He flat-out admitted he did it because of the Russian probe. I'm predicting it will be Trumpenstein's need for revenge--and Twitter--that ultimately do him in.

The *Washington Post* reports Trump has fake *Time Magazine* covers emblazoned with his profile hanging as artwork on Trump property walls. *Time Magazine* has asked Trump to remove the bogus cover; it doesn't accurately reflect the editorial slant of the magazine. No wonder Trump cries "fake news" all the time. He's the main instigator of fake news--and as always, he's projecting his penchant for fake news onto others.

Trumpenstein is already rewriting history and shoving it down our throats using social media. Puerto Rico is in ruins; twenty days after Maria and only 10%

have power and 50% are still without water. People are dying, Mayor Cruz is begging for help and Trumpestein golfs. Monster douche.

The Ultimate Revenge Brings the Monster to Life

It's Obama's fault! That's Trumpenstein's answer to every situation: Obama created ISIS, Obama wiretapped me, Obama is responsible for Assad's chemical attack on his people. "It's Obama's fault" are always the first words out of Trump's mouth.

In truth, I think this is partly Obama's fault. Gasp! No, say it ain't so! No, I haven't turned into a Republican and I will always believe that President Obama will be the greatest U.S. president in my lifetime. If anyone's face belongs on Mount Rushmore, it'd be Obama. Trump's big fat face? Please. Insert Anderson Cooper eyeroll here.

I think President Obama's epic takedown of Trump helped build the fire that brought Trumpenstein to life.

Look at the footage of the 2012 White House Press Corps dinner, the night Obama razzed Trump for Trump's relentless attacks on his citizenship. Obama had provided undisputable proof of his citizenship that week when Hawaii released the long-form of his birth record.

As always, Obama was polished and articulate even as he razzed The Donald. Obama said, "Now, I know that he's taken some flak lately, but no one is happier, no one is prouder to put this birth certificate matter to rest than The Donald. And that's because he can finally get back to focusing on the issues that matter — like, did we fake the moon landing? What really happened in Roswell? And where are Biggie and Tupac?"

"But all kidding aside," Obama continued, "obviously, we all know about your credentials and breadth of experience. For example — no, seriously, just recently, in an episode of 'Celebrity Apprentice' — at the steakhouse, the men's cooking team did not impress the judges from Omaha Steaks. And there was a lot of blame to go around. But you, Mr. Trump, recognized that the real problem was a lack of leadership. And so ultimately, you didn't blame Lil Jon or Meatloaf. You fired Gary Busey. And these are the kind of decisions that would keep me up at night. Well handled, sir. Well handled."

Trump sat in the audience, stone-faced sober. He didn't laugh and didn't shake it off. Given Trumpenstein's continued attacks on Obama, I'd say the barb had some teeth then and still does.

I think Seth Meyers, quick-witted former SNL comedian, now NBC Late Night talk-show host extraordinaire and EMCEE for that evening, delivered the zinger that might have struck the match:

"Donald Trump has been saying he will run for president as a Republican — which is surprising, since I just assumed he was running as a joke."

And the monster came to life.

It's Alive! Run For Your Life!

Thank goodness Seth Meyers continues to regale us with insightful, truthful political commentary. I particularly enjoy *A Closer Look*. Meyers isn't letting Trump get by with distraction; Meyers is calling Trump out on every ignorant and vengeful action he takes. Thank you, Seth Meyers for your continued commentary.

"I put lipstick on a pig."
-- Tony Schwartz

In the July 2016 New Yorker article titled *Donald Trump's Ghost Writer Tells All*, by Jane Mayer, Tony Schwartz, co-author of *The Art of the Deal*, says he feels deep remorse for his part in creating Trump. Schwartz says if he could rename the book now, he'd call it "*The Sociopath*."

On June 16, 2015, Donald Trump descended down from the clouds of Trump Tower and laid out his qualifications for his presidential run to a bunch of tourists and paid actors saying the country needed a leader that wrote *The Art of the Deal*. After hearing the news, Tony Schwartz responded:

Tony Schwartz
I wrote the Art of the Deal. Donald Trump read it.
5:19 PM - Sep 16 2015

In another tweet about six weeks later, Schwartz said:

Tony Schwartz
Let's be clear: Whatever else Donald Trump is it's a self-perpetuating myth that he's a good closer.
3:16 PM - Nov 6 2016

Timothy O'Brien who wrote *Trump Nation* called *The Art of the Deal* "a nonfiction work of fiction" and says Trump used the book to turn most every aspect of his life into a "glittering fable." O'Brien says The Apprentice is "myth-making on steroids."

Indeed, Trump continues to believe and spread that rhetoric: he's a great negotiator. "I'm a master negotiator," (do your own Trump impression here), "I will fix all the nation's problems through negotiation." Clearly, Trump's embraced the book *The Art of the Deal*. Of course, he does! It was part of his own self-made celebrity. Trump paid Schwartz to write it.

Edward Kosner, former editor and publisher of *New York Magazine* said of Tony, who was working there at the time he wrote the book, "Tony created Trump. He's Dr. Frankenstein."

The first article Schwartz wrote about Trump in *New Yorker* wasn't that flattering, but Trump loved it and hired Tony to write his book. Remember, to Trump, there's no such thing as bad press, and he's proven that. Tony said he wrote the book for the money. Don't despair Tony, no one blames you for Donald Trump. Writers gotta eat. And you're making up for it.

"Others see Trump as a charmingly, brash entrepreneur with an unfaltering knack for business," wrote Mayor in her interview with Schwartz, but Schwartz sees him differently. Schwartz thinks he's a pathological, compulsive liar who is self-centered, has a short attention span, with superficial knowledge and who's just plain ignorant. Schwartz confirms that lying is second nature to Trump.

Here is a passage from the book *The Art of the Deal*. Trump's said, "I play to people's fantasies. People want to believe that something is the biggest and greatest and the most spectacular. I call it truthful hyperbole. It's an innocent form of exaggeration and it's a very effective form of promotion."

Tony Schwartz says of Trump, "He is not innocent. Truthful hyperbole is a contradiction in terms. It's a way of saying, 'It's a lie but who cares?'"

159

Indeed, we watched Trump lie every day of his campaign and now we're watching that same dynamic in his presidency. Lies, lies, and more lies. Both the *Washington Post* and *New York Times* have published articles articulating his top 1000 lies since taking office.

Tony Schwartz regrets creating a character far more likable and winning than Trump really is. Schwartz says Trump is driven by an insatiable hunger for "money, praise, and celebrity."

Yes, that sure sounds like POTUS 45, Trumpenstein, a ratings whore and a monster of a douche.

The Monster Mash

Trump threw his own book launch party in December of 1987 in the atrium of his own Trump Tower. It was a black-tie and evening gown event where guests drank champagne and ate from a cake in the shape of Trump Tower. Jackie Mason, a popular and celebrated comedian, introduced Donald and Ivanka, wife number one, with the words "Here comes the king and queen." For more on *that*, see Chapter 9, King Dong.

Trump called Tony Schwartz the next day telling him he owed half of the party expenses since he had profited from the book. Trump's bill for the decadent event was rumored to be a six-figure number. Tony Schwartz, having learned a few tricks from Trump, negotiated the bill down to a few thousand dollars, then Schwartz wrote a letter to Trump offering to donate the money to a charity of Schwartz's own choosing. According to *The Art of the Deal*, that negotiating tactic was a Trump special. Trump promised to give millions of dollars to charity, but the *Washington Post* has only found evidence of about $10,000 donated from the profits from *The Art of the Deal.* Trump's non-profit is currently under investigation for fraud by New York City Attorney General Eric Schneiderman.

Tony Schwartz is donating all profits he makes from *The Art of the Deal* to charities that support the rights of the people Trumpenstein is currently trampling on.

Tony is also doing his part to inform people of Trump's madness. Follow him on Twitter @tonyschwartz and read the book he's co-authored, *The Dangerous Case of Donald Trump: 27 Psychiatrists and Mental Health Experts Assess a President.* It's on my reading list. Thanks Tony for getting the word out.

It Takes a Village

I believe the Republican party is partly to blame for Trumpenstein's rise. Mitch McConnell set the tone for obstructionism in President Barack Obama's first term. "My only goal is to make sure Obama is a one-term president."

Forget his policies or how Obama inspired and helped the American people. Mitch McConnell was one of the reasons is that Congress was stuck in gridlock. Does that make McConnell racist? I don't know. Was this about policy or the color of Obama's skin? Does immediately disliking someone for their politics make them racist? Then include Mitch McConnell--and include me!!

Trumpenstein is not the only one the Republicans made, they helped make me, too. I can define myself as almost directly opposed to all Republican issues: a woman's right to choose, healthcare for all, just for starters. When someone identifies to me they are a "Republican," I automatically know our thinking will not be aligned. Their close-mindedness leads to my own. That's why I choose not to do business with them. Or include them in my inner circle.

Is that the definition of racist--having preconceived notions of who's right and who's wrong? I don't do it based on things I can see but on what I perceive to be wrong thinking! Is that a racist? I like surrounding myself with my own kind: those that care about others and have integrity and grant equal rights to all. I avoid people who deny others' rights. I repeat, does that make me a racist or elitist? Doesn't that make me a kind human?

I'm not judging on looks, heritage or culture, all things people can't help; but I am judging. I'm judging based on thinking which I believe we have some control over. Or is this nature-versus-nurture? Are we born Democrat or Republican? Can a child really help where or who it comes from and how one's parents voted? Aren't we all a product of our environment until a certain age? I have a friend whose parents use to say, "what you do as a child reflects on us; what you do as an adult reflects on you."

Clearly, we don't all have the same advantages growing up, but at some time each of us must take responsibility for our own decisions. Trumpenstein, man-made, self-made, or Russia-made, makes decisions based on his own needs.

The Walking Dead

Republicans flat-out refused to work with President Obama on anything. Even when Obama took Republican policies and tried to get the Republicans on

161

board they still wouldn't budge. It was quite clear that they were obstructionist from the get-go. They shut down the government. They balked at every proposal President Obama brought to them. They stole a Supreme Court seat with defiance and glee and refused to confirm lower court Obama appointees. Who is paying the price? The American people and Democracy as a whole.

When it came to voting in the 2016 election, people had had enough of Republicans, and Democrats too for that matter thanks to all the Trump-Russia propaganda. Trumpenstein took advantage of the holes in both Republican and Democratic platforms and he made up a platform of his own.

Trumpenstein ran as an independent thinker--neither beholden to the Republicans or the Democrats. He had no solutions or policies. He simply repeated again and again "it'll be so easy," and "we'll win, win, win, you'll be sick of winning." He never said what we'd win. As it's turned out, we've all won a big gaping hole in our collective soul and the ire of the rest of the world.

He also said he was financing his own campaign, but corporate money financed Trumpenstein's presidential bid. And as soon as Trumpenstein got the nomination--bullied and bought his way into the nomination--the Republicans took notice and jumped on the Trumpenstein train and opened up the Republican equivalent of Gringotts Wizarding Bank.

Watching the Republicans cave, one by one, was disheartening. All the people that Trump bullied came on board, including Mitt Romney and Ted Cruz. Trumpenstein got ultimate revenge on Mitt Romney when he had him down to dinner and served him crow. I mean, frog legs. And how pathetic was it to see Ted Cruz, wife and daughters in town go kiss Trump's ... ring.

John McCain is a small hope that there are still Republicans that have a spine and will stand up to President Trump. McCain's thumbs-down vote to kill the Senate health care bill will be remembered for a generation. His speech to return to bipartisan efforts will be legion--but know that thumbs-down vote would not have made a difference if it weren't for the two women Senators from Alaska and Maine. More on them in Chapter 8, Biff Trump. Lindsey Graham is also showing a bit of fortitude and sass. We need more.

But now the spineless Republicans on the House Ways and Means Committee voted to help Trump conceal his tax returns. They know the truth, too. Trumpenstein is bought, paid-for, assembled, animated and brought to life.

Trumpenstein is a trash-talker and hater who has projected his need for revenge on the nation. The only person he spares is his friend, Vlad Putin.

How Do You Say "Monster" in Russian?

Self-made, man-made, Russia-made. There is no doubt that Russia interfered with the 2016 election. All of our intelligence agencies agree Russia hacked DNC servers, released erroneous information, and targeted voter registration rolls in key swing states. The only person who doesn't believe Russia interfered is Donald Trump.

There is nothing being done by Trump or Congress to assure Russia never again interferes in our election. In fact, Trump is moving in the opposite direction. He's appointed a council on voter fraud. He's looking to find 3 million votes he can throw out because he claims he won the popular vote, too. Should Trump's people get their hands on other data, I predict many will lose their ability to vote in the next election. Their information will be scrubbed off the voter rolls, but Russia already got a head start on that.

Trump barely squeaked by an Electoral College win. In the three critical swing states of Pennsylvania, Michigan and Wisconsin, Trump won by 77,744 votes out of 13.9 million ballots cast. TheNation.com reported that new voter ID laws in Wisconsin suppressed 200,000 votes. Trump won Wisconsin by 22,748 votes. Trump said he wouldn't accept the results of the election if he didn't win. He wouldn't accept because he knew it was rigged.

Has it been proven? That Russia actually affected the result? Not yet. But now Facebook, Twitter, and Google have all admitted that Russians spent almost $1 billion on ads across all three tech giants. It's imperative that the American people see the ads. When I hear propaganda come out of the mouth of my friends, I want to know where they heard that. Chances are, they saw a story on social media. A story written and distributed by the Russians with the sole purpose of getting Trumpenstein elected.

But I am going to trust Bob Mueller with that investigation. If he finds that Trump did collude with Russia to win, I'm going to do my part to help Trump right out of office. If Mueller finds nothing then I'm going to work with Trump, the Monster, until he learns to see all of the village people.

Trumpenstein

The Monster Needs a New Heart

Trump unveiled his budget blueprint and immediately we are going to increase spending on Military, weaponry and the Wall while eliminating funding for people, the planet, and the arts.

Trump campaigned on the Wall and the War Machine, but he also said he'd take care of everyone. Now, the Monster with no heart is cutting food programs to the poor: Meals on Wheels and school lunch programs. He's eliminating funds for National Public Radio and other cultural programs as well as funds for kids to go to college.

It truly takes a monster to take food out of the mouths of seniors and children. Who cares that we can destroy the world a million times over when our elderly and our babes are starving in the streets? Trumpenstein's never missed a meal in his life.

This is what happens when a capitalist and con artist buys himself a country. Good citizens who voted for him will be starving soon.

People with disabilities? Freeloaders! Get a job! Mentally impaired? Physically handicapped? Who cares, get a job.

Trump's currently raiding government coffers--mainly the State Department and Environmental Protection Agency--to start work on his wall. He is still figuring out how he can steal the other $22 billion from Mexico, or bully it out of them.

Trump campaigned on securing the border, and many of his voters support putting up an actual border wall. Other supporters thought he was speaking metaphorically but he is indeed getting bids on putting up an actual structure. He's like a monster with building blocks that could construct the greatest cities of the world!

Instead, Trumpenstein builds walls. Why? Because he's small-minded. He's got the brain of Abby Normal. For being such a successful businessman, he appears to be a very small thinker. If he was truly as great as he thinks he is, he would be revered by all, not just a few who hate others. But he's not. He's no Bill Gates. He doesn't work to make the world a better place for all, he works to make the place better for his family, his friends, and the very rich. His enemies and the small people he trashes and demeans without concern and often with delight.

Demystifying the Monster

What I've done to deal with Donald Trump is to demystify the monster. I'm trying to override emotion with reason. Frustration to fascination? How about pure rage to total contentment? How do I get there? Faith? Belief? Believing there's a bigger picture I cannot see? The story is still being written. But I'm looking at Donald Trump and truly believing I'm seeing an ill man. Who pits Americans versus Americans? How is this behavior even explainable?!

I've come to understand if I have a disagreement with someone, it could be because of our communication styles. We might be focused on different information with different outcomes in mind.

Maybe Trump is not a monster. We're watching his every move trying to understand his intent and style. For someone who wants only English-speaking immigrants let into the country, it's ironic, he barely speaks English. He's either conversing in 140 characters or less, or burping up a word salad of insults and lies. If we put aside Trump's need for revenge and glory and look specifically at his style of communicating, I can see a familiar communication style. It helps me understand Trump. Let me explain.

Trump is an often abrasive, always direct communication style. Contrast that with Hillary Clinton who is a thoughtful, logical communication style.

I've been teaching a communication profile for 17 years. I use my own hybrid version of Psychogeometrics, a communication profile which I first heard in 1999 on an audio program by Dr. Susan Dellinger. Psychogeometrics is based on Jungian psychology and has been in the public lexicon since the 1950s. Cross that with another program I listened to about that same time, Relationship Strategies, by Tony Allesander, then throw in a bit of the Colors and the Animals if you want. There are many communication profiles, and each breaks down the styles into four basic categories. Think shapes, animals, colors, or letters, but do think about how Trump communicates.

Understanding Trump's communication style helps me cope with his leadership style--which I assure you exists. It's just not normal.

Let's Begin with the Basics

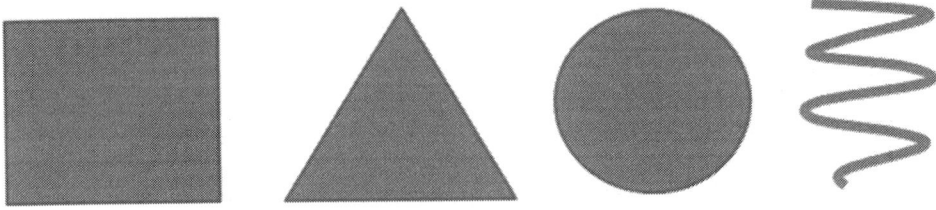

Quick, pick your favorite shape. Don't second-guess it. Which one do you like? Point to it, own it, let's see if that's really you. Because this profile is based on Jungian psychology, you're over 50% likely to have a match. Read on, and if the shape you pointed to isn't your main communication style, no problem. Each one of us is predominantly two of the communication styles. You'll know what style you are by the time you're done with this chapter.

We're going to make this easy and break this communication profile down for you into the basics: the 101 of the Shape of Communication.

When you meet someone new, or now as you're trying to put your spouse, kids, relatives, friends, co-workers, boss or the president into a category, there are two questions you must ask yourself.

The two questions are:

1. How fast do they move?
2. What do they talk about?

There are fast people and slow people.

There are people who talk about people and there are people who talk about projects.

Let's put it on a quadrant and make it simple:

Trumpenstein

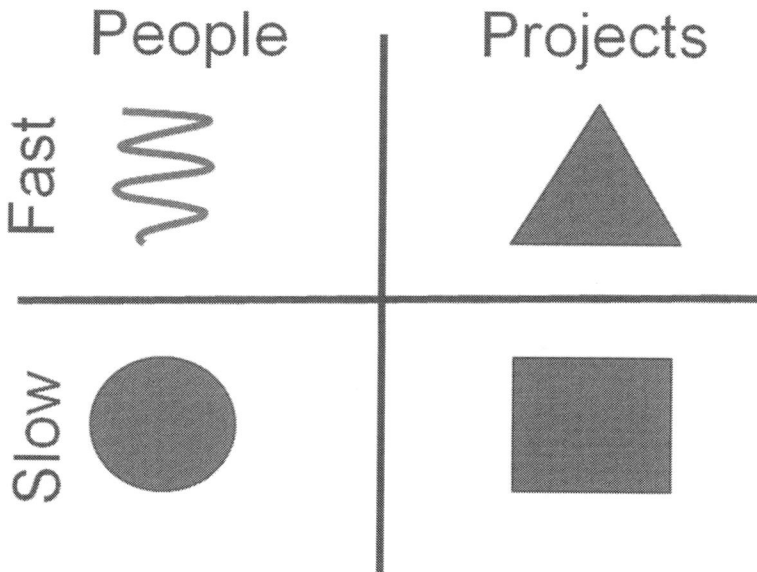

People | Projects

Fast

Slow

The fast-paced people, the movers and shakers, are the Squiggles and Triangles. The slow-paced people, steady-as-they-go, are the Circles and Squares. Then we have the people who talk about people, the Squiggles and Circles. Finally, we have the people who talk about projects, the Triangles and the Squares.

Let's Simplify

Fast-paced people people are Squiggles.
Slow-paced people people are Circles.
Slow-paced project people are Squares.
Fast-paced project people are Triangle.

Let's take a closer look at what each shape finds important and how that translates into perspectives and language.

The Project People: Triangles and Squares

Both Triangles and Squares are linear, logical, and sequential. They relate to logic and facts and numbers and statistics. They are rigid in their thinking as conveyed by the rigid structures of their shapes. They immerse themselves in projects--Triangles more so focused on getting it done--Squares, focused on getting it done right.

Even though both shapes focus on projects, the Triangles do more so from a big-picture perspective. The Squares focus on the details.

Let's look a bit more closely at each of the project people. Let's start with the Triangles. Why? Because they have the shortest attention spans and the most need for the information.

Triangles

Triangles are leaders and doers and, yes, sometimes they are bullies on a mission. What Triangles often forget or don't understand is that projects serve people. "Period," as former White House Press Secretary Sean Spicer would say.

Every project that has value does not have value in and of itself, it has value because it serves people. That is the litmus test of worthiness of any project? Does it serve people? Or animals, or the planet, if you like to argue the technicalities of the language, which Squares do.

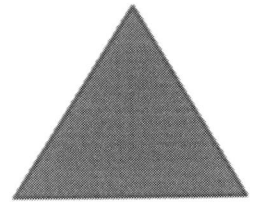

Why build a bridge? It helps connect land masses and people. Why own a business of any kind? So you can serve people.

Maybe you own a business that sells to other businesses. Maybe it's not a sexy or glamorous business. Maybe you manufacture and sell huge grates and drains to architectural firms and other builders. It doesn't take a flood for everyone to know how valuable a drain is when the water is rising. Somewhere down the line that business serves people, or they wouldn't be in business. I challenge you to find me a business that does not serve people.

If you're saying no way, I'm in it for the money, well somewhere down the line is a person handing over their cash. Instead of serving people, you are exploiting them.

Triangles forget that sometimes. People are put into categories and dehumanized. They become a task on a list, and Triangles put their self-worth into accomplishing tasks and checking items off their "to-do" list. They often stampede over the very people their project is serving simply because completing the task is what's most important.

Trump is the biggest Triangle on the planet! He's built his reputation on being a tough negotiator. He's often admitted he doesn't discuss the details, he doesn't have the attention span for the details. This makes him a delegator, something Triangles love to do but not necessarily a good leader. Trump often speaks of surrounding himself with confident people, the "best people." He's counting on them to fill in the details because his mind doesn't think that way.

For example, "Forget about the little shit" Trump reportedly told the Freedom Caucus when trying to get them to buy into his Trumpcare plan. "Let's focus on the big picture here," and in typical Triangle fashion, Trump focused on the big picture not even taking time to understand the details.

I'm a Triangle, too. A Triangle/Squiggle combination. That means I love getting projects done but understand that everything I do serves someone on some level. Trump doesn't have this understanding. He's not wired for people. How do you know? By how he treats them.

Trump treats people as part of a project, a "get-it-done" mentality that will backfire if he doesn't slow down. Trump and Ryan's attempt to ram through Trumpcare is a perfect example. Trump didn't understand the details and he oversimplified the repeal and replace option even as he demonized it.

Trump bold-facedly over-promised what he could do and is now playing the blame game: Freedom Caucus, Democrats, anyone but himself or Bully Bannon. In reality, it was Trump's grandiose thinking and communication style that led him to promise healthcare coverage for everyone, with better options, and lower premiums. I personally hope he can deliver on that campaign promise. But in true Triangle style, he pushed and pushed, and when he didn't get his way, walked away from the deal. On to the next thing--tax reform--that's a Triangle. What about the people? What people? Trump doesn't see them.

There are two main questions for a triangle:

1. How much does it cost?
2. How fast can I get it?

Not bad questions if you're ordering pizza, but when ordering aircraft carriers, Triangles need to slow the F down.

Squares: The Process People

Squares are a much-needed check and balance to a Triangle that over promises, because it's Squares who are responsible for making impossible ideas real; for writing the policies that would make Trumpcare work. For working out the details between the insurance companies, the pharmaceutical companies, the hospitals, the clinics, the doctors, the nurses, the support staff and ultimately the patient.

"Who knew healthcare could be so complicated?" said Trump the Triangle. For F's sake, Donald, everyone but you! You're the only one who didn't know providing health care to millions and millions of people was a complex endeavor. The only person who didn't know that running the government is not a reality show version of The Apprentice where you can send a ragtag crew of celebrities to get their friends to raise money for charity - and have the whole thing filmed, edited and packaged for viewing in 60 minutes of TV Time - is you!

Time out before I pull a Scaramouch and go all gutter on Trump's ass. Breathe, Girl! Ommm. Better.

Let's talk about the items on Trump's "to-do "list. His first 100 days were a whirlwind of activity. Triangle Trump needs some Squiggle energy. He needs to find someone with an optimistic bright side to every shitshow he exposes them to. No, that's not Kellyanne Conway. The bloom is off that rose. Many people are counting on Ivanka to bring positive energy and balance to her daddy's life, but it's not happening.

Trump has now brought on General John Kelly as his new Chief of Staff. Let's see what this brings. Will he be able to influence Trumpenstein? Will he keep Trump from pushing the button??!! We are all hoping and praying so, but chances not. Triangles cannot be controlled--and they pride themselves on that fact!

Power Through Intimidation and Force

Trump's threats might have worked in the business world but they don't work with Congressmen and Congresswomen. Want to know why the Trumpcare bill didn't pass? Triangles? Want to venture a guess?

Squares. Even though Squares look like introverted pushovers, they are not. And squares with Triangle tendencies are just as likely to give you a big FU. All those scientists Trump have dissed? Squares.

170

How do we know Climate Change is real? Squares. When over one million people in 600 cities joined the March for Science, we need to take note. When the nerds and geeks take to the streets it's time to listen!! They want nothing more than to be behind the scene, buried in their data, but they are sounding the alarm. The only ones not convinced by decades of data are the Triangles. And that's Trump.

There are some squares behind the scenes right now sorting through the details of Trump's financial history. If Trump colluded with Russia, the Squares will find it. Trump should be afraid of what he's hiding; Squares are relentless.

Triangles need to close their mouths and listen--and methodically adjust unrealistic deadlines and expectations. Ryan's Trumpcare bill didn't come close to being passed because the vote-driven deadline superseded the time necessary for discussion. Because as a discussion really started, it was clear the bill didn't serve people. Boom! And we're back to the people.

More About Squares

Squares, the slow-paced project people, doing their jobs under pressure as Triangles and Squiggles breathe down their necks.

Squares are the know-it-alls, and they really are. They are data collectors that go deep down the rabbit hole. Ask them what time it is and they want to tell you how to build a watch. Squares keep to themselves, and they don't want to talk to you. If they must communicate with you, they prefer to write to you. Don't bother to call, they never pick up the phone. Of all the communication styles, Squares are the toughest to persuade. They don't relate to emotions and feelings instead using phrases like "I think" and "I don't know, but I'm willing to test it out."

Squares are meticulous about their language--and yours! They will call you out on it, or secretly confirm in their heads that you are stupid. They see themselves as having superior intellect. Think "nerds on The Big Bang Theory." When you speak and work with Squares, focus on the process, the details, and the tasks needed to accomplish a goal.

Neither Squares nor Circles like confrontation and both are sensitive to tone. Squares like an even, lowered voice discussion. They don't like it when people get too animated. Triangles and Squiggles--kings and queens of drama-- can't help but let their emotions out. Think hot-blooded Italians, the Spanish, and the Irish. Heated discussions intimidate and shut Squares down, although you'll never know what they're thinking, they wear poker faces, as do Squiggles.

Squares need a long time to process information, so don't rush them. And don't hug them. Squares keep to themselves. They are loyal, predictable, and a must have for every team. Trump's team is lacking in linear, logical, sequential Squares.

But you know who is a Square? Hillary Rodham Clinton. HRC, with a degree from Wesley and a Dr. of Law from Yale; former First Lady of Arkansas; former First Lady of the United States; former Secretary of State; Democratic Nominee for President of the United States and winner of the popular vote. Hill is a Square/Triangle/Circle combo: a Square because she thinks about details. And her website contained her well-thought-out strategies with the leadership of a Triangle.

But why do I say Circle? Because Hillary's entire career has been advocating for children and families. And because she's a Square, she had created the policies to help them. All families. But she was flattened by a Triangle who had no vision for the country and didn't and still doesn't play by the rules. A Douchebag at that.

Circles Are All About the Love

Circles, team players, have a family at home a family at work and a Facebook family. Circles often work in positions that directly affect people. Remember, they are the slow-paced people people. That means Circles have all kinds of time to listen. They don't interrupt, they nod and smile and engage and play along. They understand every project they undertake serves people and they often work in healthcare, education, and human resource positions.

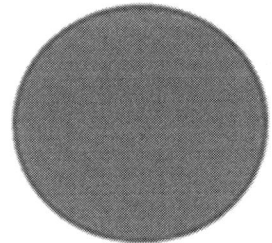

Circles have candy dishes on their desks. They go around and say "good morning" and "hello" to everyone. If you need a hug, Circles always have one to offer. Circles are empathetic and people pleasers. They don't like to let others down.

People think they are office gossips but they're not; it's just that Circles do not have boundaries on information. That means anything you tell them has the potential of being passed about. It is their number one function: Circles spread the information. Triangles often count on them to do just that, but Triangles rarely give enough detailed information. They count on Circles to deal with the details.

Are the White House leakers Circles? They might be. I'm betting there are multiple leakers who are all of the communication styles, because these leaks are deeper than a style itself, this is about the information and their motivation for sharing the information.

To me, these leakers are heroes. They are sending vital information to the American public. They are the SOS within the White House. Trump is either batshit crazy or batshit mean, either way, someone has got to let the people know. Triangle Trump is moving America away from a democracy and to an authoritarian society where government and private money is intermingled. Thank goodness all of the communication styles are capable of being courageous when the need arises. We are going to need all of them to stand up to Triangle Trump.

Circles, thanks to their attention to detail, are great event planners. Wow-- can they throw a party! But often it's a low-key event, that's until the Squiggles show up!

Squiggles--the Visionaries!

Squiggles are outgoing, gregarious, weird, and totally likeable. Squiggles have great energy and great appreciation for others. They are visionaries, they look ahead, they dream, they wonder. Right now, there are Squiggles out there dreaming up new tools and gadgets--things we don't yet know we need.

Squiggles are up, up, up - until they are not. Squiggles are natural bipolars. They work and play for as hard as they can for as long as they can and when they've exhausted all of their energy, it's as if someone flipped a switch and turned them off. They hit the wall; they collapse. When that happens, the Circles want to hug them and love on them and to nurture them back to health, but if you just leave them alone, Squiggles bounce back on their own.

Squiggles are fun and exciting. Like Triangles, they are big picture thinkers. Squiggles work well with Circles who are masters of detail.

Squiggles ask "Who is involved? Who will be there?" Who, who, who, because they are often the welcoming committee. They are tapped into a higher consciousness than most, often understanding how the project will fit into the world and the Universe as a whole.

Squiggles are the best communicators, speaking all four languages: Square, Circle, Triangle, and of course Squiggle. Squiggles are chameleons and work well with all of the shapes. They have Squiggle logic: at times they are brilliant, and of course like Circles, they serve people.

So, we know Trumpenstein is predominately a Triangle, but what is his second most common shape? This is a bit harder. Most of us have a line in common, meaning squiggle/Triangle combinations are common, Squiggle/Circle combinations are common. Triangle/Square combos are common and Square/Circle combos are common. What's not common is a Triangle with circle tendencies or a Squiggle/Square combo, but sometimes they happen.

Trump has very little circle in him. He says he's about people now that he's President, but he's never served people in his business endeavors; he serves himself.

I don't see him, Trump, as a Squiggle. He's not tapped into people and he doesn't think big enough. He thinks he's a big thinker, but big thinking to Trump is a taller building in a different country. That's not big thinking. Trump has no vision. I don't see him as a Triangle/Square, he's not detailed or patient enough.

When asked in an interview, what makes Trump tick? He responded, "My own tempo, which is fast." Trump went on to explain we each have our own internal tempo. He says some people are deliberate, contemplative, and reflective. He says "others, like me, proceed at lightning speed. I think that my speed enables me to do more. It also challenges my people to keep up with me."

What Trump fails to recognize is his strength is also his weakness. He doesn't have time to understand details, he overlooks important information. Not all decisions should be made in a snap. What little consequence his decision has on him has plenty impact on others.

Trump lacks awareness of different communication styles. In true Triangle fashion, he expects everyone to adapt to him. In chapter 21 of *Trump 101*, Trump says "keep it short, fast, and right to the point." He goes on to criticize anyone who doesn't speak in that style. He says being quick is a sign of respect for one's time. Well, letting people finish their thoughts and sentences without interrupting or projecting what you would say on to it--is a sign of respect. You can't be respected when you don't respect others.

I think Trump is a Triangle/Triangle. But seriously, who cares what his style is?! How can this information help you? How can it help me? His rhetoric makes me sick. His speech to the Boy Scouts? In-a-pro-pri-ate! This 1st Class Girl Scout was horrified! This is why I wrote the book: to release the rage. I want to understand this man and how and why he does things. I'm trying hard to understand. Here's what I know.

Each one of us is predominantly two shapes, the question right now is what two shapes are you? Because your communication style will determine how you react to Donald Trump. Remember, this book is about *your reaction* to Donald Trump.

If you are a Triangle, you can probably relate on some level to Donald Trump. If you hate him, have lost patience with him and you are tired of Trump's exaggerations and lies, you probably see him as the bombastic douche that he is. If you are a Trump-supporter, you probably love everything he's doing. Govern? Why bother when you can just sign an executive order and get it done.

If you're a Squiggle or Circle you might be deeply offended by how Trumpenstein treats people. Notice he is not adding money to the budget to give people raises. He wants $54 billion for the military but how much of that will go to our infantry men and women while they put their lives at risk every day--for about $8.50/hour!? If I knew that some of that money was going specifically to our troops in the form of higher wages, I would approve, but using that $54 billion to help contractors stockpile an arsenal of nukes that can blow up the world a hundred times over? Waste of money. It'll only take one to destroy the world as we know it.

Currently Triangle Trump is talking tough and stupid on North Korea and Iran.

"North Korea best not make any more threats to the United States. They will be met with fire and fury like the world has never seen," said Trump to the Press in August 2017 while working from his golf club Bedminster, NJ. Trump calls it "the Winter White House."

At his first United Nations address to over 100 world leaders, Trump ramped up the rhetoric, "The United States has great strength and patience. But if it is forced to defend itself or its allies, we will have no choice but to totally destroy North Korea. Rocket Man is on a suicide mission for himself and for his regime; the United States is ready, willing and able, but hopefully this will not be necessary."

And he's decertifying the Iran Nuclear Deal even though his own advisers say Iran in complying with the agreement. Despite all of our allies saying the same thing—Iran is complying with the agreement. Even Russia says he's complying. But Trump is doing his own thing: backing out by tweeting about it and then throwing it to the GOP, despite what the United Nations Security Council, the original drafters think. The UNSC includes: the United States, United Kingdom, France, China, Russia and in this case, Germany.

Some people think Trump surrounding himself with Generals is a good thing; the Generals will save us from Trump. But it hasn't proved to be an asset yet. The Generals seem to be getting on board with Trumpenstein's agenda. And without temperance, Triangle Trump could lead us straight into war.

In the end, revenge was Frankenstein's undoing. God help us all if Trump's karma comes due while he's in office. It could be the end of us all.

Man, or monster? You decide, but right now Trumpenstein haunts my dreams, lives in my closet and under my bed. None of us is safe with Trumpenstein in the White House.

What Can You Do?

1. Escape from it all by watching the Mel Brooks, Gene Wilder version of Young Frankenstein

2. Do some research on Psycho-Geometrics: psychogeometrics.com

3. Join the Girl Scouts of America! There's nothing like being a Girl Scout! #G.I.R.L. At least buy some Girl Scout cookies!

4. Join the Boy Scouts of America. And kudos to the Boy Scouts for now allowing girls, but I'm still a raving Girl Scout fan—and a First-Class Scout, 1980

5. Join Knock Every Door and go out and meet the villagers, your neighbors. Encourage them to vote

6. Really get involved with Run For Something, an organization dedicated to helping Millennials join politics

7. Join the online conversation: follow @tonyschwartz on Twitter

Everyone carries around their own **Monsters.**

Richard Pryor

Trumpenstein

Trumpenstein

Scut Trump

7. Scut Trump: Bullies, Toadies, and Victims

"Scut Farkus, what a rotten name."

"We were trapped. There he stood between us and the alley. Scut Farkus staring out at us with his yellow eyes. He had yellow eyes so help me God! Yellow eyes! In our world you're either a bully, a toady or one of the nameless rabble of victims."
-- Ralphie, A Christmas Story

If you are a fan of the classic holiday movie *A Christmas Story*, you'll recognize the name Scut Farkus--and don't forget his sidekick Grover Dill. Scut Farkus was the meanest, nastiest bully in the school. He and his toadies would beat up Ralphie and his brother Randy whenever they felt like it. Why? Because they could, and because no one stood up to him. Everyone was too afraid of Scut Farkus.

The first time we meet Scut Farkus in the movie, Ralphie the 9-year-old hero of this story, is on his way to school with his brother and friends. Out pops Scut Farkus to torment him.

In my world, Donald Trump is Scut Farkus. He pops off daily on Twitter. He's a bully and he likes it. Scut Farkus is intentionally mean and so is Donald Trump, except Donald Trump exploits his meanness for ratings and money and it's always at someone else's expense.

Trump openly mocked physically-challenged *Washington Post* reporter Serge Kovaleski. The "bully" is so ingrained in Trump, to this day, he can watch himself doing it and still openly deny it. Mental professionals refer to this as gas lighting--making you doubt something you saw with your own two eyes and know to be true.

Gas lighting is actually a bit more nefarious than that. Gas lighting makes you doubt your own sanity. It's a trick often deployed by bullies using denial, misdirection, contradiction and lying to sow seeds of doubt in what you believe to be true. Bully Trump is a master gas lighter, gas bagger, and ultimately Douchebagger.

Trump doesn't just know he's mean, he wants you to doubt it. That's not mean; that's maniacal. "I'd never do that," Trump said when reporters pointed out he'd done it; the evidence was clear. Bully Trump belittled and demeaned a person who wrote an article he didn't like. Bully can dish it out, but he can't take it.

In one classic scene, Scut Farkus and his loyal sidekick Grover Dill confront Ralphie, his little brother Randy, and a couple of his friends, Flick and Schwartz. Randy gets pushed to the ground and because he has on a huge snow suit he struggles to get up and run but can't. Scut Farkus and Grover Dill continue to terrorize the boys as "Randy lay there like a slug."

Calling All Slugs!

We cannot afford to "lay there" like slugs!! Each one of us must get up and stand up to pure meanness. We must stand up to Donald Trump. We can't let Trump and his toadies wear us down. We must stand up so Trump's mean-spirited, people-hurting policies do not become law.

Yes, Donald Trump and his gang are deconstructing and realigning the government; he's running it like one of his businesses--into the ground, and he is mean, aggressive and hurtful to others to make these changes. Trump does not have to persecute others. Trump does it by choice because Trump doesn't see others as equals. Bullies don't.

At a victory rally in Florida in December, Trump joked with his toady-minions, "We had fun fighting Hillary, didn't we?" "You were vicious, violent, screaming 'where's the wall? We want the wall!'" "Screaming 'prison, prison, lock her up.' I mean you are going crazy...you were nasty and mean and vicious, and you wanted to win, right?" He continued prodding his sheeple.

"But now, now, it's much different," he continued. "Now you're laid back, you're cool, you're mellow, right...and you're not nearly as vicious or violent, right? Because we won, right?"

Score one for the bully pulpit. But unfortunately, there has been no "mellowing." The vicious blood-sport that Trump triggered is just now beginning to rise. For the second time, White Supremacists are carrying tiki-torches and marching in Charlottesville, empowered because Trump supported them after their first rally saying, "many are fine people."

In the movie Scut Farkus eventually gets what he deserves when Ralphie snaps from excess taunting and physical violence and he finally stands up to Scut

Farkus and beats the crap out of him. Unfortunately, violence is one of the ways to defend yourself from bullies, and sometimes the only way; it's called "self-defense."

Scut Farkus cries like a baby and Ralphie has to be dragged off Scut Farkus by his Mother. Ralphie's Mom, not Scut's. Scut Farkus and his toadies run off. Ralphie is a hero and the schoolyard will be a safer place now that Scut Farkus has been put in his place.

We can't literally go to Washington, DC to beat up Donald Trump. We must define what is the "American" way. For me, I believe Americans resolve our differences with diplomacy, with words. So, we must use our words to stand-up to Donald Trump. And if that means taking a knee to protest national injustice, then I say actions speak as loud as words.

#ikneelwithcolin is about Colin Kaepernick, formerly the quarter back of the San Francisco 49ers, who became notoriously known for taking-a-knee before each football game during the playing of the national anthem. He did it to protest the oppression of people of color in the United States.

Standing Up to Bully Trump

I don't condone violence, but I am upset that Trump has thrown transgender people out of the military. It's appalling. If there was ever a time to put bully Trump in his place, it'd be now. I laughed at Kristen Beck's response to Trump.

Kristen Beck, transgender retired Navy SEAL said, "Let's meet face to face and you tell me I'm not worthy." Beck is fighting back in true warrior fashion.

Donald J Trump
After consultation with my Generals and military experts, please be advised that the United States Government will not accept or allow ......
7:55 AM - July 26 2017

Holy Crap! Notice the almost 10-minute gap in time. "The U.S. Government won't allow what?!...

Scut Trump

Donald J Trump

....Transgender individuals to serve in any capacity in the U.S. Military. Our military must be focused on decisive and overwhelming....

8:04 AM - Jul 26 2017

Donald J Trump

....victory and cannot be burdened with the tremendous medical costs and disruption that transgender in the military would entail. Thank you

8:08 AM - Jul 26 2017

To quote Stephen Colbert in his opening monolog July 26, 2017 "Trump has gone from crazy to cruel," and oh yeah, "Fuck You!"

Thank you, Stephen Colbert, for keeping us informed. And expressing our rage!

First, they came for the Muslims, then they came for the Trans community.

Trump went on to say, "I think I'm doing the military a great favor." "I think I have great support...I got a lot of votes." The man is delusional.

Kristen Beck went on to say in her Business Insider interview, "Transgender doesn't matter. Do your service." A 20-year military veteran telling bully Trump, 5-time draft dodger, to do his job. I'm looking forward to reading Kristen's book, *Warrior Princess: A U.S. Navy SEAL's Journey to Coming out Transgender.* #sisterpreach

Here's an idea: Let's put Trump in the WWE ring with Kristen instead of a pretend CNN reporter. Kristen can kick his ass on behalf of the entire nation. Throw Caitlyn Jenner in the ring and give Trump the ménage-a-trois of a lifetime. I dare Trump to grab these gals by the pussy.

We all have to stand-up to bully Trump. We have to call out his contentious attitudes and actions because currently Donald Trump and toadies are terrorizing the world.

Where to Start?!

He's shaking down Mexico for money to build his border wall--which they insist they will not fund! And after his first face-to-face meeting with German

Chancellor Angela Merkel, he took to Twitter to play tough saying they need to pony up more cash to NATO if they want our protection. What are we?! The friggin' mob?!

Donald J Trump
Despite what you have heard from the FAKE NEWS, I had a GREAT meeting with German Chancellor Angela Merkel. Nevertheless, Germany owes ....
8:15 AM - Mar 18 2017

Donald J Trump:
...vast sums of money to NATO & the United States must be paid more for the powerful, and very expensive, defense it provides to Germany!
8:23 AM - Mar 18 2017

This must be why Trump and his toadies are building up the military: so they can get small countries to pay for our muscle.

Trump is putting the pressure on China now to step-up and take care of Kim Jong-un. Yes, those conversations must happen, but Trump does it in the most public and disrespectful way.

A Dog-Dare-You of Epic Proportions!

GRRRR!!

Trump's day of playing Commander-in-Chief aboard the U.S.S. Gerald Ford "supercarrier" should terrify us all. Bully Trump intends to lead by intimidation, promising the sailors he'd build up the number of supercarriers in the fleet from its current ten to twelve.

Having them is one step closer to using them and fighting words are coming out of his mouth. In reference to the soon-to-be commissioned carrier he said, "It is a monument to American might that will provide the strength necessary to ensure peace. Hopefully, it's power we don't have to use. But if we do, they're in big, big trouble."

Trump also spouted some bullshit about "winning again, we never win wars anymore" and more bullshit as he played dress-up in a naval hat and jacket. He's itching for war and he's daring Kim Jong-un.

Trump is the reason crazy-ass Kim Jong-un is upping his nuclear arsenal and efforts. It's in direct response to Trump's tweets. Trump accuses Jong-un of

184

"playing," but it's Trump himself who's playing "who's-the-biggest-bully-on-the-block," and he intends to "win" telling Rex Tillerson to beef-up the intimidating rhetoric on his visit to South Korea.

Donald J Trump
North Korea is behaving very badly! They have been "playing" the United States for years. China has done little to help!
8:07 AM - Mar 17 2017

This tweet just serves to escalate animosity and draw lines in the sea.

Trump's been trolling North Korea on Twitter for months.

Donald J Trump
North Korea just stated that it is in the final stages of developing a nuclear weapon that will reach the United States! It won't happen!
6:05 PM - 02 Jan 17

He brought China into it as well.

Donald J Trump
China has been taking out massive amounts of money & wealth from the U.S. in totally one-sided trade, but won't help with North Korea. Nice!
6:47 PM - 02 Jan 17

Trump is encouraging China to fight this fight, and even though China has been talking about a diplomatic resolution, they are acquiescing to Trump. China granted trademarks to daughter Ivanka the very day President Xi dined with Trump at Mar-a-Lago. Will China step-up and fight Trump's fight? The last time we fought North Korea, both China and Russia fought against us. We've yet to see. Trump is putting the pressure on them.

Donald J Trump
I am very disappointed in China. Our foolish past leaders have allowed them to make hundreds of billions of dollars a year in trade, yet...
4:29 PM - Jul 29 2017

Donald J Trump
...they do NOTHING for us with North Korea, just talk. We will no longer allow this to continue. China could easily solve this problem!
4:35 PM - Jul 29 2017

Classic Trump, once again simplifying the situation into one tweet. "China can easily solve this problem," he said. But nothing is as simple as it seems.

Trump continues ratcheting up the war machine saying, "North Korea is making fools out of U.S negotiators and only one thing will work." Are you frightened yet? I'm terrified. My "let's wait and see" premise is looking bad for Schroedinger's cat. The kitten's in the air--and he's going to get nuked!!

Our Bully-in-Chief sent missiles into Syria, after warning his BFF Russia of the strike.

And in another playground-bully incident, not even an equal comparison to firing missiles at another country, ITRL, In Trump Real Life, Trump flat-out shoved Montenegro Prime Minister Dusko Markovic out of the way to get to his front-row position in a photo op at the NATO Summit.

And then Trump criticized London Mayor Sadiq Khan after a terrorist attack with all the class and style of a ten-year-old. First, Trump tweeted "WE ARE WITH YOU. GOD BLESS!" Then this:

Donald J Trump
At least 7 dead and 48 wounded in terror attack and Mayor of London says there is "no reason to be alarmed!"
6:31 AM - Jun 4 2017

What Mayor Khan had actually said was people need not be alarmed with the increase of military presence. It was confirmation that their government had the situation under control. Trump took the quote out of context then turned it on Khan in a second tweet.

Donald J Trump
Pathetic excuse by London Mayor Sadiq Khan who had to think fast on his "no reason to be alarmed" statement. MSM is working hard to sell it!
8:49 AM - Jun 5 2017

For God's sake--can't someone put this kid in time-out? Kid President is waaay more qualified to lead the country than our current man-child.

Trump continues his assaults closer to home. Trump's attacks on San Juan Mayor Carmen Yulin Cruz in the aftermath of hurricane Maria are repugnant. As always, Trump made a humanitarian disaster for 3.5 million Puerto Rican-Americans all about him. Trump is the victim.

He's also attacked his own Attorney General, Jeff Sessions. But I'm okay with that. Sessions is the main character in a horror movie. He's also having his toadies put pressure on members of Congress, specifically Lisa Murkowski from Alaska who stood strong and voted no on the repeal of Obamacare. Trump, ever the instigator behind the scene, had his Interior Secretary, Ryan Zinke, call and threatened funding to the state of Alaska. Trump doesn't have the cajones to do it himself, so he puts one of his good fellas on it. I.e. Trump empowers toady Jeff Sessions to announce Trump is kicking out 800,000 DREAMers.

There are times Trump goes so far we have to question his sanity. Trump's verbal attacks on others could all be a well-crafted ploy to distract as his toadies do damage behind the scene.

Meet the Toadies

There are many who've joined Trump's bully-pulpit gang. I've only written about a few of them here, but let's take a look at Trump's toadies and let's begin with one of his main sidekicks, Steve Bannon.

Big Stevie Bannon the Canon

Through Trump's campaign and into the White House Steve Bannon is one of Trump's top toadies and trusted advisors. But never one to share the spotlight, Trump kicked him out of the White House. I think he got too much "air-time" and credit.

The internet world has gone crazy with Bannon memes. *Saturday Night Live* compares Bannon to the Grim Reaper wreaking havoc with Trump's small mind. Cartoonists compare Bannon to Trump's marionettist--the one who's pulling Trump's strings and making him dance.

My favorite take on the Trump-Bannon relationship comes from the Occupy Democrats' Instagram account:

How Trump gets his news:

1. Trump has paranoid thought
2. Trump shares it with Steve Bannon
3. Steve Bannon shares it with Breitbart
4. Breitbart publishes an article about it
5. Trump reads the Breitbart article and shouts in amazement--that's exactly what I thought!

Who Is the True Power Behind Trump?

Trump has made it clear that he's the one "in charge." But it doesn't matter to me which one is leading the other--Trump leading Bannon or Bannon leading Trump--they are both equally disastrous and destructive. Trump talked a great game about helping regular, working-class Americans as he lied and bullied his way into office. Now that he's there, he's convinced he's helping people, but every executive order he's put forth so far helps corporations and Wall Street investors but not the little people who work for a salary. Neither Trump nor Bannon seem to care.

Bannon brags about his efforts in the "deconstruction of the administrative state." Trump and Bannon have waged war on the American government as we know it declaring it "bad and sad" and in need of redefining.

Bannon calls the Press the "opposition party" and Trump calls the media the "enemy of the people." Bannon says the Press doesn't understand the White House's agenda and "should keep its mouth shut." Could Bannon have the best interests of the nation at heart? Doesn't seem likely; his allegiance is to Trump, and he's waged "war" on establishment Republicans.

Bannon has returned as Executive Chairman of Breitbart News, an alt-right website that promotes the white race and White Nationalism. It's also known for racist, anti-immigrant, anti-muslim ideology. And here we must be vigilant and aware. Bannon has not abandoned Trump. He has set himself up to do harm, openly admitting he plans to unseat certain GOP constituents.

Bannon's a former investment banker at Goldman Sachs who started his own investment banking firm, Bannon & Co. Bannon and Trump are tossing out corporate regulation and shutting down federal regulatory agencies.

Currently Trump and Bannon are dismantling Dodd-Frank, the very law created to regulate the major financial institutions responsible for the market crash of 2007/2008. I was just one of the millions of people who lost their jobs and their homes when Main Street bailed out Wall Street. Wall Street needed some regulation...and now Bannon and Trump are rolling back customer protections. When Trump said people were going to make money he meant that his rich Wall Street friends were going to make money off of you!

Donald J Trump
U.S. stock Market up almost 20% since Election!
10:04 AM - Jul 29 2017

And the Rich Get Richer, and Richer, and Richer

Currently Trump has put together a cabinet full of millionaires and billionaires--his oldest friends and biggest donors. After bashing Hillary Clinton for making money on Wall Street speeches, Trump pledged he wouldn't be indulging in pay-to-play politics. And indeed he's not. He didn't just engage with one Wall Street firm, he bought and brought the entire friggin' financial district. They now run the White House.

"I love all people, rich or poor. But in those particular positions, I just don't want a poor person. Does that make sense?" he was addressing a rally in Iowa--organized by himself--telling them why he stacked his cabinet with stock-exchange cronies...a whole 'nother breed of gator.

Here are a few of Trump's toadies with their reported net worth as reported by Forbes, in an article July 5:

Mike Pence, Vice President	$ 800,000
Alex Costa, Labor Secretary	$ 1,300,000
David Shulkin, Veteran Affairs Secretary	$ 1,700,000
Ryan Zinke, Interior Secretary	$ 1,900,000
Rick Perry, Energy Secretary	$ 2,000,000

Sonny Perdue, Agriculture Secretary	$ 2,000,000
John Kelly, Homeland Secretary	$ 5,000,000
Jeff Sessions, Attorney General	$ 6,000,000
James Mattis, Defense Secretary	$ 7,000,000
Tom Price, Health and Human Services Secretary	$ 10,000,000
Elaine Chao, Transportation Secretary	$ 22,000,000
Ben Carson, Housing and Urban Develop Secretary	$ 29,000,000
Rex Tillerson, Secretary of State	$ 300,000,000
Steve Mnuchin, Treasury Secretary	$ 385,000,000
Betsy, DeVos, Education Secretary	$ 1,000,000,000
Linda Mahon, Small Business Administration	$ 1,000,000,000
Wilbur Ross, Commerce Secretary	$ 2,500,000,000

Does being rich make you a bully? No, those two ideas aren't mutually inclusive. Look at Warren Buffett, Richard Branson, Bill Gates, and Mark Cuban. I think you'd be hard pressed to find people who would define any of those people as bullies. I'm not saying they are all saints but they all have reputations of treating people well, and they've all made large fortunes without fleecing consumers or filing for bankruptcy. Not having respect for others and taking advantage of their financial hardships is what makes a bully.

But I digress...I was talking about the toadies.

Propaganda Barbie

Kellyanne Conway, or Propaganda Barbie as Keith Olbermann calls her, is Trump's top female stooge and the highest-ranking woman in the White House if you don't count "daughter/wife" Ivanka, as Bill Maher calls her. Counselor to the President is her official title. Someone in the White House must be a Star Trek fan! She's Trump's personal Counselor Troi, but without morality or compassion. Apologies to Marina Sirtis, the actress who plays Counselor Troi on Star Trek: the Next Generation. I follow @marina_sirtis on Twitter; she is informed, articulate and a champion of people's rights. Add her to your follow list.

Conway is smart as a whip having earned a law degree with honors from George Washington University Law School. She's known Trump for years meeting him while living in one of his buildings; she even served on the Trump World Tower condo board.

She originally attacked Trump for saying "untrue," "vulgar," and "unpresidential" comments while she was working with the Ted Cruz campaign. Conway said Trump had "actually built a lot of his business on the backs of the little guy" and he had a history of "not paying contractors after they have helped him build something." She also said, "the little guys have suffered" because of Trump.

She clearly saw Trump for the Douchebag that he is. But when asked to join his campaign she happily did, leaving her integrity and morality at the door. Kellyanne Conway might lie even more than Donald Trump, and that's a tall order to fill.

"Alternative facts" is how she spun Trump's delusion that more people attended his inauguration than Barack Obama's. Photo evidence comparing the two crowds clearly shows Trump had a fraction of the attendance. But Trump's narcissistic need to be the "biggest and the greatest" had him bragging about the crowd size. Kellyanne Conway's "alternative facts" are nothing more than lies to justify Trump's rantings. Merriam-Webster weighed in on the conversation tweeting the definition of the word "fact" and linking a trending article about Conway's "alternative facts."

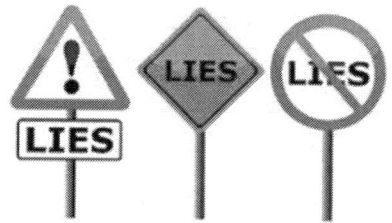

Merriam-Webster
A fact is a piece of information presented as having objective reality.
9:32 AM - Jan 22 17

The "Bowling Green Massacre," another whopper she's been known to tell, began as a phrase she "misspoke" while referring to two Iraqi citizens who were indicted on terrorism charges in Bowling Green, Kentucky. There was no "massacre" but somehow, she continues to be linked to the lie.

I really am baffled by Kellyanne. She shines up pretty--until the Trump vodka wears off--then she looks a little ragged around the edges. As Trump's trusted advisor, working with him has taken its toll. When I see her on tv, with resting blank-face, I just want to feed her and send her to bed. She looks tired to the core. Smoochin' Trump's rump must be exhausting.

Scut Trump

Douchebag Wisdom

As cartoonist Bob Thaves infamously said of Ginger Rogers and Fred Astaire, "Sure he was great, but don't forget that Ginger Rogers did everything he did...backwards and in high heels." Kellyanne is doing everything Trump is doing backwards, in high heels and carrying the biggest pooper scooper on the planet.

I wonder if her children will grow up to be as wildly conservative as she? She's proudly anti-choice. She doesn't call herself a "feminist" because she thinks "feminists" are man-haters. Man-haters in general, not so much, but there are certainly men to hate right now as Trump and the Republicans assault women's rights around the globe and are rolling back access to family planning, contraception, and birth control. These issues don't seem to concern Kellyanne.

When asked about the Women's March which brought half a million women protesters to Washington, DC on January 21st, the day after Trump's inauguration, she said "I frankly didn't see the point." Nearly three times as many women attended the March as attended Trump's inauguration and she didn't "see the point." An estimated 4.2 million women marched in over 600 US cities, the biggest march in the history of the U.S., and she "doesn't see the point." Additional tallies include almost another half million marchers in major cities all over the world. And Kellyanne Conway "doesn't see the point." Kellyanne, like Trump, clearly doesn't respect women who have opinions other than their own.

Of course, she participated in the much smaller attended March for Life on January 27th. Attendance numbers not published. I guess she finally saw the point.

Kellyanne wondered why no one called her prior to the Women's March to have a "dialogue." Dialogue about what? Donald Trump verbally attacks anyone who irks him. He has no self-control and the manners of a socially-stunted ten-year-old. He's attacked dozens of women on twitter: Rosie O'Donnell, Bette Midler, Whoopi Goldberg, Arianna Huffington, Meryl Streep, Carly Fiorina, Heidi Cruz, and of course Hillary Clinton to name a few. He's been accused of sexual assault by fifteen women throughout his life. I can't imagine how many women he's disparaged in his career. He's vulgar and condescending. She saw it in him before and I'm betting she sees it now, but it seems he's got her by the ... well you know.

Kellyanne's been pretty quiet of late. She crawls out of the "sewer," as Trump refers to it, when he needs a distraction, like Sewer Rat Barbie.

Arrrgh, you see? Who's being the douche now? Maybe I shouldn't be calling names, but the vile twisting of facts and constant, insistent blame Conway projects onto others makes her hard to look at and impossible to listen to. I'm not interested in her propaganda either. As Roosevelt said:

192

"Repetition does not transform a lie into the truth."
-- Franklin D. Roosevelt

And then there's the GOP.

Grandpa's a Bigot!

Ahhh, Mike Pence, Trump's "first hire." Could he have picked anyone so milquetoast and laced with arsenic? Anti-women? Hell yes. As Governor of Indiana he backed every piece of anti-choice legislation he's encountered. Anti-gay? Hell yes. He signed a bill allowing discrimination of others based on their sexual preference. He supports gay conversion therapy for God's sake. He willingly and knowingly continues to pursue an agenda of discrimination. He may look and sound like your beloved, friendly grandpa, but Grandpa's kinda creepy and pervy even admitting he won't have lunch or dinner with a woman without his wife's presence. What? The old hound dog can't trust himself? I'm afraid of what's hidden in his cellar. Underneath his passive facial expression, he's working his hardest to take away your rights. And he knows all about Russia. He's lawyered-up like the rest of the toadies. And the White House Ethics Committee just changed the rules so now lobbyist's money can be funneled to Trump's team for their defense. Good thing for Pence. Knowing Trump's penchant for hiring "rich" people, Pence doesn't qualify. But then again, Pence was chosen to be Trump's non-thinking side-kick.

I Do Declare

Jefferson Beauregard Sessions needs to be stopped. He was the first Republican Senator to sell his soul and board the Trump Train. He's getting exactly what he deserves now that he's getting run over by it as Trump lobs verbal shit-balls his way. No, I don't feel sorry for him, oh boo-hoo Trump has turned on him. That's what you get for watching Trump bully others; karma's a bitch.

Go ahead, Trump, fire Sessions. He's a liar, too, and his agenda destroys people. He's currently after: immigrants, alleged criminals, and the marijuana industry.

Scut Trump

Sessions is not the sweet little sprite he looks like and deserves to feel the bully pulpit even as he's exercising it against others.

Is it wrong for me to want karmic retribution? Don't we all cheer when the bad guy gets what's coming? Sessions knows what an unreasonable tyrant Trump is but still steps up to do his bidding. With sheer glee he announced Trump's decision to deport the DREAMers. #sessionssucks

Bully with a Baby Face, Paul Ryan

There's a special place in heaven reserved for Paul Ryan, and it's outside of the Pearly Gates trying to explain to the Big Kahuna why he chose to kill so many Americans by denying them health care. As Bill Paxton, #imissbillpaxton #ripbillpaxton, said in *Aliens*, "One express elevator to hell going down."

Paul Ryan is one of the privileged. He sees himself above others or others as less deserving. He perpetuates the myth that *if each of us just worked harder we would get ahead*. It's a classic Republican lie that's been spoon-fed to everyone working 40-60 hours a week for a substandard living wage, usually $7-$10/hr.

Ryan is living off a huge salary--$223,500 a year with complete health care coverage--while denying people who work 40 hours a week making $10 an hour or less the opportunity to have health care. He says people will have access to it and it's up to them to make the decision of whether they want it or not. Forget the fact that you can't afford it. If you really want it, you don't have to eat or pay your heating bill, just get insurance instead. Make that choice. It is, after all, your choice. And it's all your fault if you choose not to get it. Still can't afford it? If you only worked harder and smarter!

I'm insured by the Affordable Care Act. I've worked hard my entire life. I'm college educated with a Midwest work ethic, meaning I'm up at the crack of dawn and often work far past sunset. Make no mistake, Paul Ryan, YOU are on government health care. Yours is paid for. And I--and millions of other Americans--deserve that same consideration!

I Triple-Dog Dare You!

Go ahead, Paul Ryan, repeal Obamacare. I triple dog dare you. After you and the rest of the toadies dismantle the government and screw over your constituents, we'll see who gets tossed out on their Eddie Haskell ass. If only you had a heart, but go ahead, pump that keg, have another beer, and celebrate fucking over the poor, challenged, young and old. Invite your obstructionist friend Mitch McConnell. Hell awaits his arrival for not holding a hearing for Merrick Garland and screwing over President Obama and the American people.

Thanks to bully Trump and his toadies there is a collective stink on our nation. I fear for our neighbors, Mexico and Canada; our reputation as a peaceful, compassionate, and prosperous nation is ruined. Now we're the selfish, self-serving United States of America, in it for ourselves and bullying all other nations until they see things our way.

Trump should be sending aid to the Mexican people after that 8.1 magnitude earthquake as well as #Harvey and #Irma and #Maria victims--NOT BUILDING A WALL! I feel like I have to apologize to the world for hurricane Trump. And especially to Mexico!

Introducing Mini Me

Anthony Scaramucci, the trash-talking Mooch hawked the Trump vodka and he poured it down our throats. A miniature of Trump, right down to the signature hair and bigly hand gestures, Scaramucci was an entertaining distraction to the Russian investigation. He lasted ten days.

He, too, used to think Trump was a troglodyte, but those tweets and that criticism has been scrubbed clean from the internet...all except the record of it. It's an obvious about-face on his love and respect for Donald Trump. Rumor has it he owes a lot of taxes and he's selling a company to China. I didn't care enough to even google it or him. I won't be distracted. Russia, Russia, Russia.

Am I For Sale?

I wonder how many million it would take to make me work for Trump? There's not enough money in the world to make me like and respect him. But what would it take to make me work with him? America has big issues that need to be addressed. Kudos for "Chuck and Nancy" working with Trump to get the debt ceiling lifted and budget extended including funds for hurricane relief. Let's hope the joke's not on you. Trump isn't known for his loyalty. But what would it take for me to talk nice about Trump? I can't imagine it.

Of course, this chapter wouldn't be complete without the family, the golden baby toadies Ivanka and husband Jared. There is Eric, Don Jr., bless their hearts, what privileged fools. As you know Trump has Tiffany and Barron but they're not part of the White House scene or Trump 0.

195

Jared has been tasked with solving most of the nation's and part of the world's problems, including: reinventing the government, solving the opioid crisis, and brokering peace in the Middle East. And remember, he has to do it on a six-day work week because of his religious observations.

Jared was credited with Trump's win. He was the "data person," determining where the campaign would go next. His digital footprint is all over this presidency. And if there truly is collusion with Russia, he's headed to jail. I trust Bob Mueller to do his job.

Remember the Comrades! Heil Trump!

Paul Manafort: Trump's former Campaign Chief
Rex Tillerson: Trump's current Secretary of State
Michael Flynn: Trump's former National Security Advisor
Wilbur Ross: Trump's current Commerce Secretary
Carter Page: Trump's former foreign policy advisor

All of these men have ties to Russia, but the question is: was it collusion?

I guess that depends on your definition of "collusion." The difference between "collusion" and "collaboration" is the intent. Obviously, Trump was working with Russia to get elected. As Donny Jr. said, the Russian money has been flowing into the Trump Organization for years. Russia wanted Trump to win. Russia helped Trump win. That is no secret. There was nothing hidden. Trump asked for Russia's help to get elected from the stump. He sang Putin's praises throughout his campaign. There was no hidden agenda. It was right there in our faces. Still is. The question is: is that legal? I'm leaving that to Bob Mueller to decide. #inmuellerwetrust

Bullies in the Hallways

There are many other Trump bullies behind the scene, but bullies only stay in power when they are themselves empowered.

Is it money? Or is it something beyond that? It has to be beyond money because all of these people are loaded, well except for Mike Pence, who probably has a secret coke habit. I don't know. Notice the Trumpism?

Oops, it happened again. Yes, that's a douchey thing to say. Just because Trump employs that tactic doesn't mean I have to. I don't think Pence is a cokehead. But it is hard watching him empower Trump to be the bully that he is. And Pence is beyond complicit, he--like the rest of the toadies--is actively encouraging Trump's bully pulpit.

Trump and toadies have empowered bullies in school yards across the nation. Reports of Elementary school violence is on the rise. Playground bullies are using Trump's words to taunt their classmates and in one case lynched and nearly killed an eight-year-old bi-racial boy in New Hampshire. What kind of animals do that?! Parents everywhere should be appalled! Yes, I said it before, but let me say it again: anyone who does not stand up against this hatred is complicit.

Privileged, affluent American kids on spring break had the nerve to go to Cancun and chant "build the wall" to the Mexican people. It is beyond reproach. It's Trump's words and continued encouragement of violence and verbal assault that empowered those young adults--and they are adults! This epidemic of disrespect will only get worse with Trump running wild in the White House and now back on the campaign trail already in 2017.

What will it take to shut this bully up? Too bad we can't leave Trump out in the school yard with his tongue stuck against the flag pole, *A Christmas Story* style. That'd shut him up for a short while.

What Can You Do?

1. Watch A Christmas Story and cheer when Ralphie stands up for himself and friends

2. Watch Kid President on YouTube: any of his videos are positive and uplifting

3. Write a note to all the people who bullied you. Forgive them and thank them, they made you who you are today

4. Check-out StandForTheSilent.org, an organization dedicated to fighting bullying

5. Check-out Life After Hate

Scut Trump

What Susie says of Sally says more of Susie than of Sally

Scut Trump

Scut Trump

Biff Trump

8. Biff Trump: Rolling Back the Future of Human Rights

It pains me to write this chapter. Is there anyone as repugnant and repulsive as the real Donald Trump? Maybe it's his movie character doppelganger Biff Tannen, the liar, cheat and bully from the hit movie trilogy *Back to the Future*.

Did you know the character of Biff Tannen was fashioned after Donald Trump? I didn't either until I read an interview with Bob Gale, writer of *Back to the Future 2*. He said bully Biff Tannen was created after "loudmouth, terrible haired Donald Trump."

I watched the first movie again in October 2015 to celebrate its 30th anniversary release. Many of us did and shared it with our children. The original movie came out in 1985 with the characters of Dr. Emmet "Doc" Brown and Marty McFly being played by Christopher Lloyd and Michael J. Fox. In movie 1, Marty accidentally gets sent back in time to the year 1955 where he meets his Mom's younger self, Lorraine Baine, who falls in love with him instead of his real Dad, George McFly. Marty's future has been altered, his very existence is in question if his parents don't meet. The plot line is further complicated by Biff Tannen, local nasty guy who harasses George and Marty and fancies Lorraine. Marty has to find Doc, outwit Biff, and unite his parents at the school dance in order to get back to his life in the present, 1985.

In *Back to the Future 2*, the iconic future date to which Doc and Marty travel to is October 21, 2015. Concerned for Marty and Jennifer's children, Doc comes back and takes them to 2015. The plot twists and turns are too complex to recount here, not to mention, you should watch the movie! It's a nice reprieve from the madness that's playing out today.

Here's the nutshell version: Marty saves his kid from some bad knocks in the future, but while he does, Biff steals the DeLorean time machine, goes back to the year 1955 and alters history. When Marty and Doc return to 1985 their lives have changed: Biff Tannen has become rich betting on sports with the Almanac he'd lifted from the future. Biff is a rich, powerful thug with a 27-story tower and casino he uses to extort money from the townspeople. George McFly has been murdered by Biff, and Doc is imprisoned in an insane asylum. Biff had finally gotten his way with Lorraine who he's bullied into marrying him. Marty must spring Doc from the asylum and undo what Biff has done or forever live in an altered reality.

With Trump at the helm that's what's happened to us all. We're now living in a universe of alternative facts and altered realities. Maybe that's why Trump's twitter handle is @REALDonaldTrump. He's clearly living in an alternative universe where everyone loves him, and he won the election bigly.

Donald J. Trump believes he's accomplished more than any other president in history in his first 100 days. Only you can decide if that's a fact or an alternate fact. It certainly is Donald Trump's reality although it's not mine. Or the realities of 65 million people who didn't vote for him. Or the current 66% of all Americans who say they disapprove of the job he's doing. Those numbers from polls by the news sources Donald Trump has dubbed #fakenews: CNN, *Washington Post*, *Huffington Post*, and *The New York Times* which is flourishing thanks to the Trump bump. Exposing truths behind his lies is good business.

Congrats to my home-girl, Rachel Maddow, for the two Emmys for Excellence in News Reporting.

If you're going to watch *Back to the Future 1 and 2*, then finish the trilogy with a western tribute and watch number 3. If you don't have the time, rest assured, Biff gets what's coming to him in the end. A bright future with logic and civility is restored. Trump may have altered reality when he lied, cheated, and bullied his way into the White House, but he will get his in the end.

Relax and Let Karma Finish It

Now that Trump is in office, his business dealings continue to dog him. He has not excused himself from business profits although he swears he's excused himself from the day-to-day operations of The Trump Organization. His sons, Beavis and Butthead, are currently in charge. But as world leaders continue to book into his Washington, DC hotel in efforts to garner favor with Trump, it is quite clear Trump has not recused himself from profits from said hotel and other businesses. Mar-a-Lago is billing the government $546/night for guests of Trump to stay and meet with him. That's taxpayer dollars going directly into Trump's pockets.

Here are just a few of his questionable business dealings still under investigation:

- Ties to Russia and the 2016 election
- Refusal to release his tax returns
- Settlements for defrauding Trump University students
- Charitable foundation operating w/out authorization in New York
- Questionable donations to Vets
- Liens on his DC hotel
- Bugs in the kitchen at Mar-A-Lago
- Sexual assault accusations from 13 women

It's clear Trump has as many questionable business dealings as that of Biff Tannen in Back to the Future 2, but the most offensive thing about Biff Tannen and Donald Trump is they are both pussy grabbers.

The turning point in *Back to the Future 1* is when Biff has Lorraine in the front seat of his car and he is "going for it." Biff was up under Lorraine's skirt without consent. When George opens the door thinking that he would break in on Marty who would be pretending to get frisky with Lorraine, instead he finds Biff Tannen in the front seat and he has Lorraine trapped. Biff tells George to close the door and walk away. Lorraine looks at George and pleads with him for help. It is quite clear she's in physical and mental distress and needs help. History changes in that moment when George McFly stands up to Biff and saves Lorraine from being raped.

President Pussy Grabber

"I'm automatically attracted to beautiful--I just start kissing them. It's like a magnet. Just kiss. I don't even wait. When you're a star, they let you do it. You can do anything. Grab them by the pussy.
You can do anything."
-- Donald J. Trump

Reprehensible and Disgusting

I think if Donald Trump was grabbed in the crotch every day, he might "get it." Include Attorney General Jeff Sessions, the former Republican US Senator from Alabama who didn't think being grabbed by your genitals was sexual assault. During his confirmation hearing for Attorney General, he did finally admit that being crotch-grabbed would be described as sexual assault.

I think it's our patriotic duty to help these men understand this basic human right--no one deserves to be sexually assaulted!

Think Trump's words don't make a difference? Even 70-year-old geezers feel empowered thanks to Trump. Check out this story.

Christopher Von Keyserling, a member on the Greenwich, CT town board, was charged with fourth degree sexual assault for pinching a woman "in her groin area." He'd been emboldened by Trump's defiance of "political correctness," and the pussy-grabbing comment, obviously. He also told her it'd be her word against his. But he was wrong. The altercation was caught on camera and the woman was able to get a warrant against him.

Misogyny: A Hatred of Women

Trump's been accused of being a misogynist--a woman-hater. He'd tell you just the opposite: "No one has more respect for women than Donald J. Trump."

His daughter, Ivanka says he's been a champion of women's rights. She was booed for saying so. His actions speak louder than his words. Trump's cultivated his own reputation as a lover of women and that's what he wants all women to believe now. But double-talkin' Trump's own words and actions say otherwise.

From a 1992 interview with New York Magazine regarding women, Trump said "You have to treat them like shit."

In a 1994 interview, Trump said "I think putting a wife to work is a very dangerous thing. Unfortunately, after they're a star the fun is over for me. It's like a creation process. It's almost like creating a building. It's pretty sad." That he got right, but he's the one that is sad.

Trump's hateful rhetoric toward women continued to surface in his career, campaign, and now his presidency. He continues to attack his Democratic opponent Hillary Clinton, former U.S. National Security Advisor Susan Rice, even the gracious, talented Meryl Streep!

Donald J. Trump
Meryl Streep, one of the most overrated actresses in Hollywood, doesn't know me but attacked last night at the Golden Globes. She is a.....
6:27 AM - Jan 9 2017

Donald J. Trump
Hillary flunky who lost big. For the 100th time, I never "mocked" a disabled report (would never do that) but simply showed him.....
6:36 AM - Jan 9 2017

Donald J. Trump
"groveling" when he totally changed a 16 year old story that he had written in order to make me look bad. Just more very dishonest media!
6:43 AM - Jan 9 2017

Donald Trump, we all saw it with our own two eyes. You were mocking him. You're a bully that knows no bounds.

Trump's Twitter rant was in response to Meryl Streep's speech at the Golden Globes mentioning his mocking of a disabled reporter. She went on to say, "This instinct to humiliate, when it's modeled by someone in the public platform, by someone powerful, it filters down into everybody's life. Because it kind of gives permission for other people to do the same thing."

We are now seeing the consequences of Trump's words play out in our everyday lives. When a 70-year-old pervert in a small town in Connecticut has been empowered to pinch a woman in her privates, I fear for our young women, and men!

Yes, our destinies are ever entwined between men and women thanks to how we, the species, procreate. And that in itself is a problem with this White House and this President. They want to make women the "bad guy" ironically. This White House would love to overturn Roe v Wade, outlawing access to abortion, while currently denying federal funding to family planning information--including contraception!

They want to lay all burden on the woman. Trump said regarding abortion there had to be some sort of punishment. Whether he meant on doctors who performed them, or the women who had them, he said nothing about the bastard that impregnated the woman! He quickly walked that back. Perhaps Ivanka was whispering in his ear. Or not. She's admitted she has no influence on him, even though she is his advisor.

Trump once said he opposed exceptions to having an abortion in cases that a woman's health would be in jeopardy because it would become an excuse to seek an abortion: "You have a cold, and you're going to end up having an abortion."

He needs to have a cold and end up with a frontal lobotomy!

Trump has been so openly hostile towards women and so repulsive in his treatment of women that 5 million people protested--worldwide!

And Trump insulted the 500,000 women who marched on Washington, D.C. January 21, the day after his inauguration.

Donald J. Trump
Watched protests yesterday but was under the impression that we just had an election! Why didn't these people vote? Celebs hurt cause badly.
7:47 AM - Jan 22 2017

They did vote, Donald Trump. Three million more people voted for Hillary than did Trump! THAT's why they were out in the streets, protesting the actions of an abuser.

Grabbing women by the privates? Not okay. Kicking people out of the country?! NOT OKAY! That's just one of many big issues the Women's March protested. Maybe it did affect Trump. Later that same day, Trump was a bit more level-headed:

Donald J. Trump
Peaceful protests are a hallmark of our democracy. Even if I don't always agree, I recognize the rights of people to express their views.
9:23 AM - Jan 22 2017

THIS is the Donald Trump we want to see! This is the Donald Trump we want to negotiate with! This man sounds reasonable. This man learned something. Yes, it's like applauding a chimp learning to speak banana, but it's progress. He sees us! He acknowledged another view. This is the Trump I want. Not the Donald Trump that picked up the radical anti-woman Republican agenda once he won the nomination.

That's one voting stat I still struggle to understand: more college-educated white women voted for Trump over Hillary. What was that? A white knight dream? The belief that someone would ride up and save them, elevate them, take them to the castle to live?

I'm a college-educated woman who voted against Trump. But I can see Trump fans wanting to believe him. But he's got to stop shoving the Republican agenda down our throats.

I want Trump to sit back for a moment and think, not just of the 62 million that voted for him, but of the 65 million that voted against him. Don't our ideas still matter? Can't he let up on his either/or, big bully image and work with the world? Does he have to start World War III with his boastings, bombast and threats? Can't he just do what he said he'd do and put America first?

Look at me, begging for mediocrity, for keeping the peace. In another reality America would be leading the world in feeding the people, building communities, seeking earth-friendly policies, putting people and clean jobs together. In a Hillary Clinton as President reality we'd be working together. Riiiight. I'm sure the Republican would be trying to impeach her over emails.

Bitch!

When I was in high school, I was bullied. The boys called me "Bitch." Not a bitch, just "Bitch," as if it were my name. They yelled it after me as I walked down the school halls. They'd say it to my face as they passed me going class to class. It wasn't one person, or two people who did this, it was about 20 boys from both my Junior class and the Senior class who did it. I couldn't pass from one class to another without two or three of them saying "Bitch" to my face.

They were relentless. Some days they would stand in packs in the student center and yell it out together, laughing, egging each other on as I ducked in just long enough to grab books from my locker. Most days I carried all my books, so I wouldn't have to walk past them. I took the long way around, circumventing halls I knew they were in. They took turns, but there was always someone stepping up to launch the next attack to my face or yell it behind my back.

No big deal, you're thinking, but it was. My graduating class had forty people in it, the senior class had 40 people. I was being verbally assaulted by half of my class and half of the senior class, a quarter of the Junior/Senior class. But we didn't call it assault back then.

I tried to see the humor in it. I tried not to take it personally. But it was quite clear that I wasn't being teased, I was being harassed.

At first the girls laughed about it. My sister stuck up for me. She was a Senior at the time. Her best friend was sister to my best friend. They all stuck up for me. They tried to reason with the guys and then confronted them about backing off. They told me to ignore them, but it just didn't stop. It went on for months.

The experience was profoundly altering who I would become although I didn't know or understand that at the time. I tried to understand, and I wondered what I had done to deserve it.

I thought about killing myself, and not just in passing as in "I wish I were dead," but as in "if I take a bottle of sleeping pills and wash it all down with a fifth of vodka" it'll all be over. And it wasn't idle rhetoric. At age 17, I didn't understand how big the world was or what opportunities were ahead, I only knew that I dreaded every day having to walk into that school and hear people I'd done nothing to, call me Bitch.

I grew despondent. I dropped out of school activities and my grades slipped. My parents were worried. They knew something was wrong but didn't know what. I begged my sister not to tell them. I told her I could handle it. I wanted to handle it and tried to stay optimistic. But the bullies' relentless attacks were doing me in.

It came to a head one day in the student center when a bunch of the guys pushed me onto a 5' round table and then lifted that table to the ceiling, trapping me in a one-foot space in between. I told myself again and again that it was all in fun, not to take it seriously, they didn't mean it, I could handle it, but I couldn't and didn't.

They put me down when the Principal showed up. A girlfriend had gotten him. That's when it spilled—how bad things had gotten. The principal had heard

Biff Trump

the shouting and name calling on several occasions, but had ignored it. Since I had kept my mouth shut, he really didn't know.

The five or six main culprits were called in to the principal's office. I finally told my folks. We talked about taking me out of school and sending me to high school 20 miles away in the next school district. My folks even spoke with the parents of the boys.

And what happened? For the next few weeks the boys whispered "Bitch" behind my back. As I picked up my books, went class-to-class, and did school activities. And finally, finally, blessedly, it calmed down and stopped.

It started up again just briefly in my Senior year, but the girls shut that down quick. They had stayed silent the first time around, but this time, they all stuck up for me. The last I heard of it was graduation day when someone left a note in my locker that said, "Have a nice life, Bitch!"

This election, and most especially Donald Trump's bullying, has brought all of that back to me and has proved to me how profoundly important it is to speak up!

I've been a "good girl," a kind girl my whole life. I've cared more for the needs of others, putting them over my own needs. And I've played nice and fair and even let people take advantage of me because I didn't want them to think I was a bitch. I tried to stand up to the guys back in high school; I found it easier to duck and run, counting the days until I could get the hell out of Dodge. But now it's time to stand and speak. And today I don't mind being called a Bitch one bit. Sometimes a Lady just has to be.

A Cause for Melania

Melania once said her platform would be "cyber bullying." That's not ironic, she's living with it every day as her husband sends out his mean-spirited tweets. We all are living with Trump's cyber bullying. Melania is a witness to his every day bullying. She's living with the consequences of his every day bullying. She looks a little bullied herself, who knows? Yes, I can say that. If Donald Trump can say about Hillary "I don't think she's faithful to Bill, who knows?" I can say that about Melania. Come talk to me, Girl, in any of the six languages you supposedly speak. I saw with my own two eyes as your husband bullied you on Inauguration Day.

Trump is moments away from taking the presidential oath. As he waves to the crowd, you can see from the movements at the back of his head, he says

Biff Trump

something to Melania. She was beautiful, beaming a smile as her husband acknowledges the crowd, then Trump appears to say something to her--and then--her immediate reaction: she goes from happiness to disillusionment in one second flat. But don't just look at a picture. Google "Melania Trump's face Inauguration Day" and watch a video.

To this day I'm baffled: what could Trump have said to Melania to make her face fall like that in the blink of an eye?

- You're the first to go--you and all the other illegal immigrants (seems harsh)
- You're fired (no, too obvious)
- You and me tonight, Baby (Yep, my money's on that one. No one in their right mind would want to do this man)

Abuse by Neglect?

Or, is there another reason why Melania's face fell flat, and her spirit withdrew so quickly? I didn't notice until it was pointed out to me by The Sun at thesun.co.uk/news. Trump didn't dis her with a zinger, he didn't zing her at all. A wider shot of the video shows where Trump's attention truly was. Ivanka.

Trump made eye contact with his daughter, not his wife. He didn't so much as acknowledge Melania. Has she been abused by neglect?

I once saw an interview with Melania, one of her first while Trump was still running for office. She had said not to feel sorry for her. I wondered at the time why we would possibly pity Melania? Then the #FreeMelania hashtags started to surface.

Candice Bergen wore a "Free Melania" shirt while promoting her new movie. When asked, Bergen said she had one date with Trump when she was 18 years old and in college. She described him as "a good-looking guy" and a "douche." See? I'm not even close to the first; even back then he was a Douchebag.

Given Trump's verbal abuse of other women, I've inferred Trump must also be a bully at home. But is the "silent treatment" verbal abuse? It's the sign of a poor relationship, for sure, but is it abuse? And who else is he abusing? Besides Jeff Sessions and General Kelly and Rex Tillerson and… the list goes on?

Perhaps Sarah Huckabee Sanders? Big, beautiful Sarah Huckabee Sanders who is melting before our very eyes--Momma Boo-Boo style. A steady diet of lies and stress will do that to you. Or maybe Trump is playing his own version of White House make-over Honey Huckaboo style. Let's turn off the cameras, run Sarah over White House hurdles until she drops 30 or 40 pounds. He did it to former Miss Universe Alicia Machado or as Trump referred to her "Miss Piggy." Who's to say he's not size-shaming Huckabee behind the scenes? She clearly had dropped weight and gotten a make-over once the Press cameras were allowed again in the White House briefing room. For those who don't know, Trump turned off the cameras on White House briefings for weeks in June 2017. And Sarah Huckaboo Sanders' personality make-over is almost complete; she pukes lies daily and disparages anyone who questions Trump or the regime. Kellyanne taught her well.

Gleefully Embracing His Inner Bully

Trash-talking Trump destroyed every opponent on the way to the Oval. He didn't just go after them, he made it personal even going after their wives. He was particularly merciless against Senator Ted Cruz who he dubbed "Lyin' Ted." Ted took it and took it and took it and took it and took it and took it...you get the picture. He questioned Trump's character and temperament for office. He was one of the last Republicans to stand-up to Trump and then one day Trump attack Ted Cruz's wife, Heidi. Trump tweeted he'd "spill the beans" on her. I believe the story was in regards to Heidi Cruz having issues with depression. Trump was publicly shaming her.

Here's irony: now that Trump's elected many more women are suffering from depression!

I was proud of Ted Cruz that day when he stood up for his wife; he called-out the bully. Insert applause track here. But wait, get ready to boo.

After all the mean and immoral things Trump said about him and his wife; after the lies Trump told insinuating Cruz's father had something to do with the assassination of JFK, nothing was as disappointing as Ted Cruz's visit to the White House. Ted Cruz had stood for common decency, but, after all the hateful, hurtful rhetoric, Cruz took Heidi and his two girls for dinner and everyone played nice. I guess anything goes in love and war and business and politics.

And then the bully turned his attention to Hillary Rodham Clinton.

Donald J Trump
Crooked Hillary Clinton is spending a fortune on ads against me. I am the one person she doesn't want to run against. Will be such fun!
8:41 AM - Apr 17 2016

Then bully Donald Trump fired up his stooges. "What shall we call her? Crooked Hillary? He made his choice and then he unloaded. The bully called her crooked during his entire campaign. He shouted it, his cronies shouted it, his minions repeated it like lemmings going over the cliff and out of their minds. And Bully Trump egged them on.

Here are all the times over the campaign that Trump bullied Hillary--on Twitter. There are many other instances in interviews and rallies.

As reported from New York Times' list of "People, Places and Things Donald Trump has Insulted on Twitter." Each tweet is set-off with commas. Visit nytimes.com/interactive where all tweets are active links to the original tweet.

This is abusive! Read for yourself. These are all the insults directed toward Hillary Clinton, Democratic Presidential Nominee during the campaign:

"Crooked", "unfit to serve", "Crooked", "Crooked Hillary's corruption is closing in", "decades of lies and scandal", "Guilty - cannot run", "Crooked", "a big mistake", "Crooked", "should not be allowed to run for president", "Crooked", "Crooked", "unfit to be president", "Crooked Hillary", "Bad judgement!", "We must not let #CrookedHillary take her CRIMINAL SCHEME into the Oval Office", "launched her political career by letting terrorists off the hook", "Crooked", "Hillary said she was under sniper fire (while surrounded by USSS.) Turned out to be a total lie. She is not fit to lead our country", "Crooked H", "wants to take in as many Syrians as possible", "Crooked", "Crooked", "Crooked", "Crooked", "Crooked", "Crooked", "Crooked", "Crooked", "FAILED ALL OVER THE WORLD", "loves to lie", "She'll say anything and change NOTHING!", "a Wall Street PUPPET!", "Crooked", "Crooked", "has never created a job in her life", "Crooked", "Crooked", "a foreign policy DISASTER", "you have failed, failed, and failed", "no solutions, no ideas, no credibility", "too weak to lead", "the most corrupt person to ever run for the presidency of the United States", "If we let Crooked run the govt, history will remember 2017 as the year America lost its independence", "So CROOKED", "Crooked", "Crooked", "Crooked", "Crooked", "Such a dishonest person", "Crooked", "crooked", "Crooked", "Crooked", "Crooked", "SO CORRUPT!", "Crooked", "should be in jail", "Crooked", "Crooked", "PAY TO PLAY POLITICS", "Crooked",

"Fraud", "Crooked", "Crooked", "unfit to run", "disgraceful behavior", "Crooked", "Hypocrite", "Hypocrite!", "nothing Hillary has said about her secret server has been true", "If I win-I am going to instruct my AG to get a special prosecutor to look into your situation", "there's never been anything like your lies", "Crooked", "has only created jobs at the FBI and DOJ!", "Crooked", "Crooked", "Owned by Wall St and Politicians", "nasty to Sanders supporters behind closed doors", "Crooked", "suffers from BAD JUDGEMENT!", "Crooked", "Crooked", "terrible!", "failing for 30 years", "not getting the job done", "Crooked", "failed all over the world", "all talk, no action", "a typical politician", "taking the day off again, she needs the rest", "copying my airplane rallies", "puts the plane behind her like I have been doing from the beginning", "Crooked", "Crooked", "said horrible things about my supporters", "SO INSULTING to my supporters", "Crooked", "very dumb", "Unfit to serve as #POTUS", "totally confused", "just gave a disastrous news conference", "Lyin'", "Crooked", "Crooked", "Crooked", "Crooked", "doesn't have the strength or the stamina to MAKE AMERICA GREAT AGAIN!", "doesn't have the drive or stamina to MAKE AMERICA GREAT AGAIN!". "Crooked". "Crooked". "has BAD JUDGEMENT". "brainpower is highly overrated, decision making is so bad". "Crooked". "Crooked". "called African-American youth "SUPER PREDATORS"". "Crooked". "will NEVER be able to solve the problems of poverty, education and safety". "SABOTAGE OF THE INNER CITIES". "CORRUPTION". "No policy" "only knows how to make a speech when it is a hit on me", "using the oldest play in the Dem playbook", "all talk and NO ACTION!". "using race-baiting". "She should be ashamed of herself!". "pandering to the worst instincts in our society". "fear-mongering!". "lies". "crooked". "LIE!". "Crooked". "Crooked". "Crooked". "Crooked". "not a talented person or politician". "Crooked". "Crooked". "Crooked". "Crooked". "not fit to be our next president!". "Anybody whose mind 'SHORT CIRCUITS' is not fit to be our president! Look up the word 'BRAINWASHED.". "Very dangerous!". "Crooked". "unfit to serve as President". "bad judgment". "incompetent". "Crooked". "Crooked". "Crooked". "A PATHOLOGICAL LIAR!". "Crooked". "100% owned by her donors". "Crooked", "Crooked". "Crooked". "Crooked". "Crooked". "has very small and unenthusiastic crowds in Pennsylvania". "Crooked". "Crooked". "Crooked". "Crooked". "a formula for disaster!". "Crooked". "Crooked". "a lose cannon". "extraordinarily bad judgement & instincts". "Crooked". "Crooked". "Crooked". "Crooked". "Crooked". "very long and very boring speech". "Crooked". "Crooked". "no one has worse judgement". "corruption and devastation follows her". "owned by Wall Street!". "unfit to lead the country". "Crooked". "Crooked". "wants to flood our country with Syrian immigrants that we know little or nothing about". "Crooked". "Crooked". "a liar!". "incompetent". "Crooked". "Crooked". "Crooked" "betrayed Bernie voters", "Crooked", "Crooked". "Crooked". "Crooked". "judgement so bad". "Crooked". "Crooked". "Crooked". "not at all loyal". "Crooked". "Crooked". "BAD JUDGEMENT". "Crooked". "killed jobs!". "Against steelworkers and miners".

"destroyed jobs and manufacturing". "Crooked". "Crooked". "Crooked". "Crooked".
"Crooked". "look at all of the bad decisions she has made". "led Obama into bad
decisions!". "Crooked". "will sell our country down the tubes!", "bought and paid
for by Wall Street, lobbyists and special interests", "Crooked", "Crooked", "has
made so many mistakes" "Crooked", "embarrassed herself and the country with
her e-mail lies", "a DISASTER on foreign policy", "Crooked", "email lies", "negative
ads are not true", "Crooked", "fraudulent", "Sad!!", "Having ZERO impact",
"Crooked", "Crooked", "Lyin'", "Crooked", "not qualified", "Crooked", "Crooked",
"Crooked", "Crooked", "not qualified!", "Crooked", "Crooked", "WEAK leadership",
"Crooked", "lies", "Lyin' Crooked", "Crooked", "Crooked", "sooooo guilty",
"Crooked", "lied to the FBI and to the people of our country", "incompetent",
"dishonest", "very bad judgement", "Crooked", "Crooked", "Not fit!", "Crooked",
"BAD JUDGEMENT!", "Her temperament is weak", "unfit to serve as President",
"Crooked", "As usual, bad judgment.", "A total disgrace!", "Crooked" "guilty as hell",
"will NEVER be able to handle the complexities and danger of ISIS", "Crooked",
"Crooked", "Crooked", "Crooked", "As Bernie Sanders said, Hillary Clinton has bad
judgement. Bill's meeting was probably initiated and demanded by Hillary!",
"selling out America", "Not capable!", "Presidency would be catastrophic", "bad
judgment", "ill-fit", "Crooked", "Lying", "Crooked", "Crooked", "no sense of
markets", "such bad judgement", "Crooked", "Crooked", "Crooked", "Crooked",
"bad judgement", "Disgraceful!", "Crooked", "All talk, no action!", "Crooked",
"would be a disaster", "Crooked", "may be the most corrupt person ever to seek
the presidency", "Crooked", "will be a disaster for jobs and the economy!",
"defrauded America", "Corrupt", "dangerous", "dishonest", "judgement has killed
thousands, unleashed ISIS and wrecked the economy", "Crooked", "bad
judgment", "failed policies", "totally unfit to be our president", "really bad
judgement and a temperament", "Crooked", "Crooked", "Crooked", "Crooked",
"Crooked", "Crooked", "will be a disaster", "Crooked",, "Crooked", "Crooked", "total
fraud!", "Crooked", "record is so bad, unable to answer tough questions!",
"Crooked", "poor leadership skills", "bad judgement", "unfit to be president", "very
bad and destructive track record", "Crooked", "Not honest!", "Reading poorly from
the telepromter!", "Crooked", "Bad performance", "doesn't even look
presidential!", "no longer has credibility", "Crooked", "too much failure in office",
"Crooked", "Lyin'", "Crooked", "has made so many mistakes", "BAD judgement!",
"Crooked", "temperament is bad", "Crooked", "zero natural talent", "decision
making ability-zilch!", "very stupid use of e-mails", "fraud", "Crooked", "Crooked",
"Crooked", "Crooked", "bad judgement and temperament", "Crooked", "CROOKED",
"Crooked", "suffers from plain old bad judgement!", "Crooked", "Crooked",
"Crooked", "Crooked", "her judgement has been proven to be so bad!", "not
qualified", "Would be four more years of stupidity!", "Wrong!", "reckless and
dangerous", "Crooked", "very dishonest", "Crooked", "Crooked",, "Crooked",

"Crooked", "has no chance!", "ISIS, China, Russia and all would love for her to be president", "zero imagination and even less stamina", "Crooked", "Crooked", "a fraud", "Crooked", "Crooked", "Crooked", "Crooked",, "can't close the deal with Bernie Sanders", "Crooked", "Crooked", "Crooked", "Can't believe she would misrepresent the facts!", "Liar!", "Crooked", "can't close the deal on Crazy Bernie", "Crooked", "Crooked", "Crooked", "has bad judgment!", "Crooked", "Crooked", "pushing the false narrative that I want to raise taxes", "Crooked", "Crooked", "Crooked", "Crooked", "Crooked", "corrupt", "bad judgement", "Constantly playing the women's card - it is sad!", "ZERO leadership ability", "Crooked", "said she is used to "dealing with men who get off the reservation." Actually, she has done poorly with such men!", "Crooked", "Crooked", "perhaps the most dishonest person to have ever run for the presidency", "Crooked", "one of the all time great enablers!", "Crooked", "unqualified to be president", "incompetent", "has been involved in corruption for most of her professional life!", "Who should star in a reboot of Liar Liar- Hillary Clinton or Ted Cruz? Let me know", "not presidential material", "a major national security risk", "such bad judgement", "lied last week", "doesn't have the strength or stamina to be president", "totally flawed candidate", "stupidity", "pathetic", "SAD!", "LIED at the debate last night", "We need a #POTUS with great strength & stamina. Hillary does not have that", "lied" "disloyal person", "no strength, no stamina", "weak and ineffective", "does not have the STRENGTH or STAMINA to be President", "will be soundly defeated", "won't call out radical Islam", "afraid of Obama & the emails", "SHE HAS NO STRENGTH OR STAMINA", "weak", "corruption is what she's best at", "no strength or stamina", "totally incompetent as a manager and leader", "she looked lost", "her record is so bad", "the trade deal is a disaster, she was always for it!", "100% CONTROLLED", "Just can't read speeches!"

You just skipped right over that last three pages, didn't you? Stop. You need to read these tweets, as ugly as they are. All of this came straight from bully Trump.

Do you understand? Donald J. Trump is a bully--by choice. He chooses to be this man. He claims he's so smart? Well, if he truly is smart then he knows he is mean. And a misogynist.

Doesn't Make Him Right

But please know this: just because Donald Trump repeated it a thousand times calling Hillary crooked? It does not make it true and it doesn't make him right! Those bullies at my school, calling me bitch, didn't make it true and didn't make them right!

What Susie Says of Sally Says More of Susie than of Sally

Substitute Donald Trump for Hillary Clinton in each one of these tweets and I bet we'll have a better understanding of Trump's own life, not Hillary's. Hillary Rodham Clinton was bulldozed by the Trump machine and with a little help from his Russian friends, Trump took over the White House.

My story has a happy ending of sorts. Five of my classmates apologized. I mean, came to me after graduation, and truly, genuinely, from the bottom of their hearts apologized for treating me so poorly. Even though damage had been done, having them acknowledge the hurtfulness of it made a difference. I value these men for coming forward and their apologies, too. They helped make me who I am today, and I consider all of them my friends.

I can't imagine there will be an apology coming from Trump. His response to his "pussy-grabber" comments? It was "locker-room talk," a "private conversation." He dismissed the comments like he dismisses women in general.

If You Can't Say Anything Nice...

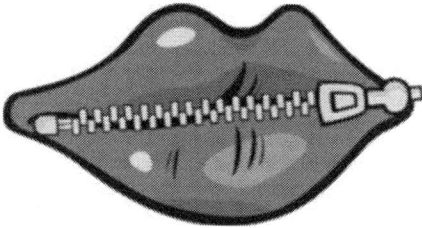

Too bad the man doesn't know when to keep his mouth shut. I share the tweets and quotes below because I know the strong, confident women mentioned can take it. I also think these women will support my effort to motivate others to take action. Trump is the true loser; the man looking in the mirror. He's the one that is unattractive both inside and out.

Donald J Trump
.@arianahuff is unattractive both inside and out. I fully understand why her former husband left her for a man--he made a good decision.
9:54 AM - Aug 28 2012

Donald J Trump
I feel sorry for Rosie's new partner in love whose parent are devastated at the thought of their daughter being with @Rosie--a true loser.
11:45 AM - Dec 14 2011

217

Rosie retaliated by calling Trump "an ass." Colossal ass doesn't even scratch the surface. What would possess a grown man to take to Twitter and act like a scorned teenage girl? Who gives a crap what he thinks about Arianna Huffington or Rosie O'Donnell, they are both accomplished, authentic women.

His attacks on Mika Brzezinski were a scene straight out of *Mean Girls* and oh so juvenile.

Donald J Trump
I heard poorly rated @Morning_Joe speaks badly of me (don't watch anymore). Then how come low I.Q. Crazy Mika, along with Psycho Joe, came...
7:52 AM - Jun 29 2017

Donald J Trump
...to Mar-a-Lago 3 nights in a row around New Year's Eve, and insisted on joining me. She was bleeding badly from a face-lift. I said no!
7:58 AM - Jun 29 2017

It's hard to believe that this man with his abhorrent behavior has been elected to the highest office in the land. If Momma Trump was alive today she would be ashamed.

Equal Opportunity Abuser

I want to like the President of the United States, but I will never like or respect a man who says such vile things to and about women. He gets his digs in on men as well; he's an equal opportunity abuser. To this day, he tries to make Barack Obama his own personal whipping boy--blaming him for *everything*!

Trump's wiretapping claim against Obama? Clear subterfuge; pure bullshit!

Donald J. Trump
Terrible! Just found out Obama had my "wires tapped" in Trump Tower just before the victory. Nothing found. This is McCarthyism!
6:35 AM - Mar 4 2017

Donald J. Trump
How low has President Obama gone to tapp my phone during the very sacred election process. This is Nixon/Watergate. Bad (or sick) guy!
7:02 AM - Mar 4 2017

And what is up with Trump's criticism of Arnold Schwarzenegger?

Donald J Trump
Wow, the ratings are in and Arnold Schwarzenegger got "swamped" (or destroyed) by comparison the ratings machine, DJT. So much for.....
7:34 AM - Jan 6 2017

Donald J Trump
being a movie star--and that was season 1 compared to season 14. Now compare that to my season 1. But who cares, he supported Kasich and Hillary
7:42 AM - Jan 6 2017

Schwarzenegger's reply was masterful:

Arnold @Schwarzenegger
There's nothing more important than the people's work @realdonaldtrump.
7:03 AM – Jan 6 2017

Arnold @Schwarzenegger
I wish you the best of luck and I hope you'll work for ALL the American people as aggressively as you worked for your ratings.
9:03 AM - Jan 6 2017

Aw, snap! Good one, Arnold.

It'd be humorous if it wasn't so real and disheartening. Trump's number one concern is still his image.

Here is Trump using a classic Trumpism to crap on Bette Midler.

219

Donald J Trump
While Bette Midler is an extremely unattractive woman, I refuse to say that because I always insist on being politically correct.
10:59 AM - Oct 28 2012

Donald J Trump
I refuse to call Megyn Kelly a bimbo, because that would not be politically correct. Instead I will only call her a lightweight reporter!
6:44 AM - Jan 27 2016

Trump went on to say about Megyn Kelly, after she'd grilled him with questions during one of the first debates, she had "blood coming out of her eyes, blood coming out of her... wherever." And then as always Trump took to Twitter to get abusive.

Again, from the New York Times' list of "People, Places and Things Donald Trump has Insulted on Twitter."

Trump on Megyn Kelly, Anchor, Fox News

"You have no idea what my strategy on ISIS is", "get your facts straight", "BAD", "highly overrated", "so average in so many ways!", "crazy", "sick", "Never worth watching", "the most overrated person on tv", "is always complaining about Trump and yet she devotes her shows to me", "crazy", "Highly overrated", "her bad show is a total hit piece on me", "Crazy", "Crazy", "Can't watch Crazy Megyn anymore", "Without me her ratings would tank", "Get a life Megyn!", "lightweight reporter", "I refuse to call Megyn Kelly a bimbo, because that would not be politically correct", "lightweight reporter", "so average in every way", "lies", "dopey", "highly overrated", "bad!", "very bad at math", "the most overrated anchor", "really weird, she's being driven crazy", "don't watch her show", "I don't watch", "had her two puppets say bad stuff", "should take another eleven day 'unscheduled' vacation", "lightweight", "highly overrated", "really off her game", "not very good or professional", "really bombed tonight"

And let's not forget the racial slurs against Elizabeth Warren, U.S. Senator from Massachusetts

"Sad to watch", "bombed last night!", "Pocahontas", "Pocahontas", "wanted V.P. slot so badly but wasn't chosen because she has done nothing in the Senate", "Pocahontas", "a very weak Senator", "Goofy", "Pocahontas", "Goofy", "the least productive Senator in the U.S. Senate", "Goofy", "goofy", "one of the least productive senators", "Very racist!", "Goofy", "has a nasty mouth", "one of the least productive U.S. Senators", "Goofy", "All talk, no action!", "Total hypocrite!", "lowlife!", "Goofy",,

220

"she doesn't have a clue", "If it were up to goofy Elizabeth Warren, we'd have no jobs in America", "goofy", "failed Senator", "gets nothing done", "lied", "Our Native American Senator", "goofy couldn't care less about the American worker", "does nothing to help!", "using the woman's card", "didn't have the guts to run for POTUS", "Goofy", "phony Native American heritage", "didn't have the guts to run for POTUS", "Goofy", "phony Native American heritage", "has done nothing!", "one of the least effective Senators in the entire U.S. Senate", "Goofy", "All talk, no action -- maybe her Native American name?", "Does nothing", "weak and ineffective", "Goofy", "phony Native American heritage", "Goofy", "has a career that is totally based on a lie", "Hillary Clinton's flunky", "Goofy", "goofy", "a fraud!", "goofy"

Regarding the infamous sitting U.S. Supreme Court Justice Ruth Bader Ginsburg, Trump said "her mind is shot," and he called for her resignation. Because why? She knows the law and spoke out against him.

I'm not sorry to say it, Trump fans, your dude is an epic Douchebag. And if you can't see what's wrong with what he's saying, then look in the mirror, you're a Douchebag, too.

What Have You Got to Lose?

I mentioned Trump's assault on physically challenged individuals including conservative columnist Charles Krauthammer, who had referred to Trump as a "rodeo clown," but what of Trump's assaults on the African-American community and the LGBTQ community? Trump courted the African-American community with the campaign slogan, "What have you got to lose?"

We're still tracking what chaos Trump is unleashing on the Black community, but he and Jeff Sessions are ramping up the prison system for people of color. They are undoing Obama's initiatives supporting Police Departments with training. Instead Trump is giving our Police Departments military equipment.

Trump signed his own executive order rescinding Barack Obama's Fair Pay and Safe Workplaces order of 2014 that kept federal contractors from discriminating against people based on sexual orientation or gender identification. Did you get that? Trump's Commerce Department has removed protections for sexual orientation and gender identification. Trump's White House did not recognize Gay Pride Month in June. They've rescinded rules allowing transgender people the right to use the bathroom they identify with. Trump and clown posse have removed the category "LGBTQ" from the census, turning back gay rights by a decade. And Nikki Haley actually voted against a United Nations resolution that would keep gays from being executed. Oh. My. God.

Obama's Fair Pay and Safe Workplaces order also made gender-based fair pay practices more transparent. Trump reversed that order, ironically, on Equal Pay Day. Makes sense: Trump's female staff members earn on average 63% of what their male counterparts make. That pay gap tripled under Trump.

Obama's Fair Pay and Safe Workplaces order also gave women a voice if they had been sexually harassed at work. But all those protections are now gone. Thanks to Trump.

De-Regulation! Except in Your Bedroom!

Why is it that the only thing the Republicans want to regulate is what goes on in our bedrooms? Why do they care who's keeping whom warm at night? It's not their business. As Katie Byron would say, "There's your business, my business, and God's business." Especially for those hypocrites reporting to love the Bible - it's not your job to judge and condemn others. It's not your business! Mind your own damned business and I'll mind mine. And as for judging, that right belongs to your God. For those of you persecuting others, do not pass the Pearly Gates, and go straight to hell.

Bill O'Reilly has been fired from the Fox News Network for sexual harassment of multiple women. The network has paid out more than $13 million over the years to keep the allegations quiet. Maybe Trump will now appoint O'Reilly as head of the U.S. State Department's Office of Global Women's Issues like he put Scott Pruitt in charge of the Environmental Protection Agency, and Rick Perry in charge of the Department of Energy. Each of them wanted to do away with the organization they are now running. "Deconstruction" is the word the White House is using.

O'Reilly can work directly with all the women who accused him--and Trump--of sexual impropriety! Trump said of O'Reilly, "I don't think he's wrong." Notice Trump didn't say he didn't do it, he said he didn't think O'Reilly did anything wrong.

There are currently over 20 women alleging Trump assaulted them to some varying degree including: voyeurism, shaming, groping, kissing, rape. Read the story "A Running List of All the Women Who've Accused Donald Trump of Assault" published in October 2016 by the *Huffington Post* and written by Catherine Pearson, Emma Gray, and Alanna Vagianos. Read the accusations for yourself.

Douchebag Wisdom

I applaud each and every one of these women for standing up to pussy-grabber Trump. I thank them for their bravery. Each of them has a story to tell. I support them in their journey and will stick up for victims of sexual assault everywhere.

Trump's reaction? He said at a campaign rally in Gettysburg, "All of these liars will be sued after the election is over." But the only one being sued right now is Donald Trump. Warning: karma is coming for you. It's disguised as a woman. And she's pissed.

I'm shocked to say I have a girlfriend who voted for Trump. Since we only see each other occasionally, I didn't find out until a few weeks after the election. At the time I was still in the first stages of grief and shock; I was depressed but hadn't yet moved to despondent. Her admission blew me straight into anger. She must be joking!! What would ever possess her to vote for such a pig?!

This woman and I practice yoga together. She's a trauma survivor with her own story to tell--and now a trauma coach for others for God sakes! She's about love and light, and forgiveness and healing. To say her whispered confession floored me is an understatement. How could someone who embraces the philosophies of yoga vote for a man so obviously opposed to anything remotely Zen, or human for that matter? She said she meditated on it and thought his business experience might take the country in a different financial direction.

She also said, "You know he's not really a Republican, right?" You could have fooled me--and the rest of the nation now as he crams Republican ideology up our vaginas! Yes, I know that was harsh, but you get the picture, women are being forced to "take it." Old, white men are making policy for women across the country, and in some cases around the world. The only solution is to stand up for each other.

I wanted to be supportive, but I didn't understand. Why vote for the bully? What could have possessed her?

Then I realized I was being the douche. How dare I judge her? Maybe she was being victimized as well, Stockholm Syndrome style. If Trump's bully techniques had raised powerful, old memories and feelings in me, maybe they had done that for her. Maybe she, too, had something to overcome. Maybe she wanted to believe he could be a better man. I wanted to believe he could be a better man but wasn't naïve enough to think Trump could change.

How could she have known that he would roll-back women's rights in his first one hundred days? And that's just the tip of the iceberg. And yes, she regrets her vote. As do many.

Actions Speak Louder Than Words

In addition to what I've already mentioned, here's how Donald Trump is harming women in our nation and around the world:

1. Trump reinstated the Mexico City Policy which prevents the U.S. Government from funding international non-governmental non-profits if they counsel women on reproductive options that include abortion. The Helms Amendment of 1973, passed shortly after Roe v Wade, already prohibits any federal money for abortion funding: goodbye contraception availability, hello more unplanned pregnancies

2. Trump defunded Planned Parenthood: goodbye access to basic   women services such as annual pap smears and contraception. Contraception! And yes, abortion when needed. Now Trump has made it easier for employers to deny their female employees insurance that includes birth control. Millions of women will now have to pay for their own birth control while insurance companies raise the prices

3. Trump got pro-life Neil Gorsuch on the Supreme Court: say goodbye to a woman's right to choose

And in the height of hypocrisy, President Pussy-Grabber proclaimed April 2017 as National Sexual Assault Awareness and Prevention month. Is he quite mad or simply moronic? How can he think any of these orders help women? They don't.

What these executive orders against women prove is Trump's need to destroy any law that President Barack Obama put his signature to. It doesn't matter how worthy the law, or how many women the law helped. Trump can't see past his hatred for Obama, and women will suffer.

Trump's budget cuts alone will eliminate a grant by the Department of Justice used to help victims of sexual assault and domestic violence. The Department of Justice says more than 300,000 instances of rape or sexual assault are reported yearly. Trump's budget cuts will eliminate contraceptive services and supplies to millions and millions of women around the world.

Trump just used Betsy DeVos to roll back title IX protections for survivors of sexual assault on college campuses.

Tell me again how "No one has more respect for women than Donald J Trump"?

At least Biff Tannen knew he was stupid. He just lied and bullied his way through every situation. Donald Trump thinks of himself as a genius. He doesn't even know that he doesn't know. He is that stupid.

It's up to us, women (and men) everywhere, to help educate this moron! I agree with Rex! Our Secretary of State, Rex Tillerson, called Trump a "fucking moron" after a meeting regarding national security. Thanks for saying so; we agree.

A big shout-out to Senators Lisa Murkowski of Alaska and Susan Collins of Maine for voting "no" on the healthcare-killing bill. And of course, our hero, Senator John McCain of Arizona.

> *"The problem is not just what we don't know, but*
> *what we do know that ain't so."*
> *-- Mark Twain*

There are four major categories of perception and intelligence--as first explained to me by my Freshman-year bandleader on a total rant.

This 2x2 matrix has been studied by many and here is my interpretation of how Donald Trump fits in. But remember, this book is not about Donald Trump as much as it is about your reaction to Trump. The bigger question is: where do you fall on the quadrant?

	Know	Don't Know
Know	Q1	Q2
Don't Know	Q3	Q4

Douchebag Wisdom

There are people who:

- Know that they Know, Q1
- Know they Don't Know, Q2
- Don't Know that they Know, Q3
- Don't Know they Don't Know, Q4

Trump thinks he's in Q1: he knows that he knows. "I'm a great negotiator." And although Trump has been in Q1 at times throughout his business life, he is now actually in Q4: he doesn't know he doesn't know.

It's the Trump Effect meets the Peter Principle. Trump has risen to his level of incompetence, but he says things like "I know more than the Generals do." I think that's clear evidence that Trump thinks he's in Q1 but proof that the man doesn't know that he doesn't know. He's really in Q4.

I want to believe that when Trump is signing these executive orders that he doesn't know what he's signing--he doesn't know he's signing away women's rights. He certainly doesn't pay attention to detail. He simply wants to sign them to get them done. The question is: does Trump know what's he's signing, what he's doing, does he know--or not know--how stupid and destructive he's being?

Congratulations and welcome to Q2!

"Who knew?"
-- Donald Trump

"Who knew healthcare could be so complicated?" Are you F'in' kidding me? Seriously? The whole nation knew, Donald Trump. The only person who didn't know was you. Again, Q4, don't know that you don't know.

But with the declaration of this one question: who knew healthcare could be so complicated, Donald Trump now knows that he doesn't know. He's now entered Q2. And that's where he needs to be--all the time.

He says over and over again that he surrounds himself with the best minds, but what holds Trump back is his unwavering belief of what he already knows.

When asked about his differing opinion on North Korea with Rex Tillerson, Trump said he was "stronger" and "tougher." He made it clear he had the final say on what military action would be taken. Earlier that same day, Trump challenged Tillerson to an I.Q. test after finding out Tillerson called him a "fucking moron." Trump says we all know who'd win. We certainly do--not the American people.

And we're back to Q1 and Twain, "The problem is not just what we don't know, but what we do know that ain't so."

Trump believes so much that hasn't proven to be true: there's been a spike in murder rates around the country, China is a currency manipulator, removing illegals will make us safer, we have the highest corporate tax rate in the world.

Trump rarely admits to Q2, knowing he doesn't know. He says he surrounds himself with smart people, but that's not the same as saying "I don't know." I think there is little that falls into Q3: Trump doesn't know that he knows. I haven't seen any unconscious behavior that leads me to believe he is enlightened at levels he's yet to understand.

As rich as Trump is, he has a very limited perception on people and cultures. He knows how to slap his name on a building without actually building it. He knows how to be a bully. He knows how to blame others. And he knows how to treat people with respect and common courtesy, he just doesn't care to do it. But that's a whole 'nother chart.

The Trump Paradox: Bringing Out the Worst in Us

During Trump's campaign, an eighteen-year-old college student stood up at a political forum in New Hampshire and told Donald Trump that she didn't think he was "a friend to women." What did the mean-spirited, belligerent, thin-skinned old man Trump do? He stewed on it all night, and in the early morning light he attacked her on Twitter. He called her an "arrogant young woman" and accused her of being a "plant" from a rival campaign.

Donald J Trump
The arrogant young woman who questioned me in such a nasty fashion at No Labels yesterday was a Jeb staffer! HOW CAN HE BEAT RUSSIA & CHINA.
6:39 AM - Oct 13 2015

What she was is a woman brave enough to stand up and ask the question.

Then the Trump Twitter trolls piled on and continued Trump's attack, making it personal and threatening. The young woman feared for her safety. This

227

is what happens when Trump targets a private citizen who publicly challenges him. He initiates and intimidates and encourages his followers to do the same.

He may pretend he's in Q4, he doesn't know the effect his tweet will have on his followers and the young woman, but he's in Q1, he knows what will happen, he knows. He knows.

Whether he's playing dumb or is dumb, the perception is--our President is dumb.

So how do we deal with the next four years of Trump? God forbid!! The next year of Trump? Even if he's not impeached, he's one swing away from a stroke. He doesn't look well. Bless his poisonous heart. Until that time, what do we do?

We make a stand and take a stand! Find your voice and get active. Resist, for yourself and those who agree with you, and those that have been victimized and assaulted.

How do you deal with a bully? You do what Hillary Rodham Clinton did: you stand up! You confront them. And you don't let them alter your perception of you. Stand your ground. One thing I do wish Hillary would have done--in addition to standing up to Trump--was clarify her beliefs. Much of her campaign put Trump's own words back in our faces. I was already appalled. I would have appreciated a bit more "positioning" and "messaging" from Hillary. I knew she had it together. Her website was a masterpiece of spelling out her voting record and where she stood on the policies. The nation deserves to know how competent and prepared Hillary Clinton was and still is. #GiveEmHill Can't wait to read the new book, *What Happened*. We know what happened, the trolls got in the way.

Pizza-gate? Ridiculous, obviously fake news, and yet Trump passed the story on but cried anytime anyone published nonsense about him. Fake news, fake news, Trump continues to shout even though he's part of that. Obama wiretapped his phones? He's not just spreading fake news, Trump is the source; he's making this crap up. He got his Masters at Trump University--Bachelor of Bull Shit and a Masters in Business as in giving us all the business.

But we're discerning individuals--we can see through the crap. We all know:

A Set Back is a Set Up For a Come Back

Don't wait to be empowered; you are empowered on your own! Let Donald Trump be your role model for what not to do.

Don't despair and don't give up. Believe in yourself! You decide how you want to respond. And you go forward, knowing that just because someone says it is so doesn't make it so. You don't need to know everything to prosper. You just need to be aware of Q4, what you don't know you don't know.

You must be open to new perspectives and new ways of thinking and dealing with your emotions and behaviors and those of others. You can make a difference. You do make a difference! The Universe is not the same without you.

Spoiler Alert!

At the end of *Back to the Future 3*, Doc says to Marty and Jennifer, "It means your future hasn't been written yet. Your future is whatever you make it. So, make it a good one, both of you."

And in this turbulent, tumultuous, uncertain future just remember...

Roads? Where we're going, we won't need roads.

So, What Can You Do? So Glad You Asked!

1. Watch the movie Back to the Future 1, 2 and 3

2. Don the costume, a Pussy-Power Hat: The Pussy Hat project started with Krista Suh, a 29-year-old screenwriter living in LA who was planning to attend the Women's March in D.C. Krista was looking for a visual way to enforce her message, so she and her friend Jayna Zweiman and Kat Coyle, owner of the Little Knittery in Atwater Village, CA launched a small project that turned into a global movement. Krista Suh knitted the first pussy hat. Then with the help of Kat, her knitting instructor, the Pussy Power Pattern was created. It's been duplicated, replicated, and knitted up by thousands of supporters. Add cape and boots and you have one powerful superhero outfit

3. Go with a bit more bite and show your support for the LGBTQ community

4. Support high school duo Jules and Gabe in their Quest to "send Trump pussy." For $3.99 you can have an anatomically correct pussy sucker sent to Trump at the White House. Contact Jules and Gabe at hello@sendtrumppussy.com. 50% of proceeds are being donated to Planned Parenthood. Nicely done!!

5. Maybe a traditional sucker is more your style - Check out Smith & Sinclair's "Trump sucks" lollipops. Smith & Sinclair take issue with Trump reinstating the Mexico City Policy. All profits raised will go to the international Planned Parenthood Foundation. Visit the UK company site here: http://www.smithandsinclair.co.uk/shop/trump-sucks

6. Give to Planned Parenthood! Join the #fight4birthcontrol

7. Get yourself a Nasty Woman 6-pack of magnets by Kate Grenier

8. Send a Bag of Dicks to those that need a reminder: Douchebag Trump or Pence

9. $9.99 bagofdicks.com

10. Join a Girl Power organization like

11. GirlScouts.org

12. GirlUp.org

13. Become a friend of the Women's March Facebook page and stay up-to-date on events designed to empower and inspire

14. Take part in the conversation! Become the movement: facebook.com/womensmarchonwash/

15. Go to the official Women's March website, womensmarch.com/100/action1/, and download a list of actions you can take to take a stand

16. Run for office!

17. Check out Emily's List, a political action committee focused on getting pro-choice Democratic women into office

18. Join the conversation: follow the real influencers on Twitter
    a. @HillaryClinton
    b. @RepMaxineWaters
    c. @KamalaHarris
    d. @AnaNavarro
    e. @Maddow

    f.   @ChelseaHandler

    g.   @mariannewilliamson

    h.   @sarahksilverman

19. For the Wiccans: a binding spell for Trump

    Get the spell on the Official Bind Trump Facebook page: facebook.com/groups/officialbindtrump

20. Read Hillary's new book: *What Happened*

21. Or better yet, listen to Hillary read the book herself! I cried at the last story

22. Join NOW, the National Organization of Women, the largest organization of feminist grassroot activists in the United States, chapters in every state

23. Continue to March, Dance, and Sing

Biff Trump

Pour yourself a drink, Put on some lipstick, and Pull yourself together.

Liz Taylor

Now,

Get caught trying.

Hillary Clinton

Biff Trump

Biff Trump

King Dong

9. King Dong: King of Trump World

"Every critic, every detractor, will have to bow down
to President Trump."
-- Omarosa Manigault

Omarosa Manigault, former participant on Celebrity Apprentice, now Trump's Director of African-American Outreach continued in that particular interview, "It's everyone who's ever doubted Donald, whoever disagreed, whoever challenged him. It is the ultimate revenge to become the most powerful man in the universe."

That, to me, defines Donald Trump, King Dong.

Trump had no desire to run for president; he ran to be King. He ran, not because he cares about the little people, the common people, but because he cared about the people who dissed him. He became president out of sheer spite and revenge, so others would have to bow down to him.

Now that he's taken the White House, the respect Trump doesn't earn he thinks he can command, or declare. Sorry, Donald, all the money in the world has not afforded you: respect, class, looks, brains, compassion, a sense of humor, or manners.

Rogue POTUS Staff
Pres. Trump is already making waves at the office. Wants to be "the President who will be remembered as a King." His words, not ours.
9:02 PM - Jan 25 2017

So, tweeted @roguepotusstaff shortly after Trump took office. According to their Twitter profile, @roguepotusstaff is the "unofficial resistance team inside the White House." They "pull back the curtain to expose the real workings inside this disastrous, frightening Administration."

The validity of this account is questionable; it is hard to filter the fake news from the real. We don't know who is behind this Twitter account, but Trump himself has already declared it: he thinks he's King: King of New York Real Estate, the King of Illegal Immigration, the King of Debt.

Donald J. Trump
I am "the King of debt." That has been great for me as a businessman, but is bad for the country. I made a fortune off of debt, will fix U.S.
11:55 AM - Jun 21 2016

At campaign rallies across the country he declared again and again, "I alone can fix it." It'd be interesting to watch this man learn on-the-fly how democracy works--if it weren't so tragic! Being president of his own company is nothing like being president of the United States. For the first time in his life, he truly does answer to someone else. For the first time in his life, he answers to everyone else. He didn't understand the scope of the job, because he never respected the job, evidenced by how he treated the man before him, Barack Obama. To this day, King Dong lays blame at Obama's feet. You name any problem that Trump has yet to figure out and Trump will find a way to cast blame back on Obama.

Trump blamed his own incompetence of choosing Mike Flynn for National Security Advisor on Obama--after the Obama team had warned him of Flynn's contact with other countries. They were aware of his questionable ties to Russia.

That's probably why King Dong wanted him. Flynn could be the scapegoat for all the Russia talk. Currently the Russian investigation is heating up. Trump is tweeting Flynn to "stay strong," which we now know after the disastrously bastardly pardoning of known racist Sheriff Joe Arpaio is code for "I'll give you a pardon." But you decide. It's safe to say, Donald expects Flynn's loyalty. Kings do. We'll see who prevails over time. Apparently, Flynn has a "story to tell." We'll see if he tells it or relies on Trump to reward his silence.

Donald Trump thinks he's the "King of" and the "best at" everything. Trump brags about being top of his class at Wharton Business School (he wasn't), the best baseball player in New York (you're joking, right?), and as he's said many times proving just the opposite is true, "I have the best words."

Donald Trump is a privileged white man who's bought himself a country and he intends to rule it.

The King Has No Clothes--and No Heart

Does Trump have malicious intent? At one time, that question intrigued me, but not anymore. Who cares what his *intent* is as he's crapping over the country and all its people? He's breaking up families with his deportation forces and persecuting others based on religion. Trump says he's fighting for "the little guy" but he's enacting policies that will hurt the little guy. His mouth says one thing--and then says just the opposite--but he's empowering goons to take action.

"I am your voice," he told his fanatics, his sheeple. But he's not my voice! And he's not the voice of the 65 million others who voted for Hillary Clinton. And he's not the voice of the over 90 million people that didn't vote. They let someone else's vote be their voice. And Trump is not my voice as he uses his position to defend White Supremacists and flame and embolden the worst of humanity.

Trump fans like that he's tough on immigrants and Muslims and Hispanics and African-Americans and Native Americans and women and LGBTQ, pretty much anyone who's not white and male, but where does Trump draw the line? You think this president is not coming for you? If you're average, just working hard and trying to get ahead, look out, because King Dong is preparing to syphon money straight from the poor and middle class to the accounts of big business which will in turn line the pockets of the CEOs while they destroy a planet for the sake of money.

It'll start in little, nonchalant nothing-to-see-here ways, but he' comin' like a King Kong-sized gorilla, stompin' and crappin on anything or anyone in his way.

The very first executive order Trump signed in his first 100 days in office rolled back legislation making it easier and less expensive for first-time home buyers and those with modest means to buy a home. He took that money out of the pockets of people and put it squarely in the pockets of the banks. With a flash of a pen and a flouncy autograph for showmanship, he made it more expensive for the average person to buy a home.

I don't think Trump truly sees the little guy, or if he does, he sees them as expendable. Over 24 million people could lose their health care coverage with the Trumpcare bill. He doesn't care. He labels people as his "enemy," puts them in a category, a detention center, or deports them. He blames and shames everyone or anyone who doesn't agree with him.

Trump has delusions of grandeur; he thinks he's King. He thinks he can now control and manipulate a system he's taken advantage of for decades. His litigious ways leak into and onto everything and everyone who gets in his way. He'd rather sue you then pay you. He thinks his way is the only way, the best way. He's not open to other people's suggestions.

Karma for the King

Karma's a bitch, and King Dong is feelin' the bite. All that time and energy Trump spent spreading rumors and falsehood about Obama's birth certificate is coming back around like a karma boomerang of Trump's own making. Can you say "Russia, Russia, Russia." Except Obama just had one self-titled King, Donald Trump, shouting about a birth certificate. Now, President Dong is up against an entire nation demanding he be accountable for his actions, beginning with Russia's interference in our election. All those times Trump questioned and badgered Obama with questions of his legitimacy to be president? Know the entire nation questions Trump's legitimacy except Trump supporters who don't question anything about their self-declared King.

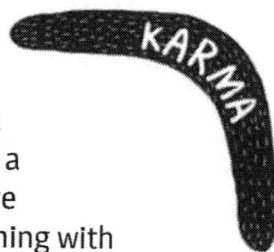

Donald Trump, Starring in King Dong!

Donald Trump's created a King Kong image of himself; he's larger than human. He's a beast. He's larger than life.

In the 2005 Peter Jackson movie version of King Kong, a movie director (played by Jack Black) discovers King Kong on Skull Island where they happen to be shooting a movie. Black's character talks the crew into capturing King Kong and taking him to New York City where he writes Kong into a Broadway show, billing him as: the "8th Wonder of the World." King Kong has become a chained animal in a circus, or in this case, an off-Broadway play. Greed, the drive for money, is behind the exploitation of the animal.

The parallels are similar, except Trump is a willing participant! It's with purpose Trump thumps his chest and bellows, billing himself as a wonder-of-the-world, the "greatest" and the "best," a King.

Trump believes he's entitled to that view from the top of the tallest building. He's taken over the White House and we are all being subjected to his "kingly" idea of America. But I don't care how many times this man thumps his chest and roars his mighty roar, he is not royalty! And there is no royal family!

King Dong is the result of dark money into politics. It's called Citizens United and it refers to the monumental case brought by the conservative Koch brothers, founders of the 501c organization, as they sought to pour their money into the federal election against then Democratic presidential nominee Hillary

Clinton. This 2010 decision, Citizens United vs Federal Election Committee, changed the face of politics forever.

Previously, we only had to worry about corporate lobbyists infusing election campaigns with money. Now anyone with money can declare themselves a Super PAC and start spending.

Now that King Dong is in the White House the dark money will try to keep him in.

His policies are remarkably un-American, anti-immigration, and reprehensible. Trump's base knows exactly who he is and what he stands for. Their views match Trump's. But there are those who voted for him, believed in him and thought they were voting for positive change that are going to be hurt the most. Slashing billions and billions out of the 2018 budget, out of food assistance, healthcare and college funding will lead to a very poor and stupid generation.

All of us lose in this current version of the 2018 budget except for the very few at the top, King Dong's loyal cabinet, and of course the royal family.

I don't believe King Dong knows how to fix our economy. I don't trust he is a good businessman. He lacks vision and how he's made his money is suspicious to me.

If King Dong won the election without Putin's help then let him release his taxes and prove it. Barack Obama did, after all, release his birth certificate, not that it shut Trump up, but it was the proof that he craved. I want to see Trump's taxes and who ultimately paid for his campaign. That'll be my proof that I've misjudged him. Show me his money and I'll tell you who he's loyal to. It doesn't take an independent investigation to figure that one out.

King Dong, release your taxes. Prove you're not in Putin's pocket. That would lift you a notch in my view, in a nation's view. As you're fond of saying, "What have you got to lose?"

Lead, Follow, or Make It Up as You Go

I've heard people call Trump a genius. I've heard Trump say he heard Putin called him a genius, although the word Putin used was "colorful." The point is, some people think what comes out of Trump is planned, that he's intelligent and strategic and his bluster and bravado is just a role in the part of a supreme plan.

I wonder if he's mentally ill. Temperamentally unfit, batshit crazy. Doesn't matter how you label it, if I cared what happened to him, I'd be worried. King Dong's radical behavior is unsettling. I mean come on!!? Who shoves another person aside? To get to the front of the pack? I'm referring to the Prime Minister of Montenegro who Trump shoved aside as if he was a 3rd grader at his first G7 NATO Summit.

And, who shoots off missiles over "the most beautiful piece of chocolate cake" or threatens to "totally destroy" another country with "fire and fury"? Who pulls out of the Paris Climate Accord then says he'll come back in if it is skewed more favorably to the U.S.?

Either an oblivious man or a deliberately dismissive, sick man. Or a man who thinks he's King.

Did you notice that Trumpism, by the way? Calling someone "sick" demeans them. It judges them. It condemns them. We must be conscious of these assumptions. We must keep the lines of communication open with each other. "Diplomacy" can't just be a word for how we address other countries, it has to be how we address each other as citizens, as fellow human beings. This is a lesson King Dong has yet to learn.

@realdonaldtrump

Trump lumbers around the White House and his "summer" and "winter" White Houses, tweeting out the essence of who he really is. His Twitter handle is: @realdonaldtrump.

Donald Trump has played many roles throughout his career, including a brief appearance on Wrestlemania but he's most famous for playing the role of a successful businessman on TV. Trump has carried that TV showmanship and wrestlemania spirit with him to the Oval.

The wrestlemania tweet of Trump pummeling a man with the CNN logo for his head? Strange and telling. His retweet of a video of him swinging a golf club with the ball hitting Hillary Clinton in the back of the head? Demented and dangerous. The man that just retweeted these IS the president of the United States. Trump is up all hours of the night obsessed with how he is being covered by the media. His priority is his image.

Trump would appear a lot more kingly if he didn't let loose every thought in his head. He doesn't censor his language or consider the consequence. Mere days after peaceful protester Heather Heyer was killed by a White Supremacist in Charlottesville, VA--plowed into by a Trump supporter driving a Dodge Charger--Trump retweeted a picture of a Trump train smashing headlong into a CNN reporter on the train track.

It took Trump days to acknowledge what was happening in Charlottesville because he is still on his vendetta against the Press. Did he even acknowledge the loss of Heather? If so, it got buried in all his White Supremacist double-talk.

Time out and a prayer for the family of Heather Heyer, and especially her Mom. When they go low, we go Heyer. "If you aren't outraged, you aren't paying attention."

King Dong approves violence. Can Trump be that intentionally stupid, or does he just not care or is that really who he is? Trump clearly did not want to anger his white, angry, racist supporters. He admonished "many sides" in his comments against racism, failing to lay blame with haters, the KKK, and White Nationalists. He didn't rebuke them because he'll need their votes, if he's not impeached and imprisoned first. Trump is not versed in the laws of civility nor does he care. Twitter is how he talks to his kingdom and television is how he gets their reply.

The King Makes the Rules

King Dong's created a world where he is above the law. He hasn't disassociated himself from his businesses and he's deliberately obstructing justice as the Russian investigation intensifies. He's putting us all in danger with his own radical rhetoric.

He doesn't know what he doesn't know, but he's still making the rules:

Rule 1: Follow the rules

Rule 2: Don't question the rules

What rules, you might ask? Any rule the King wants....

The Associated Press reported the Trump Organization asked the government to grant dozens of special visas to allow foreign nationals to work at two of his Florida resorts. He preaches "buy American; hire American" but he ignores his own rules. Rules are for you, the common people, the little people, the ordinary people who pay taxes. And he will continue to make and break his own rules...

...until the judicial branch of government shuts him down.

Thank goodness, we have a judicial court system to check King Dong's executive orders. His travel ban was a blatant attempt to limit all travel from Middle Eastern, Muslim countries except for the ones that Trump is doing business with!

King Dong didn't like it when judges questioned his rules and in particular, Rule #2: Don't question the rules. When the 9th Circuit Court upheld the injunction that blocked Trump's travel ban, Trump tweeted:

Donald J. Trump
The opinion of this so-called judge, which essentially takes law-enforcement away from our country, is ridiculous and will be overturned!
8:12 AM - Feb 4 2017

Trump has no understanding of, or respect for, the judicial or democratic system. He's been quite upset with the rulings of the court regarding his unconstitutional travel bans. Thank God for the judges because this so-called POTUS thinks he can do anything he wants.

This isn't the first time Trump attacked a federal judge. Remember, Trump's been involved in over 4000 lawsuits. When Judge Gonzalo Curiel said there was enough evidence in the Trump University case to proceed with a hearing, Trump took to Twitter and questioned Curiel's heritage and presumed Curiel's bias against Trump because of his divisive rhetoric on building a wall. Judge Curiel was born in Chicago. King Dong didn't bother to get the facts.

Sally Yates, former US Deputy Attorney General until Trump fired her, is not obeying Rule #1 and daring to break Rule #2 has warned Trump is trying to "dismantle the rule of law, destroy the time-honored independence" of the Department of Justice. She went on to say in her op-ed that if we're not careful "our justice system may be broken beyond recognition."

There's nothing more King Dong would like to do: dismantle democracy and do everything his way. THAT's called a dictatorship or authoritarianism. I don't care what you call it, it's not democracy. Let him be King of his own real estate empire in his head. But he in not King of America. Sorry, King Dong, you may have bought the Republican party, but you can't buy the American people. But now that he's in office, King Dong's assault on our court system is part of a multi-pronged attack.

But this particular attack on our judicial system began when Mitch McConnell would not allow a confirmation hearing for President Obama's appointee, Merrick Garland. That strategy paid off; they hijacked the Supreme Court. Neil Gorsuch, Trump's appointee tilts the court conservative. Gorsuch is already showing his pro-corporation, anti-choice biases. With Gorsuch on the court a woman's right to choose is in jeopardy.

Trump is currently stacking the lower courts with conservative appointees--seats, once again, hijacked from Obama and the Democratic party. Trump is on track to fill over 100 judgeships, a move that will shape the morality of our country for decades to come.

King Dong makes war with anyone who questions his rules, opposes them or exposes them. His on-going feud with the Press is an epic battle between authoritarian rule and democracy. It's the battle between good (the Free Press) and evil (authoritarians opposed to the Free Press). I'm not a fan of Fox News but I defend their First Amendment right to report stories--as long as they are factual and accurate! That goes for all the news sources.

But the King wants to control what you read and watch. He hates the Press. He's tweeting suggestions of pulling NBC's license because he doesn't like their news, but thank goodness, the Press doesn't work that way. The Press have their own set of rules and, unlike the big moguls at the top, are not for sale. Rules? What rules? The Press makes their own rules in this quest for information and truth. I applaud the Press, especially as Trump continues his assault on their character. They dare to call him out.

The Washington Post, in their pursuit of transparency of government and information, changed their masthead to read "Democracy Dies in Darkness." I was so impressed I bought an online subscription.

FAKE NEWS or Fake King?

Donald J Trump
The FAKE NEWS media (failing @nytimes, @NBCNews, @ABC, @CBS, @CNN) is not my enemy, it is the enemy of the American People! Sick!
4:32 PM - Feb 17 2017

And then again 16 minutes later without the word "sick!" As if that one word made a difference.

Donald J Trump
The FAKE NEWS media (failing @nytimes, @NBCNews, @ABC, @CBS, @CNN) is not my enemy, it is the enemy of the American People!
4:48 PM - Feb 17 2017

Democracy dies when 62 million people believe Trump's words over that of reporters and journalists, dedicated people just doing their jobs. Trump has demonized them again and again. I can't wait to read Katy Tur's book, *Unbelievable*, about her time covering the election. Trump would purposely single her out at his rallies as he vilified her profession.

We're seeing increased violence towards our Press Corps, thanks to King Dong. King Dong still stands at rallies and singles out the press. Any story King Dong doesn't like he labels as FAKE NEWS. He's also claimed that the "leaks are real, but the news is not." It's hard to keep up but Trump's disregard for reporters is having an effect.

Greg Gianforte, a Republican contender for Montana's open congressional seat, on the night before the election, body-slammed a reporter from the Guardian. He didn't like a question regarding health care and totally lost his shit. Unfortunately, he won the election the next day. I want to think it's because 70% of voters had already cast their ballots in early voting. I hate to think that we've lost our sense of decency and morality and that this man is the best the people of Montana can do. Heaven help us all if they really didn't care. And heaven help our journalists because Trump has declared them "the enemy of the people."

Who Is the Real Enemy?

King Dong continues his effort to squelch First Amendment rights: Freedom of the Press. He's threatening to change libel laws so news sources can be sued for what they print. Trump has lost this battle in court before, but now that he's president, he thinks he can push it. He thinks he's infallible. He thinks he knows best. His rules.

Jeff Sessions, or as King Dong calls him, beleaguered Jeff Sessions, is looking for ways to press journalists on their sources. When asked explicitly whether he planned to prosecute reporters he said he couldn't say "no." We don't imprison reporters in the U.S.! This isn't Russia! We give them a Pulitzer prize and take down the greedy, dirty Douchebags they expose.

And we don't arrest peaceful protesters, yet the Republicans, empowered by Trump, have proposed legislation in 18 states that make peaceful assembly and protest unlawful. This is legislation that strikes at the heart of what it means to live in America. I don't need Trump to "be my voice." I'm my own voice--and I am pissed! As long as I am not breaking any laws, it is my right as a citizen of this country to stand and protest--or take a damned knee! I repeat--is this Russia?! But Trump feels confident we'll all follow his rules.

On matters of national security, King Dong sent Stephen Miller, Senior Policy Advisor, to say Trump's national security decisions "will not be questioned." He, too, has forgotten the meaning of democracy and the role of the President. Even scarier, Miller says "President Trump is the most gifted politician of our time. He's the best orator to hold that office in generations." This he said to Fox News host Laura Ingraham.

I believe Trump's the most gifted con man of our time.

King Dong infamously said during a GOP debate, "They're not going to refuse me. Believe me." Trump's remark was in response to the host asking him what he'd do if the military refuse to carry out orders considered war crimes, such as torture and targeting family members of terrorists.

Follow the rules; don't question the rules. Trump has currently surrounded himself with military men, three Generals: Kelly, Mattis, and McMaster. Hopefully their honor to nation is stronger than their allegiance to Trump's ridiculous, racists rules.

The day King Dong called our men and women in uniform "my military," my skin crawled. It is *our* military, King Dong; they fight for the nation. King Dong sees them as pegs in a IRL game of "Who Sunk My Battleship?" King Dong gives away covert intelligence, telling other world leaders the location of our submarines, taunting North Korea suggesting we're not afraid of a pre-emptive strike?! And threatening North Korea with "fire and fury"? And then announcing, "the calm before the storm" and telling Tillerson and the world there is "only one way" to deal with North Korea.

Trump's predilection to settle conflict through violence and intimidation scares us all. Kim Jong-un doesn't play by King Dong's rules. And it seems that Kim Jong-un is the more rational between the two dictators. Kim Jong-un responded to Trump's tweets and comments about "fire and fury" calling Trump "mentally deranged" and a "dotard." A dotard is a weak or senile old person. I had to look it up so I'll spare you the time. Score one for Kim Jong-un. Nailed it.

And the Ratings Are In

The King of Ratings is the title King Dong most craves. He'll do or say anything to get those ratings. The more absurd, the better.

When King Dong didn't get the ratings he thought he deserved for his inauguration day, he pitched a fit. From Trump's perspective he saw a million to a million and a half people that day on the Mall and he was sure it was the biggest inauguration crowd, ever. The picture tweeted by the National Parks Department showed a picture of a crowd roughly one third the size of the crowd that attended Obama's 2009 inauguration day celebration.

King Dong told Sean Spicer to *get out there and set those reporters straight!* So, Sean Spicer said it was the "largest crowd to ever witness an inauguration. Period."

Sorry King Dong-along, I have two eyes and you can't fool me. The crowd was obviously a portion of the size that celebrated Obama's 2012 victory and a fraction of the size that celebrated Obama's historic 2008 victory. I don't believe King Dong's lies! He's gasbagging me and gaslighting me, the American people, and those that voted for him.

Gaslighting is just one out of a list of 20 symptoms from Shahida Arabi's book *POWER: Surviving and Thriving After Narcissistic Abuse.* I feel like I've been witness to all of these symptoms in Donald Trump:

1. Gaslighting
2. Projection
3. Nonsensical Conversation from Hell
4. Blanket Statements and Generalizations
5. Aggressive Jabs Disguised as Jokes

Is this behavior intentional? Or is it mental illness? And how long will the Republicans lead us down this path? They are co-conspirators in King Dong's reign. The longer it goes on the more dangerous King Dong becomes.

Don't believe me? Read Amy Siskind's The List. Every week she puts together a succinct, fact-based list of actions King Dong and court are taking. If you read nothing else I've suggested, know the facts, read The List.

America First: World Second

Countries all over the world see King Dong differently. He was well-received in the Middle East, not so much in Europe. He played nice with the Saudis but not so much with the Europeans. It was an embarrassment when he used his NATO speech to try and fleece our NATO allies. Trump's a thug like the Russian oligarchs he admires. And speaking of doing business with the Russians--they're not our friend and therein lies the rub. The Russians are quite clearly King Dong's friends. An AP/NORC poll found 7 out of 10 Americans are at least moderately concerned that Trump or associates had inappropriate ties to Russia with good cause.

It looks to me as if Trump is bought and paid for by the Russians. The Russians have pumped millions of dollars into his businesses. Most every member of his royal family and his closest advisers have ties to Russia. *Newsweek* reports Jared Kushner received a $285 million loan from Deutsche Bank, a German bank with ties to Russia, one month before the 2016 election. Kushner did not disclose the loan to the Office of Government Ethics as required. But don't expect information like this to be addressed. Walter Shaub Jr., now former Director of the Office of Government Ethics resigned citing Trump's multiple conflicts of interest.

Trump quite clearly stated he wanted a better relationship with Russia while on the campaign trail. And he's been doing business with the Russians for years!!! He's boasted again and again how successful and well-received his 2013 Miss Universe pageant in Russia was. He signed a letter of intent to be part of Trump Tower Moscow. Allegedly, The Donald would get $4 million up-front, with no up-front costs to him, a percentage of sales, and a spa named after Ivanka. Puke. Sorry, that was a bit douchey. Who wouldn't want a spa named after them? Insert Anderson Cooper eye-roll, again. Don't hurt yourself. See what I mean? I become the douche.

But Trump's lies are hard to understand. "I have nothing to do with Russia -- No deals, no loans, no nothing," said King Dong--but Don *Jr.* has stated again and again Russia is a big source of revenue for them. The facts are staring at us. We don't need the taxes to prove he does business with Russia. He obviously does. But the question is: is that illegal?

248

No, really, stop and think about this. Obviously, Russia wanted Trump in the White House as opposed to Hillary Clinton who was a formidable threat to Putin due to her experience as Secretary of State. This is what Robert Mueller is investigating: did Trump and his team actively work with the Russians to hijack the election. Are the 2016 election results valid and true? This is the question we must all ask of ourselves. If you believe Trump had nothing to do with this, then go about your business and dismiss it, and if you think Trump had something to do with this, then go about your business and prove it. But stay informed. From my perspective, every connection he recruited for his campaign has/had ties to Russia. This is what we get when we let an ultra-elite capitalist into the White House.

I don't know the law. I'm trusting our intelligence community, and Robert Mueller, former FBI Director and our duly appointed independent counsel on all things Russia. I trust this man and these institutions to get to the bottom of the Russian scandal.

And they are. The top four intelligence agencies have all agreed with "high confidence" that Russia interfered in the election. That would be the National Security Agency, Federal Bureau of Investigations, the Central Intelligence Agency, and the Director of National Intelligence.

If these agencies and commissions find Trump was not in collusion with Russia, then I will let it drop. Period. Because I trust democracy and believe there are still honorable people serving in Congress, although I don't see many Republicans that I respect.

The Russian investigation is the biggest issue to me. It legitimizes this president for me. It validates our election and our democracy. Follow that up with taxes. I also want an accounting of where Trump's money has come from. "I'm really, really rich" King Dong got his money from somewhere.

I hope each one of the Republicans on the House Ways and Means Committee who voted to keep Trump's taxes private gets voted out of office. Or better yet, get tossed out for obstructing justice. Seriously, what are they all afraid of? Why not get to the bottom of this. Why not prove he's as successful as he says he is? Why not come clean with the American people and share his taxes? Imagine how many of us Democrats he could shut-up. If only anything he said was true.

God Save the King!

I want King Dong to be the best president he can possibly be. For you, for me, for our country, for the entire world. I want him to succeed!

I hope and pray, yes, I pray, that he reads this book and has a Grinch and Scrooge moment. Keep reading, those chapters are coming up. I didn't vote for Trump but I'm going to support him IF I agree with the policy!

But, alas, there is very little happening now that I support. Yes, friends, this is what "alas" feels like. A little like prolonged disappointment. Can you imagine if King Dong was a kindly man, a serving man...but he's not.

Putting public education into the hands of Betsy DeVos? This has disaster all over it! Who stands to lose? My kids who need help with school loans to attend college. Millions of students all over the country who attend public schools. Millions of people who need help paying off student loans. Millions of teachers who work for peanuts and pay for supplies out of their own pockets.

"What do you got to lose?" Trump asked on the campaign trail. Everything, King Dong! Opportunity! For education, a good job, a small house, money for retirement, the American dream.

Who wins? Trump, because for-profit scam universities like Trump University can now hose their students and not be accountable. DeVos and her family will financially benefit because her money is invested in businesses that make money collecting school loans, or so I've read.

In Trump kingdom there are winners and losers. Which one are you?

Donald J Trump
Every time I speak of the haters and losers I do so with great love and affection. They cannot help the fact that they were born fucked up!
7:12 PM – Sep 28 2014

King Dong, in one of his many #100day celebration interviews, said he was "disappointed" with congressional Republicans for not passing legislation to repeal and replace the Affordable Care Act within the first 100 days. "It's a very rough system," he said. "It's an archaic system.... It's really a bad thing for the country." Translation: the system is bad.

Then Trump said Mitch McConnell failed to get the bill through the Senate. Meaning, Mitch is bad. Trump himself called the bill "mean." The bill is bad. When Trump doesn't understand, he calls it "bad" or "sad" and moves on. And in some cases, he wants to change the rules, King Dong style. He has said on a number of occasions that the Senate should switch to 51 votes to get healthcare and tax cuts approved.

When King Dong can't win, he changes the rules. That has been his normal MO. And on this point, we must also be diligent. King Dong has assembled a Voter-Fraud Commission tasked with finding three million cases of illegal voting for Hillary Clinton. Trump doesn't accept the fact that he lost the popular vote. King Dong, along with his Republican cronies, are asking for voter information from every state. I personally don't want Trump to have that info. My voting record is NONE OF HIS BUSINESS!

King Dong's court is also making it harder for minorities to vote knowing the majority of them vote Democrat. Republicans are enacting extremely stringent identity laws, closing precincts in highly Latino and African-American districts, and gerrymandering voting districts. Voter suppression in Michigan, as many as 200,000 people unable to vote due to new I.D. laws, could be the reason Clinton lost that state and the election. She lost Michigan by 10,704 votes. Oh, and don't forget King Dong does not believe in Russia's interference which means he has done nothing to prevent their meddling in 2018. And that's exactly how this King will stay in power.

Truth is, Trump knows three things:

1. Golf courses
2. Real estate
3. Branding/Bullshit

That's a small world, except for the bullshit, which Trump spreads liberally whenever he can. I think King Dong believes every word he's saying. He's surrounded himself with only people that support his views. *VICE* reports King Dong gets a "propaganda document" twice daily with only good news about him and his presidency. *CBN News* reported "nearly all" of Trumps staff attends Bible lessons with a pastor who compares Trump to biblical heroes. Brain-wash much?

The day Trump's Cabinet settled around a large conference room table and each paid homage to him was baffling. Person after person was given an opportunity to kiss the royal rump as Trump let the news cameras in and let them roll. "We thank you for the opportunity and the blessing you've given us," gushed then White House Chief of Staff, Reince Priebus. I guess he didn't have enough pucker power or staying power. He was let go by The Mooch a few weeks later.

Trump's Royal Cabinet: The Rich Leading the Rich

The "deconstruction" of the government is under way. Steve Bannon, the white nationalist that helped crown the King is now back at the helm of Breitbart News where he can continue Trump's damaging agenda.

Son-in-law Jared Kushner has been tasked with fixing everything! Peace in the Middle East, the US economy, criminal justice reform, the opioid epidemic. Remind me, when did we elect Kushner?

We've got Scott Pruitt, a climate change denier as head of the Environmental Protection Agency; the agency he sued 13 times as Oklahoma's attorney general.

Rick Perry's now in charge of the Department of Energy, a branch of government he thought should be eliminated before he took over and discovered what they did.

Steve Mnuchin is rolling back Dodd-Frank. Ben Carson's bringing his "poverty is a state of mind" philosophy to HUD, the Housing and Urban Development program. His big plan? Kick people to the curb to help motivate them to get a job because after-all poverty is all in your head!

For a full list of Trump henchmen, I recommend John Nichols' book, the *Horsemen of the Trumpocalypse*. It's a jaw-dropper, head-shaker and sneer-maker.

I heard Neil deGrasse Tyson say one night to Bill Maher, "The universe is under no obligation to make sense to you." It was a mind-opening moment. The universe of King Dong does not make sense to me. Tell me again how this King is going to make my life better?

"A president can have no conflict of interest," Trump is fond of saying. But everything Trump touches is a conflict of interest. "I'll be the first to run for president and make a profit," he said in 2000.

And he's already begun. In 2016, Trump paid himself with Republican donor dollars for: the use of his own 757, his smaller jet, his helicopter, his Trump Tower office space, his own clubs for hosting his own events.

Trump was charging the Secret Service $130,000/month rent at Trump Tower for the privilege of protecting him and his family. Instead of offering them space for free, Trump charged the Secret Service more than any other tenant. That's more American taxpayer dollars extorted from our pockets by the man who's declared himself King.

In just the first nine months in office, Americans have paid the Secret Service over $100,000 in golf cart rental fees to Trump properties just to follow his old, fat ass around his golf courses.

The Emoluments Clause prevents a leader from obvious and blatant financial gain. And Trump is blatantly making money on his properties. It's reported his profits on his DC Hotel alone exceeded $2 million.

And the Republicans in the House in an effort to extort the American taxpayer, prevented a vote on a bill which would have banned federal spending at Trump businesses. Shameful! I can't believe my tax dollars are being funneled to Trump's personal bottom line, but it's true. The Daily Beast reports Team Trump and the GOP have spent over $1.7 million at Trump properties since Election Day.

No wonder he's already campaigning for 2020. Being President is profitable!

"Pay Trump Bribes Here"
-- Robin Bell

The Emoluments Clause begins: "No title of Nobility shall be granted by the United States." There is no King of America!

The Clause then goes on to say, "And no Person holding any Office of Profit or Trust under them, shall, without the Consent of the Congress, accept of any present, Emolument, Office, or Title, of any kind whatever, from any King, Prince, or foreign State."

"Seven days after Trump announced his intention to seek the highest office in the land, he formed more business entities than he had on any previous day, available information indicates," states a September 10, 2017 article by Michael Tanglis of Salon.com. "All the entities were related to Trump projects in Indonesia. A few months later, Trump was joined on the campaign trail by a delegation of Indonesian politicians--who openly acknowledged they were there because of Trump's investments in their country. One had previously been caught on tape soliciting a $4 billion bribe."

And this is just the tip of the mixing-business-with-politics iceberg. The article goes on to say, "In total, Trump has formed at least 49 business entities since he announced his bid for the presidency. He continued to form businesses not only after winning in November, but also after assuming the presidency in January."

Currently foreign dignitaries are booking themselves into Trump properties around the globe trying to glean favor. Trump has not put his holdings in "a blind trust" as he said he would when he was running for office. He is openly and unapologetically profiting from his position as President--just as he intended.

Shout out and kudos to Robin Bell, artist and filmmaker extraordinaire, for "bringing light to this situation" with his brilliant light-art display over the doorway of Trump International Hotel D.C. which read: Pay Trump Bribes Here. Google it. The photo makes me smile every time. Because it's true.

Bell has also projected "Emoluments Welcome" and an excerpt from that same clause over the doorway to the hotel. Check out his work at @bellvisuals and #resist.

But those examples are Trump-change. King Dong knows the real money includes trademarks from China and Russia, building towers in Moscow, getting oil from the Middle East, and promoting his own properties and brand. He has not removed himself from his businesses. King Dong is a capitalist above all.

The Fay Wray Effect

Most days I pity Melania Trump. In my head she's been captured and ensconced high up in Trump Tower by the mighty King Dong. But I don't know that. I know nothing about her other than Donald says she speaks six languages. Dong and Melania's relationship can best be described as "awkward." Melania doesn't seem to be into the role as much as Donald, but just like Fay Wray, perhaps her role is to tame the savage beast.

Daughter Ivanka and personal counselor Kellyanne Conway also play their own versions of Fay Wray. Fay Wray, despite being terrified of the beast, does come to trust him and love him, at least in the movie version. No doubt there is real affection and loyalty by all three women to King Dong. Both of his exes also speak well of him, mostly. They sometimes make me wonder, what do I not know about the King? He must have some redeeming qualities. Doesn't he?

Kellyanne Conway admits she caters to Trump's King complex. She says being a woman helps, saying she presents ideas demurely and with a smile. Ivanka still calls him "Daddy," according to the King himself. I don't want to know what Melania calls him. But it's obvious to all we must cater to this King, because when the King ain't happy he tweets it out at 3 a.m.

Ding Dong the Kong is Gone

King Kong was eventually shot down from the top of the tall, tall building where he perched trying to escape his strange environment.

Trump's a beast on the loose. The Russian scandal is closing in, he's not happy with Congress or their accomplishments, but he's not going down without a fight. He's blaming everything and everyone in his path. He's a national disaster bigger than #hurricaneharvey, #hurricaneirma, #hurricanemaria, the wildfires in California, Washington, Oregon, Montana and Idaho, and the Mexico 8.1 earthquake.

I think our former First Lady, Michelle Obama, said it perfectly:

> *"The presidency doesn't change who you are. It reveals who you are."*
> *-- Michelle Obama*

President Trump, King Dong, has clearly revealed who he is. King Dong is a man-made disaster of epic proportion. We'll be recovering from #hurricanetrump for years.

But this book is not about King Dong, this book is about you. If you are unhappy with King Dong's performance, what do you intend to do? What is your role within the kingdom? Are you ready for it?

What Can You Do?

1. Watch the Peter Jackson version of King Kong. "Beauty" may have killed the beast in the movie, but the need for adoration will be the undoing of our King Dong

2. Read trumptwitterarchives.com to get a true sense of who this man is

3. Vote! Participate and get your voice heard. Your vote is one drop in the ocean. It becomes an ocean with your vote, then another, and another until collectively every single drop becomes a force to be reckoned with

4. Join VotingRightsAlliance.net, they help ensure every vote counts

5. The ResistanceManual.org/organizations gives you step-by-step ideas on ways to #resist

6. Get the 411: follow Scott Dworkin at the Democratic Coalition

7. Join the fight for common-sense gun regulation at Everytown.org

8. Give to Grassroots Leadership, a civil and human rights organization working to end prison profiteering, mass incarceration, deportation and criminalization

9. Be a part of Amnesty International and defend victims of violence, harassment, and discrimination in U.S. and abroad

10. Give to the International Rescue Committee and help displaced people around the world

11. Support the Nature Conservancy, an organization that protects ecologically important lands and waters around the world

12. Join onwardtogether.org and help people organize, get involved, and run for office

ThinKING
Rule Your Own Head

King Dong

King Dong

Grinch Trump

10. Grinch Trump: Hope for a New Trump or New Me

You're a mean one, Mr. Trump,
You really are quite rude,
You'll pick a fight with anyone,
Your language is quite crude, Mr. Trump,
When you open your mouth to speak
You prove you are quite unglued.

You are a loser, Mr. Trump,
Your words contain nothing but lies,
You sit atop Trump Tower,
Plotting against those you despise, Mr. Trump,
Your need for adoration and revenge,
Will surely lead to your demise.

You are a liar, Mr. Trump,
You blame your staff, the Congress, fake news,
You speak nonsensical sentences
With the intent to abuse and accuse, Mr. Trump,
But thanks to the news, you have educated and
informed voters you cannot confuse.

You are a Douchebag, Mr. Trump,
Seeing and hearing you makes us gag,
You bullied your way to the White House,
Made promises that were vague, Mr. Trump,
The 3 words that best describe you are,
Using your own words: disappointing, terrible, and
sad.

Opening Scene

Wideshot: The Trump stands by the window in Trump Tower looking down
at the ant-sized people below.

Narrator: Every person on the sidewalk valued their personal sovereignty a lot, except for The Trump, who lived high above in Trump Tower; he did not.

The Trump values money, above rights and personal freedoms,

He gave little thought to the masses, their emotions or reasons.

The Trump was a loner, this much is true,

How he'd been elected to the presidency, neither he nor the people had a clue.

Enough Cutesy!

I'm not going to rhyme this entire story--just know, to Donald Trump, it's about power and glory. Oops, hard to stop rhyming.

This is my favorite chapter.

Yes, I'm still hopeful, but probably not in the way you're thinking. Trump didn't get this far without a few good traits as well as wealthy friends. I've heard he can be quite charming. It appears to me, however, he's charming to your face even as he works behind the scenes to challenge our human rights: who we love, how we love, when we procreate, what God we worship.

It's quite astounding to me that people still support Trump. He says one thing and does another. He makes people doubt their own ears and eyes, yet people follow him blindly. And no one supports him more blindly than Cindy Lou Who, or Lil' Kellyanne Conway.

Kellyanne Conway is Cindy Lou Who holding the hope of the nation. She worked tirelessly and relentlessly to get Trump elected. Kellyanne originally worked on Ted Cruz's presidential campaign but readily jumped on board the Trump train after Cruz dropped out of the race.

Kellyanne Lou Who has been a fierce advocate for Trump even making up whopping lies such as "alternative facts" and the "Bowling Green Massacre." Now that Trump is in the White House she still believes in him and strongly defends her loyalty. When The Morning Joe anchors, Mika Brzezinski and Joe Scarborough, suggested she might secretly oppose him, Conway declared her allegiance.

Grinch Trump

Kellyanne recognizes something in Trump that not everyone sees. She must be tired of Trump's missteps and buffoonery, but she is unwavering in her support. I think she truly wants Trump to be a better person, she wants him to fix the world through capitalism, and she blindly will follow, support and defend him.

Kellyanne and I actually agree on something: I want Trump to be a better person, too, but I will not follow him blindly.

A Golden Moment

Meryl Streep surreptitiously brought up Trump at the Golden Globes: she condemned people who mocked others, tactfully referring to the time Trump mocked a reporter who is physically challenged. When Trump tweeted smack at Meryl claiming she had attacked him, Kellyanne came to Trump's defense.

Journalists should "look at what's in his heart," Kellyanne said. When CNN *New Day* host Chris Cuomo referred to that 2015 rally when Trump mocked a disabled *New York Times* reporter, Conway insisted that's not what he was doing.

"That is not what he did, and he has said that a thousand times. Why can't you give him the benefit of the doubt? Why is everything taken at face value?" she asked when Cuomo referred to the video of Trump's mocking gesture. "You can't give him the benefit of the doubt on this? He's telling you what was in his heart. You always want to go with what's come out of his mouth. Look at what's in his heart."

It's like telling Cindy Lou Who there really is no Santa Claus. I'm sorry Kellyanne, what comes out of a man's mouth is what's in a man's heart! And what's come out of Trump's mouth is leading most of us to wonder--is he drunk?!

A Drunk Man Speaks a Sober Heart

Donald Trump IS drunk on power and admiration. He continues his "victory" tour and at every rally on every day Trump plays to the worst traits in his crowd.

Like Kellyanne, I want Trump to be the best man he can be, but that's the problem, Trump needs a Grinch moment to become a better version of himself. He could have said, "The whole world misunderstood what was in my heart when I made those gestures" and left it at that, but instead he came back with personal insults and attacked Meryl, calling her over-rated. Trump's not capable of a rational response. And Kellyanne Lou Who enables him.

Marching to the Beat of Her Own Drum

Kellyanne Lou Who still believes in loyalty and logic, her own unique logic, and she quite clearly still believes in The Trump. Could she possibly see something in The Trump that I am not capable of seeing? Or has she simply drunk of The Trump punch? She certainly sounds like Trump, flip-flopping narratives for the audience. While being interviewed about the search and rescue happening in the #hurricaneharvey flood, she praised Fox News reporters for their efforts to speak to the victims. She chastised CNN reporters for the same thing.

In Trump world and Kellyanne world "facts" are the words that come out of their mouths. Whether those words are based in truth is irrelevant. But after all this time, Kellyanne must still believe in him. She obviously still has hope.

The only person more hopeful than Kellyanne is Ivanka, devoted daughter and willing participant in The Trump's rule.

Ivanka Lou Who

Liddle Ivanka Lou Who is never far from Trump's sight. She's rumored to be a stabilizing presence in Trump's life, but I think she knows Dad is batshit crazy and is there to keep an eye on him. The problem is, like Kellyanne, she and husband Jared are dedicated to pushing forward Trump's agenda. If not Trump's agenda, then Dad's agenda. They want him to be successful. But even they, celeb name "Javanka," seem surprised at times by Trump's actions, and with their silence they are condoning Trump's ignorance, intolerance, and his blatant manipulation of the facts.

But they couldn't possibly see it that way! They believe in The Trump; they see good in The Trump. She truly believes in him and said to a women's panel in Berlin, "He's been a tremendous champion of supporting families and enabling them to thrive." She couldn't understand why the crowd booed and hissed.

Ivanka doesn't see what he's doing: taking birth control from women, taking equal rights from LGBTQ people, and condoning social injustices against minorities.

She's in the Trump bubble. She answers every question in every situation as if she were on stage competing in the Miss Universe Question/Answer portion. And what do we all want? Smile now. Wait for it... "World peace." That was probably douchey on my part to say, but, come on, Girl, put some authenticity into it. Okay, now stop. See, here it is, an opportunity to give her the benefit of the doubt, not criticize her. ... I'm trying to understand Ivanka but...well, read her own words below.

Ivanka's own books are quite telling. She's cut from the same cloth: privilege. And she uses the same tool, manipulation, to her advantage. She may be pretty and soft-spoken, but it's obvious she's been influenced.

"Perception is more important than reality," she said in her book *Women Who Work.* "If someone perceives something to be true, it is more important than if it is in fact true. This doesn't mean you should be duplicitous or deceitful, but don't go out of your way to correct a false assumption if it plays to your advantage."

Given Ivanka's perspective on perceptions over reality, perhaps she needs a Grinchy heart-opening moment as well. In an interview with one of the numbskulls from Fox News, she said "I believe with my heart and soul, as my father does, and this administration does, that no one can best the American worker."

Well then, fight for the American worker!

But Ivanka sells clothes, shoes and handbags to the masses. Matea Gold of the *Washington Post* said, "We traced her current line of products to five specific countries, Bangladesh, China, India, Indonesia, and Vietnam. There's also customs records that show that, back in 2013, some of her shoes were made in Ethiopia."

Ivanka, like her father, manufactures almost all of her products overseas. There have also been news stories about terrible working conditions within factories that manufacture her products...and this is where *Saturday Night Live* comes in: Ivanka's "complicit." Why is she not stepping up and pushing for more money for those employees in her own factories? Why are there not better work conditions?

Seriously? How much money does Ivanka Lou need in the bank? She can afford to pay those workers better wages but she doesn't! She willingly and knowingly makes a choice not to. She could put cash in their pockets, directly, with a pay increase. That cash would flood the streets, spinning the wheels of businesses from the bottom up. Instantly.

But Invanka Lou believes, like good old Grinchy-Dad, that tax breaks for the corporations will mean higher profits so they can pay their workers more. Or that's the story again that The Trump is pushing down our throats. But that doesn't happen. Money does not go to the workers. Money is pocketed by CEO's and investors, leaving *nothing* to trickle down to the workers.

Ivanka Lou has the power and position to change the curve. Right here, right now, today. Imagine if she gave every worker in her factories—women who say they don't even make enough to visit their families on the weekend--more money? She'd be a hero. And "Liddle" Ivanka Lou Who could lead the way. See? Now that's just petty.

"Liddle" refers to the name Trump used to disparage Bob Corker, the Republican Senator from Tennessee. "People like Liddle' Bob Corker have set the U.S. way back." For me to use it now is a jab at both Trump and Ivanka. It's snarky. I can have a meaningful conversation about Ivanka without being disrespectful, can't I? Looks like I've got some growing to do. What if Ivanka could, too?

What if Ivanka lead by example and brought operations back to the U.S? Ivanka Trump could show her Daddy how it's done. Bring those jobs back to the United States. Daddy declared the week of July 17, 2017 "Made In America" week. So now it's up to Ivanka Lou Who AND The Trump to have a heart-opening moment.

"Buy American; Hire American" is Trump's latest attempt at branding and brainwashing the Whos. But Trump does what's best for Trump. The real question is Ivanka; the real hope lies with Ivanka. Will Ivanka open her heart and her handbag? Stay tuned, we'll find out after this commercial break.

We've All Been Trumped

"I can be very presidential," The Trump says, but The Trump is a crybaby and a whiner, "No politician in history...has been treated worse or more unfairly," he said in his address to the United States Coast Guard.

Trump's forgetting the never-ending grief he gave President Obama for eight years. The Trump deserves every critical word levelled at him. It's his karma for being a world-class ass to his predecessor. He, himself, set the standard for scrutiny and Douchebaggery.

A Heart Opening Moment

I'd pretty much given up on Trump, and then a glimmer of hope!! Two days before Trump's 100th day in office, he admitted he missed his former life. He actually said being president was "more work than his previous life" and he thought it would be "easier."

Wait. Wow. Start up those presses! Did The Trump just admit that this job is hard? Did The Trump just realize that there are things he doesn't know? "Making business decisions and buying buildings don't involve heart. This involves heart. These are heavy decisions" Trump said.

Did Trump just indicate he had a heart? Is he truly seeing and considering people for the first time in his life?!

Trump thinks his previous endeavors, buying buildings, didn't involve heart. Maybe his truth is that he's never involved his heart before; he's never even considered all the people his countless business decisions have affected. That's because Trump focuses on projects and not the people he effects with those projects.

A true Grinch moment would be Trump learning that all projects serve people. It is not the project itself that is of value; it's a valuable and worthwhile project because it touches people's lives.

There are countless people who have been hurt by Trump's business decisions. The Trump doesn't see them. This chapter could be entitled *The Trump Hears a Who*, except Donald Trump is not the bumbling lovable Horton fighting to help the Whos be noticed. Trump is the conniving money-hungry monster who doesn't give two shakes about what happens to the people.

But What If?

Can you imagine what it would be like if Trump grew a heart? All that money, all that influence going to help others? What if Trump had as much morality as money? What if Trump's guiding principles were decency and diversity? What if he treated others with respect instead of disdain, joining us together to celebrate and to create a better world for all? What if there were no winners or losers?

This Is Our Hope

- ♥ What if, instead of deporting all the immigrants he offered them a chance to pursue the American dream? What if he afforded them the same opportunity that he and his father had? After all, Trump's not Native American.

- ♥ What if Trump embraced the philosophies of Pope Francis and transferred that $25 billion it'll take to build that wall into building a bridge, friendship and e-commerce between America and Mexico?

- ♥ And now, after the devastation of hurricanes Harvey, Irma, Maria and the West Coast fires, what if Trump built houses for the hundreds of thousands of Americans who've been displaced and are now homeless?! And how about embracing Mexico?!

- ♥ What if Trump fed all the starving children in the world? What if he could see little Bana al-Abed, the eight-year-old Syrian refugee who tweeted Trump asking him for help?

- ♥ What if Trump could match every kid on the planet with a rescue puppy or kitty and save both people and animals at the same time?! He'd be a hero.

- ♥ What if he took care of our Veterans, honoring their actions--not with his words and propaganda, but with true action putting money where his mouth is? Better yet, why send our children, our brothers, our sisters, our husbands, and our wives into war in the first place? What if Trump acknowledged every day the sacrifices our military families make? And put money into raises for all the enlisted personnel?

- ♥ What if Trump pursued relationships with other countries that included diplomacy and mutual trust? What if he was a respected world leader with the assets to better the planet and every living thing on it? What if he believed climate change was real? What if he believed in clean energy and helped the U.S. lead the clean energy revolution?

- ♥ What if he didn't spend all his time courting Russia but instead courted the people of this great nation. All of us.

What if?

The truth is Donald Trump is a businessman and he deserves credit. Not respect: credit. Respect is for people that you admire and aspire to be like. Giving Donald Trump credit is nothing more than acknowledge what he's done. He has built an empire; an empire he's used to swallow-up the White House and the complicit GOP. I give him credit for that. But I can't respect him because I don't like how he did it. He earned his "billions" at the expense of others, and that's what I take offense to.

I'm hoping and praying that Donald Trump will learn and grow for the sake of all living things on this planet. The only thing it takes is an open mind and open heart. But unfortunately, Trumps burst of clarity about the pressures of the job and his expectations didn't last long.

Just days after the statement admitting being president was hard, on day one hundred of his presidency, Trump was back at it with his degrading, derogatory ways. Like a true ratings whore and adoration junkie, he threw himself a rally and took pot-shots at the attendees of the White House Correspondents' Dinner. He blasted the Press and called them "incompetent, dishonest people"; he took aim at anyone who didn't kiss his hairy orange douchey tushy.

The slight crack in Trump's heart closed.

"Let Trump be Trump" is what he's fond of saying. Too bad Trump is such a damned mean racist. Don't think so? The Trump has been known to read a poem at his rallies called "The Snake," by Oscar Brown Jr.

"On her way to work one morning, down the path alongside the lake,
A tender-hearted woman saw a poor half-frozen snake.
His pretty colored skin had been all frosted with the dew,
"Oh well," she cried, "I'll take you in and take care of you."
Now she clutched him to her bosom, "You're so beautiful," she cried.
"But if I hadn't brought you in by now you might have died.
Now she stroked his pretty skin and then she kissed and held him tight
But instead of saying thanks, that snake gave her a vicious bite."

In the final verse of the poem, when the woman asks the snake why he bit her, the snake replies: he's a snake. That's what snakes do. Trump looks at immigrants and refugees as if each was a snake. "They are murderers and rapists."

Grinch Trump

That's Trump being Trump. He calls them like he sees them, people say. That's Trump. Yes, Trump, The snake.

And truly disgusting was the rally where he told the story of the illegal immigrant who sliced up a beautiful teenage girl with a knife. "They don't want to use guns because it's too fast and it's not painful enough." This is just vile propaganda used to incite violence against a race of people; a story Trump made up to justify his hatred of ... snakes.

Trump truly needs a Grinch moment.

Donald Trump needs to open his eyes to the suffering he is causing. People need our help! And especially those hit by fires and flooding and hurricanes. The Trump talks a big game, but when it truly comes down to it, will Trump open his heart and his wallet? It's not enough for him to open his big fat mouth. He must follow with action. He must put some systems in place to help with housing and food--but NOT prisons or internment camps or ICE detention centers.

Trump's heart needs to grow on this! So does yours and so does mine.

There is Profit to be Had in Helping Others

Refugees and immigrants from South America, Mexico, Europe and the Middle East need our help. This is not an "either/or" scenario: security or immigration. We can have both.

I say let them in. Vet them, yes, but let them in. Help refugees and immigrants become part of our nation and our communities. We have plenty of open space--if Trump doesn't frack it all up.

Cities are communities that create jobs. Trump could have all his buddies build houses and cities *with* the people, not *for* them! With "cities" come enterprise. Entrepreneurs will spring up. That's capitalism. Some people will farm and feed the others; some will take care of the sick, children and elderly; others will create their own version of cheap-ass ties made-in-China and sell them to make a profit.

You see, with people comes business; with people comes capitalism. Trump says he believes in the free flow of capitalism. Then let it flow. And let those people flow in.

Job Killing or People Killing Regulation

Trump says he is killing "job-killing" regulations. If so, then companies need to police themselves and each other. There has already been oil spilled on the sacred lands of the Standing Rock Sioux.

And then a win for the people! A judge in October 2017 ruled against Dakota Access and for the Standing Rock Sioux. Donald Trump, Grinch, must be having a fit. He doesn't care about Native American rights. He has no qualms about commercializing or taking their land. I've heard the rumors that Granddaddy Trump was a squatter.

I know there are people out there who have hope. I want to be one of them. I want to be inspired and I want to believe. But every time I see Trump or hear Trump I realize he is not going to change--AND real change has to come from me.

> *"Change will not come if we wait for some other person or some other time. We are the ones we've been waiting for. We are the change that we seek."*
> *-- Barack Obama*

It's My Heart That Needs to Grow!

What is my intent with this book? Is it to hurt or to heal? I know I'm writing to get a new perspective, and I certainly have done that. I'm hoping I've done that for you, too.

Maybe Trump's just an old fart, an old man stuck in the old days and the old ways. Maybe he's not intentionally crapping over everyone, he just doesn't know better. He doesn't use the internet, he doesn't use email. He doesn't read! He gets all his news from cable TV.

Trump's negotiation skills are questionable. He's always negotiated with power and money, and that's not true power. True power is earned through diplomacy. Trump has none. He writes about negotiation but speaks mostly about money, power, and revenge. He seems willing to sacrifice anyone who opposes him. He's a mobster throwing his own under the bus. Look out Cindy Lou!!

Who's A Good Boy?

I confess, while watching *How the Grinch Stole Christmas* every year while growing up, I was much more concerned with The Grinch's dog, Max, than I was with The Grinch himself. Max, like every faithful dog, stares lovingly at The Grinch and excitedly and expectantly at the Whos. No one is more faithful to The Trump than his little dog Mike Pence.

Mike Pence is Max. He looks at The Trump with blind devotion. Every photo op, every press conference there is Mike Pence staring lovingly at Trump. I often wonder what medication he's on. There is literally nothing Trump can say that puppy-eyed Pence will not pick-up, chew on, swallow and shit-out to the people.

I always assumed The Grinch couldn't be all bad-- he had a dog for goodness sakes!! How someone treats their pet is a testimony to their temperament. Dog lovers are usually good, solid people! Dogs are work; they require effort. They eat a ton and leave a ton of waste behind. They require exercise and attention. And lots and lots of affection.

And they are so worth it! The companionship and friendship of a dog is like no other. Dogs--and cats--bring out the best in us. You've got to watch a short Keith Olbermann video about dogs and Trump. Olbermann, who grew up in an allergic household never had a dog--until recently. He described that event-- getting his first dog--as a rebirth. Anyone who has *ever* had a pet will understand.

> *"Until one has loved an animal, a part of one's soul*
> *remains unawakened."*
> *-- Anatole France*

The real Donald Trump has never had a dog. Maybe that's why he doesn't care about yours! He's deleted information about protections for animals from both the United States Department of Agriculture, USDA, and the U.S. Food and Drug Administration, FDA, websites.

No longer will information be available to the public on violators of The Animal Welfare Act or the Horse Protection Act. Breeders, puppy mills, zoos, research facilities, and circuses no longer will be accountable for how they treat their animals. And the Food and Drug Administration is no longer policing pet

271

food companies so beware of fillers that can be added to your pet's food for the sake of their bottom line.

Maybe if the real Donald Trump got a dog he'd have that soul-awakening moment that we're all hoping for. It might be Trump's only chance for true love.

Eckhart Tolle Quotes
Dogs offer the precious opportunity, even to people who are trapped in their own egos, of loving and being loved unconditionally.
5:26 PM – Aug 25 2017

Yes, dogs literally give a crap--*but they don't give a crap about how rich you are!*

Can't wait to read Keith Olbermann's book, *Trump is Fucking Crazy.*

A Grinch Moment of My Own

I've been too busy to despair. My anger over Trump's policies has fueled me to write this book. To stay quiet would take me to a deep, dark depression. I know, I tried to put the election behind me and move on with my life, but depression settled over me like mud caked to my heart and soul.

I don't trust Trump to work for the good of us all. We cannot afford to slump into a muddy depression. We all must remain tuned-in and engaged. As hard as it is to watch The Trump's reality show, we must remain positive, believe, and have faith. And we must tune into the daily blessings that surround us.

I was visiting my daughter in Hawaii on the North Shore of Oahu as I worked on this chapter, The Grinch, the chapter of hope. The book has weighed heavy on my heart at times. Being tuned to Trump news 24/7 is exhausting and disheartening. My daughter, her boyfriend and I were on our way to the beach; the ocean lay before us, breathtaking in its color and vastness. I was struck by its size and energy. Bill Withers' song *A Lovely Day* came on the radio and my heart and head exploded with joy and gratitude. Music and the ocean gave me a new perspective and my heart, and my head grew, times ten, in that moment that day.

It's not enough just to bitch. I must, we must be a blessing to others. We must turn to each other and say, "have a lovely day" --and mean it! We must ignore Trump's actions and words and honor our own code. How do you treat people?

Chelsea Handler summed it up beautifully!!

Chelsea Handler
This presidency has made me nicer, kinder, and less likely to tell someone I just met, to "fuck off." So, there's that.
7:46 PM - Aug 23 2017

Yes, there's that! A heart-opening moment applied to our fellow wo/man. THIS is the gift of a Donald Trump presidency: we each get to define how we're going to treat others. And I applaud Chelsea Handler's decision to take time from her show, so she can go meet some people. She's crass and uncouth at times but totally authentic. I adore her and look forward to her escapades and stories.

Yes, I can be a bitch, a douche, and darn right mean, we all can. But at what cost? What cost to ourselves and the others around us?

Have I been respectful to Donald Trump? No. No, I have not. But how can I respect someone when I oppose everything that they're doing? How can I be kind to a man who doesn't show kindness?

Maybe I don't have to. Maybe my job is to serve the people Trump's unkind to, the people he is victimizing.

Another Grinch Moment

And maybe it's bigger than that. Maybe my job is to shower them with blessings: speak words of kindness on them and for them, wish them a better life. I've been doing that for years for my family and friends. I knew in a moment, I needed to include more people.

In one of the darkest moments of my life, I started making a bedtime wish list. I was engulfed in depression. Life and circumstance had piled on and I couldn't seem to catch a break. I felt out of control and hopeless. I'd given up thinking I could get caught-up let alone get ahead or make a difference. I was way past being able to "pull myself up by my bootstraps."

Douchebag Wisdom

I'd gotten a new night light for my bedroom, a dome-shaped projector that cast dozens of stars across the ceiling and walls. I'd spent many years as a kid wishing upon a star. As a Girl Scout, I'd spent hours under the stars in Clear Lake, Iowa at Camp Gaywood, renamed Camp TingleFoot. As a farm girl, it was a nightly ritual. First come the lightening bugs, then come the stars. My reaction was instinctual when the stars first appeared above my bed. But I couldn't think of one wish for myself. I'd lost my faith. I was under water. Why bother?

But the stars called. And I did something that I still do today: I made wishes for my kids. I wished for them great friends, good health, good jobs, and fun and joy. I wished for my folks, my brother and sisters and my nieces and nephews. If I was still awake, I'd include my friends.

I know now I must include wishes for strangers as well. That's called compassion. Wishing the best for others.

And as I wish well for others, I lift myself, too. Yes, my heart is big enough to spread blessings and well wishes on everyone. That includes wishes right now for every person and animal displaced by hurricanes Harvey, Irma, Maria, the wildfires and earthquakes.

I wish for them:

- Safety, for themselves and their loved ones
- Water and food!
- And the assurance that someone cares!
- An immediate bed, pillow, and blankie
- Clothes (for our victims of flood and fire)
- A roof over their heads
- A quick recovery
- Enough money and help to rebuild their lives
- Family and friends and strangers and angels to see them through

The wishes are as limitless as the stars. If you're a Christian, substitute the word "prayers" for "wishes." To me they are the same.

Grinch Trump

The hurricanes are collective heart-openers for the nation. The Trump says he saw it, but he didn't see the people. He didn't get it. He still doesn't get it! His response to Puerto Rico, lifting the Jones Act for only ten days?! Is ... unconscionable ... uncivilized ... unGodly. What the F is wrong with this man? Puerto Rico and the U.S. Virgin Islands need him now, but Trump's itty-bitty douchey heart is putrid and black. It's about profit and who owes who what.

And what is going on with the Puerto Rico recovery efforts? Stories about #hurricanemaria recovery efforts have been replaced with a new Trump stink bomb daily, it's hard to break through the chatter, but the island remains devastated. And the body count rises. Over 900 bodies have been cremated due to "natural causes," according to an article in *Newsweek*. Translation: few are watching, and people are dying.

Yes, that's what happens when you have no food or water, naturally. You die. Now imagine an even slower death, happening before our very eyes, but no one sees it, no one wants to believe it. People, starving before our very eyes. Our neighbors, now without medicare and Medicaid and living off beans with no heat.

Why can Trump not see them?! Us!

You know what that means. That means you must have your own Grinch moment. Yes you!

Serve. However, you can. In your own unique style. "Resist. Persist. Insist. Enlist," as Hillary would say. Get involved. Believe change can happen and that people can grow. Open yourself to new ways of thinking and be the best version of yourself you can be. And above all, don't be a Grinchy douche.

How Can You Start?

1. Watch the cartoon version and Jim Carrey versions of Dr. Seuss's *How the Grinch Stole Christmas*. Be like Cindy Lou Who and believe

2. Tweet Donald Trump with a wish that his heart will grow three sizes in a day

3. Hug your dog or your cat!

4. Adopt a pet! Or volunteer at a shelter

5. Give money or time to the Humane Society of the United States HumaneSociety.org

6. Get your pet in on the protest action. Get a "My dog is smarter than the president" dog paw magnet, $6.99 on Amazon

7. Follow *Merch for March* on Facebook and get a t-shirt: Never trust a president that doesn't have a dog

8. Help families around the world get pet goats and cows for milking at Heifer International. Heifer.org

9. Make a contribution to the Make A Wish Foundation. Wish.org

10. Give to the American Red Cross. RedCross.org

11. Open your heart to the incarcerated, support CLASP, Community Legal & Advocacy Services Project

12. Join Van Jone's #LoveArmy, at VanJones.net Love + Power!

13.

I believe in the good things coming

Nanko and Medicine for the People

Grinch Trump

Grinch Trump

Scrooge Trump

11. Scrooge Trump: Ghosts of Past, Present, and Future

"Only when all the trees are cut down and all the waters polluted will man understand you can't eat money."
-- Cree Indian prophecy

"I'm really, really rich."
-- Donald Trump

How many times has Donald Trump bragged about his personal wealth? Unlike Scrooge, who liked to keep to himself and count his money in private, Scrooge Trump is still on his "Make Trump Think He's Making America Great Again" tour where he's touting and counting his self-proclaimed list of accomplishments, "promises kept." He's splashed his face in-our-face across billboards, banners, social platforms, radio, and tv.

Trump and entourage attempted to air a 30-second "100-day achievements" commercial, but the networks refused to air it. It contained controversial statements of "achievements," slamming of the news media calling them FAKE NEWS, and the declaration that America is winning, and Donald Trump is making America great again.

The content of the ad is an absurd and false presumption to at least 60% of the U.S. population who disapprove of Trump's accomplishments so far. The numbers are no doubt higher when you poll our foreign allies after Trump's 9-day diplomatic tour where he bowed down to the Saudi's and talked down to his NATO and G-7 peers.

The airing of Trump's ad would have been irresponsible. It was White House propaganda straight and simple. Trump's people cited First Amendment rights, but it wasn't censorship as his people cried. The networks refused Donald Trump and chose not to disseminate Trump's divisive, deceiving message.

Trump is currently using taxpayer money to fly himself around doing "victory" rallies. And he's already launched his re-election campaign: win again. Only one problem Donnie: we're NOT winning now!

The more people tell Trump they disapprove of him, the more he needs to host rallies that feed his ego. His most recent rallies are about taxes. Texas is under water, Puerto Rico is devastated, and California is burning, but Trump's talking taxes.

You can bet old Scrooge hated paying taxes. You know Trump does. He's bragged about paying "as little as possible" and we know for many years he didn't pay taxes at all thanks to loopholes Trump said he'd fix.

Trump will be reducing taxes for the wealthy but the poor and middle-class will have to continue to pay. We can assume Trump's lowering taxes for himself. Axing the "death" tax alone will add $1 billion to his estate. The mere fact Trump won't release his taxes tells me he has something to hide. Now that he's pushing for major reform, seeing Trump's taxes is even more important.

A Scrooged-Up Budget

Have you seen or heard of Trump's budget?!

If you're old and/or poor, expect a long, slow death. He's eliminating billions of dollars in "safety net" services for the old, the poor, and the physically challenged--$1.8 trillion over the next ten years.

Trump also signed an executive order in October 2017 stopping payments to the insurance companies that subsidize health care policies for the poor, intentionally sabotaging Obamacare. Premiums might go up as much as 34% says ABC.News.

Scrooge, no doubt, would be proud of Donald Trump. Trump has a reputation for taking financial advantage of people: investors, contractors...remember those Trump University students? Days before Trump took office he paid $25 million to defrauded students to make them shut-up and go away. We don't hear from people who he's made rich, but we will soon as the stock market continues to rise padding the pockets of the already wealthy.

Trump will be doing everything he can to give major tax cuts to his buddies. Current estimates say Trump's tax cuts for the wealthiest 1% will add $2.2 trillion dollar to the deficit over the next ten years. But the people who helped him buy himself a nation must be paid. Trump eliminating the "death tax," the money paid by the heirs of an estate, will put millions of dollars into his own children's pockets.

But Trump, like Scrooge, is about to meet a ghost.

America Trump First!

Both Trump and Scrooge think that money makes the world go around. The question now is: will Trump have a Scrooge moment and realize the error of his selfish ways?

Trump said he's going to use his greed to serve the American people. That was a campaign promise. You might consider that a "Scrooge" moment where Trump intends to help the American people put more money in their pockets. That sounds presidential, but know that Donald Trump serves himself first.

In Charles Dickens' classic story, *A Christmas Carol*, Ebenezer Scrooge's old business partner, Jacob Marley, is now dead and wandering the Earth weighted down in chains due to his miserly deeds and ways. He pays Scrooge a visit warning him not to repeat his mistakes. Marley tells Scrooge he'll be visited by three ghosts: the Ghosts of Christmas Past, Present, and Future.

All you Walking Dead fans, think zombies.

With the help of these time traveling ghosts who whisk Scrooge back-and-forth between poignant, memorable scenes in his life, Scrooge gains a new perspective. Scrooge begins sharing his money with the other characters in the story, most notably his employee, Bob Cratchit, whose sickly son, Tiny Tim, needs an operation.

Trump's Own Ghost of the Past

"As for you, nephew, if you were in my will, I'd disinherit you!" said Scrooge to his nephew, Fred.

That could have been Donald Trump talking to his own family, for real, according to David Cay Johnston in his book, *The Making of Donald Trump*. Johnston, a Pulitzer-winning journalist has studied Trump for decades. My condolences, Dave: tough gig. Entertaining for sure, until somebody gets hurt.

Donald Trump *is* Ebenezer Scrooge. He is a disgustingly selfish, revengeful human being. Trump knowingly and intentionally cut off health insurance from his own grand-nephew who suffered from seizures and was eventually diagnosed with cerebral palsy. Here's a portion of the story as reported by Johnston.

In 1999, Trump's Father, Fred Sr., passed away. According to Johnston, Fred Sr. had written a will after the death of his oldest son, Fred Jr., in 1981. That will left the majority of Fred Sr.'s wealth to Donald and his surviving siblings. Fred Jr.'s family was largely cut out. Fred Jr.'s family sued saying Donald Trump had undue influence in that decision since Fred Sr. was suffering from dementia at that time he wrote the will.

While Fred Sr. was alive, medical insurance and coverage had consistently been provided to Freddy Jr.'s family through Fred Sr.'s company. This coverage was so crucial for Fred Sr.'s grandson who suffered from seizures that Trump Sr.'s lawyer sent a letter to the insurer after Fred Sr.'s death in 1999 stating all costs for the child's care should be covered regardless of caps on the plan.

Despite his father's wishes, Donald Trump took action and canceled the coverage. Trump is quoted as saying, "Why should we give him medical coverage? They sued my father, essentially. I'm not thrilled when someone sues my father."

Eventually Trump settled the lawsuit. Did Baby Trump end up with medical coverage? We'll never know. The settlement agreement is sealed.

Schrodinger's Kitten. Let me explain. We do not know the outcome of that particular case. It could have had a happy ending with the kid getting coverage and the kitten landing softly and easily, or it could have ended disastrously with the kid getting kicked off coverage and the kitten crash-landing in a pile of rubble and debris. We don't know the conclusion--so we make one up in our heads. I want to believe Trump did the right thing and settled the lawsuit by taking care of his grand-nephew, but we don't know. Kitten's in the air.

Currently Trump and the Republicans are trying to knock 24 million kittens--people off of health care. Would Trump mercilessly screw over his own nephew? Because if that's true, he'll screw over yours--and you! And these adorable kittens!

Trump, like Scrooge, sees people as a means to an end. That "end" is money. He's bragged again and again he'd be the first man ever to make money off the presidency. He wasn't joking. He's deliberately doing it now--and laughing all the way to the bank.

Emoluments Clause? What Emoluments Clause?

Most certainly Trump plans on helping his friends get richer. He's already rewarded many of them with positions in his administration but first and foremost is Donald J Trump. The house always wins. Period.

The Ghost of the Present

"Darkness is cheap, and Scrooge liked it."
-- Charles Dickens

Ed Darrell wrote in his bog, Millard Fillmore's Bathtub, that Trump's entire platform can be reduced to these three words: Darkness is cheap. Darrell says that expression represents the entire GOP platform. I agree.

Darkness Is Cheap: So Is Donald Trump!

Trump's budget is appalling: severe cuts to "safety-net" programs that benefit the poor, youngest and the most elderly. After repeated claims he would not touch Medicare and Social Security, he's slicing them to shreds. The Republican-led House of Representatives is leading the charge. There's even a nasty rumor that Republicans want to slash Federal Emergency Management Agency funding, FEMA funding, to pay for Scrooge Trump's border wall. But thank goodness Congress did manage to pass a bill providing some hurricane aid. Although what is happening in Puerto Rico and the U.S. Virgin Islands is a travesty beyond compare. Trump keeps stoking the propaganda machine declaring Puerto Rico on the mend. Thousands of troops there, good news, good news, everyone loves Trump. Trump is to be exalted.

But Puerto Rico is dying! People are dying!! The elaborate videos showing Trump "in action" is just a self-serving bullshit reality concocted by the Trump Administration while 63% of Puerto Rico is still without drinking water and 83% are without electricity!

And Trump is talking about Puerto Rico's debt. Shameful. And anyone who doesn't keep pushing Trump to do more is complicit. But hey, no doubt many believe, like Trump does, that this is Puerto Rico's own damn fault.

Donald J Trump
...Such poor leadership ability by the Mayor of San Juan, and others, in Puerto Rico, who are not able to get their workers to help. They...
5:26 AM – Sep 30 2017

Scrooge Trump

Donald J Trump
...want everything to be done for them when it should be a community effort.
10,000 Federal workers now on island doing a fantastic job.
5:29 AM – Sep 30 2017

Republicans believe you should work. If you can't afford food or health care, that's your problem. You aren't trying hard enough. You need to get a better job or a second job. Wiped out by a hurricane? You aren't trying hard enough. Where's your entrepreneurial spirit? It's all in your attitude.

It reminds me of the story of the two traveling shoe sales reps. The first came to a town where none of the people wore shoes. "Bummer," he thought, "there's no potential here. No one wears shoes." So he left without a sale. The second shoe sales rep came upon that very same town and thought, "Terrific! What potential! No one wears shoes!" And he quickly sold his inventory.

In normal circumstance the moral of the story is simple: your potential to prosper in any situation is based on your attitude and how you see the world. Do you see the potential in the situation or not?

But these are not normal times—and the Puerto Ricans don't need shoes! They fucking need water—and food—and medicine—and electricity—and shelter...and then shoes.

But not one of these Republican fools knows what it's like to be destroyed by or hurricane or understands what it's like to work for $10/hr or less. And they don't care. They got "theirs" and to hell with anyone else. The sad thing is most of these Republicans will profess to being Christians even as they condemn you to poverty wages and straight to a life of living hell. They say they worship a kind, forgiving God, but their God is truly money.

This to me is the Republican way. They think only of themselves and not of others. Take Paul Ryan. Paul Ryan is now making $223,500/yr. The average rank-and-file congressman and woman make $174,000/yr. Ryan and his family have health care provided by the taxpayers who pay his salary and his benefits long after his (dis)service to the country is over. Ryan is one of the congressmen taking away our health care.

I don't begrudge Ryan and his peers their exorbitant salaries. I certainly don't think they earn it, but I don't begrudge them. Ryan's not a Douchebag because he makes roughly $107/hr. He's a Douchebag because he doesn't want

285

YOU to make $10/hr. He doesn't want to raise the average minimum wage over $7.25/hr. That's only $15,000/yr. Who can live on that?

Here's what I don't understand: Why is capitalism "good" and anything that sounds like people coming together to help other people is "bad"?

With Capitalism, trade and industry are controlled by private owners for profit, rather than by the states. Socialism refers to social ownership where political theories and movements are regulated by the community as a whole.

Capitalism shouldn't just be about making oodles and scads of money. It should be about taking care of yourself and others.

I know Mark Zuckerberg and Facebook are under close scrutiny because of Russia's interference in the 2016 presidential election *and* their slow admission to that fact, but you need to understand Zuck's purpose. "My hope was never to build a company. I was driven by a sense of purpose to connect people and bring us closer together." I don't believe Zuckerberg ever intended Facebook to be a tool used by Russia to elect Donald Trump. Nor did Twitter or Google. But all three platforms were weaponized with information created by Russia to hurt Clinton and help Trump. Altogether, Russians spent almost $1 billion across the three platforms throughout the 2016 election.

Let's hope these companies are proactively addressing this issue ahead of the 2018 election; we know Trump is not. He's counting on the system being rigged in his favor. We need Zuckerberg to connect us with truthful information! These tech companies need to work for the people and the good of the planet.

There is no one saying you can't make a profit off others. That's what capitalism is: I have something you want or need and you're willing to pay me/exchange something for it. Healthy capitalism is good, I agree with that and want that. To me--striving in business is my pursuit of happiness--the American Dream. And I want health and wealth and prosperity for all--including me! And if that makes me a socialist, then I'm okay with that. To me, that's democracy. The two coming together. Seems to me that businesses operate better when they have the best interests of people in mind.

Biz Stone, co-founder and creator of Twitter, summed it up beautifully:

Biz
We are caught in an inescapable network of mutuality...whatever affects one directly, affects us all indirectly.
2:09 PM – Aug 13 2017

Feeding the World

I'm proud to be a farm girl from Iowa. What do my folks do? They help feed the world. What one person does directly and indirectly affects others.

I grew up on a dairy farm. We drank whole milk straight from the bulk tank. Every few days, Nappy, our milkman, would arrive and drain the tank, haul it to the dairy that would treat it, package it and get it into the stores for others to buy.

Our farm was self-sufficient. We raised cattle and hogs and chickens. We had plenty of meat, eggs, and of course milk and butter. We had a garden and grew a lot of our own vegetables. We grew the alfalfa and oats needed to feed and bed the livestock. Like many farmers, my dad and mom worked hard, sun-up to long, long after sunset to keep the farm, animals and us kids thriving. I understood from a young age what one person does for a living can have a positive effect on another. Or lots of others.

That's what my parents taught me. I hope I've taught my children the same: one person does make a difference. One farm, one factory, one company can make a difference. We're here to serve each other.

Millennial's get it. Many seek jobs and careers that combine love of people and the planet. Take Adventurist Backpacks, co-founded by husband/wife team Kelly Belknap and Matilda Sandstrom, friends of my daughter. When traveling in Europe, Kelly and Matilda would fill up their backpacks with fresh food they could make into individual meals; they'd then share the meals along the way with anyone they thought needed one. They were so humbled by their experience, they parlayed their good fortune and gratitude into Adventurist Backpacks, a company that offers a simple, light-weight, comfortable and fashionable backpack.

And with every backpack they sell, they provide 25 meals to families in need! They straight-up give back. "What we wanted to do with Adventurist Backpack Co. is to integrate giving back, not only as an afterthought, but as an integral part of the company. And sure, the world may never be perfect, but that

287

doesn't mean we can't try to do our part to make it a little bit better." Kelly Belknap

Can you imagine if every business owner on the planet had that philosophy? We wouldn't need to have government regulation, there would be no need for the Paris Climate Accord or the Clean Power Plan, but that's not the case. Profits have driven corporations to indulge in planet-killing practices that harm people. How much better would the world be if every business and every person on the planet was here to serve others? Good luck, Adventuristbackpacks.com. I wish you great success. #travelwell #dogood

The Trump Paradox

Trump claims he wants to help people, but his policies and actions directly contradict that. And I am indignant on behalf of all the people he's screwing over, directly and indirectly. I'm one of them! Thanks to the Affordable Care Act, Obamacare, I have insurance for the first time in 15 years. Being self-employed and divorced, I could not afford coverage. Now I can. Thank goodness Republicans have not yet been able to repeal Obamacare. What will I and 23,999,999 people do without insurance?

As the villain said to James Bond, "I expect you to die."

Die I surely will, but with Trump and Republicans it will come sooner than later for many. To think America is the only civilized nation not to take care of its people is…is… un-American! We help ours. Don't we?

Ghosts of Present Day

Obviously, no one has shown our bombastic douchebag of a president how to act, so it's up to us, the people of our country and the entire world to teach this man:

- How to learn
- Manners
- Compassion
- Restraint

Even Melania Trump is on board with change. I think her officially-launched anti-cyberbullying campaign is aimed at her husband. She told CNN's Anderson Cooper that she has repeatedly told Donald to get off Twitter, especially after midnight.

"Twitter is such a powerful platform. He can make a difference. He can change the world," she said. "Using Twitter, I think he should use it for good. I think he should use it to uplift others."

I agree! If only he would. If only he could have a Scrooge moment and realize we are all connected, directly and indirectly. If only he could learn something new.

The first thing Trump needs to do is read the *Power of Now*, by Eckhart Tolle. Since we all know Trump doesn't read, let me share one of the most important concepts from the book. Here it is, conveniently condensed in a tweet.

Eckhart Tolle Quotes
Nothing ever happened in the past; it happened in the Now. Nothing will ever happen in the future; it will happen in the Now.
5:18 PM – Aug 30 2017

Ebenezer Scrooge woke up to the NOW and realized he could share his money with the people around him. He realized this moment in time, happening right now is where we can determine our future. If Scrooge can understand that, Trump can wake up to that reality, too.

At 3 a.m., the morning of November 9th,2016, president-elect Trump took the stage at the New York Hilton ballroom and said, "For those who have chosen not to support me in the past, of which there were a few people, I'm reaching out to you for your guidance and your help, so that we can work together and unify our great country." That sounded like humility and compassion. At least that's what I wanted to believe.

I truly do think Trump wants to make America great, but the whole "again" thing is what's throwing everyone off.

America is great, right now. We've made tremendous strides on human rights issues in the last decades. Our social media technology has connected us and we're now able to communicate as individuals en masse, which unfortunately has created problems of its own. This should be a time of prosperity but we've got some big issues to solve. Climate change for example.

Scrooge Trump

This is what Trump needs to learn--what we all need to learn! Making America great is not just about money! It's not just about jobs. Making America great is about honoring the Declaration of Independence.

"We hold these truths to be self-evident:

that all men are created equal; that they are endowed by their Creator with certain unalienable rights; that among these are life, liberty, and the pursuit of happiness."

And that includes women. Humans! Of all shapes and sizes, colors and flavors. Making sure every person in this country has those freedoms *will keep America great.* Right now. Today. And tomorrow, and next week. We are creating our future daily.

If only Trump could learn this. But his proposed 2018 budget is predicted to slash $473 billion from Medicare and $1 trillion from Medicaid over the next ten years. Those are just numbers to Scrooge Trump. He doesn't realize every single number represents a human being. One that deserves the same opportunity he was afforded. A human being that has a family, friends, and co-workers. These are real flesh and blood issues we need to discuss. And we need you, Scrooge Trump, to open your wallet and feed the people.

But first, you've got to see them. Perhaps your ghost is still coming.

Ghost of the Future

You know how the book *A Christmas Carol* ends. Scrooge has an awakening and consequently opens his heart and his wallet. After the visit from the three ghosts, Scrooge does the right thing and gives his employee, Bob Cratchit, a raise, saying, "Well, my friend, I'm not going to beat around the bush. I'm simply not going to stand this sort of thing any longer. Which leaves me no choice, but to raise your salary."

Bob Cratchit is shocked and delighted. Tiny Timmy will get his operation and the book has a happy ending.

And We're Back to the What Ifs... ?

So, let's play the "What If" game. What if all the good things Donald Trump promised truly came to pass?

What if Donald Trump could...

$$ provide healthcare for all people at a lower cost? "Everyone's going to be covered," he said again and again. "We're going to have lower premiums," he said. "We're going to cover pre-existing conditions," he said. What if that truly came to pass?

$$ take care of women's healthcare needs? Including access to both birth control and abortions if necessary! "Nobody has more respect for women than I do," Trump has said. What if he proved that to be true? What if he made women's issues a priority?

$$ care of our Veterans? What if he could reduce their wait times to see a doctor and provide mental health services to address the large number of suicides. What if he could help them integrate back into the work world with solid jobs? What if he provided them housing and took care of their families?

$$ give all our military personnel pay raises and especially higher wages for those of our enlisted men and women making $10/hour as they risk their lives for our freedom.

$$ broker world peace instead of ramping up the war machine to sell more weapons? What if Trump decreased the risk of nuclear war by putting more money into diplomatic solutions? What if Trump believed in peace through collaboration?

What if Trump DIDN'T...

$$ build the damned wall?! Think about how much money we'd save NOT building it!

What if Trump would instead...

$$ build shelter for all of the world's misplaced and forgotten? Not just high-rise, elite structures for the rich, but small houses and communities were all people were bed with warm blanket and a pillow? Trump's a builder. Why can't he build   affordable housing? There is honor in helping others.

$$ pledge to feed every hungry belly on the planet? The technology exists, but the mental and moral brain power needed to make that a reality has been squashed because of wars, greed, and profit.

291

Scrooge Trump

$$ put his efforts into increasing food benefits as opposed to slashing them?

$$ saved the National Parks as opposed to selling them to the highest bidder?

$$ model Justin Trudeau as opposed to Vladimir Putin? We wouldn't have to question Trump's morality. It'd be on display for the world to see.

$$ listened to former Mexico President Vicente Fox who suggested Trump might   make better use of $25 billion by:

- Providing clean drinking water to the entire planet for 3 years
- Ending world hunger for 1 year
- Hiring 50,000 teachers for a decade
- Paying for college education for 250,000 students

Vicente Fox also made it very clear, once again, that "Mexico will not pay for the Fucken wall." So, what if Trump used that money to rebuild--oh, I don't know, say Houston?! Rockport? The Virgin Islands?! Puerto Rico?!?! Or any of the other towns wiped out by hurricanes Harvey, Irma, and Maria and the wildfires out west.

I Want to Believe

This book ends where it starts, with my desire to believe.

I want to believe that Donald Trump can and will rise to the office of President of the United States. We know he can look presidential, but can he act presidential? Shoving himself to the front of the line during his first NATO meeting was the act of a fourth-grader and a bully. Not calling out White Supremacists is the act of a coward courting a small slice of his campaign base. It's also unconscionable. Threatening North Korea and decertifying the Iranian Nuclear Deal is a clear poke in the eye.

Who will hold Trump accountable when he acts like a bully and pretends he's the King? The Republicans certainly aren't. They are enabling his behavior. That means--we all must!!

We must tweet him back and call him out when he deliberately belittles heroes like John Lewis and John McCain. We must use Twitter to tell Trump we will not tolerate his hate speech! And we must report him to Twitter when he's crossed the line and his account should be suspended. i.e. taunting North Korea.

Donald J Trump
I spoke with President Moon of South Korea last night. Asked him how Rocket Man is doing. Long gas lines forming in North Korea. Too bad!
5:53 AM – Sep 17 2017

Donald J Trump
Just heard Foreign Minister of North Korea speak at U.N. If he echoes thoughts of Little Rocket Man, they won't be around much longer!
10:08 PM – Sep 23 2017

How did North Korea respond to that last tweet? They took it as a declaration of war--and it is!! Our words create our realities. When Trump tells the world via Twitter that North Korea "won't be around much longer," that is a veiled threat. Trump is deliberately provoking North Korea. THESE are the tweets we must report. And I'm quite disappointed in Twitter's response calling Trump's tweets "newsworthy," but I'm going to continue to report him.

On the same morning as the first tweet above, Trump retweeted a video of himself swinging a golf club and hitting Hillary Clinton in the back of the head with a golf ball. Seriously?!

Seriously sick. Donald J Trump--delete your account! #Douchebagdonaldtrump

But Still, We Must Believe

We must believe we can train Donald Trump, then work like water on rock to make that happen. We must be relentless with our feedback, to Trump and especially to our Representatives. We must believe that our voice--our vote--counts. We must move forward with positive intent and bring about positive change in this President, his present, and our future. Right now. For future's sake.

I want to believe that "deconstructing" the government and that privatizing certain aspects of government are new approaches to commerce which will bring prosperity for all. Although this seems like a terrible idea and more like an authoritarian blending his private business with government for his own personal profit. We must hold Trump accountable. We all need to "win."

I want to believe that Trump will use his power, wealth and influence to help build bridges for communities and walls on houses that hold people of all shapes, sizes, and flavors--all equal in their pursuit of the American dream.

I want to believe. But, let's get real. Trump has been in office over 250 days and I am truly terrified for people everywhere. It's clear, Trump doesn't believe all people are equal.

News flash to Donald Scrooge Trump:

There are no illegal people! There are people. Period.

But I can't count on Trump learning that truth. After 70 years on the planet, I don't believe he can. So, if I can't believe in Trump, I'm going to believe in myself. And I'm going to believe in you, my fellow wo/man. Even before Harvey, Irma, and Maria blew in and changed the consciousness of a nation, we had individuals stepping up and doing the right thing.

Chicago Mayor Rahm Emanuel invited "undocumented citizens" to Chicago as he declared Chicago schools a "Trump-free zone." That's what I'm talking about! We do not need Trump to catch the kitten, we'll catch each other...ourselves.

If You Can't Believe in Trump, Believe in Yourself

Each of us must form our own conclusions about Trump: can you believe in him or not? But if you can't believe in Trump, believe in you! You can and do make a difference. Each of us must believe in our ability to affect positive change. We must take a stand and take action knowing what we do will cause a ripple effect that can change the world. We must not let others wear us down. We must be brave. We each must rise.

You may shoot me with your words,
You may cut me with your eyes,
You may kill me with your hatefulness,
But still, like air, I'll rise.
-- Maya Angelou

And what do we do when we rise? We VOTE!

You Must Vote

Yes, you! The one reading this book. This is your shavasana—and when you get up off your mat you must register to vote and then vote!

Let me explain. Most yogi masters will tell you that shavasana, resting corpse pose, is the reason we do yoga. It's a meeting of mind and body onto your mat. A good instructor brings a class together, people in all shapes and sizes joining together in one hour of time, each to strengthen themselves, collectively strengthening the energy of a room, a city, a state, a nation and the world. Yes, yoga helps you to think that big.

After an attentive 60-minute practice, shavsana is the reward. For me it's like Jello setting-up. My body and mind come together at a higher level of consciousness.

I hope this book is your yoga class of the mind. I hope I've bended and twisted you into thoughts you might never have had. And I hope you can meet yourself, now, at the end of this book, in quiet contemplation. I hope your energy and your conviction sets in and I hope that when you get up off your...mat, you go vote. That is the American way. It's how we make a difference. It's how you make a difference.

Like Air We Rise

The Butterfly Effect is real. Whether you believe it or not, we are all affected, one by the other. When Trump spits on one of us, he spits on all of us. And when Trump lifts one of us, he lifts all of us. Does Trump have the compassion and self-restraint to lift the world?

We do not know what the future holds. Each movie villain listed in this book has their own natural evolution: Biff Trump and Scut Trump get what they deserve; DarthTrump and TrumpFace are still at large terrifying the Universe; Frankenstein self-terminated and Godzilla and King Kong were blown to bits; the Grand Nagus is probably out doing an illegal deal right now; but the Grinch and Scrooge grew beyond their original levels of understanding and became heroes.

Scrooge Trump

Douchebag Wisdom

Donald Trump is just a man, even though he's made himself the executive producer, director, script writer, and star of a bizarre reality show that includes everyone on the planet. But still, just a man. That means he has the capability of becoming a better man. Remember, what Susie says of Sally says more of Susie than of Sally. We must let Trump know it is NOT okay to belittle and demean others. It's up to us to help him live his best life and include us in it--all of us!

Trump has the opportunity to be a hero for all of the Bob Cratchits and Tiny Tims of the world. But if he doesn't step up, it is up to us. Each one of us. Choose a cause and get involved. Where is your passion? What most excites you or angers you?

- ○ Women's rights
- ○ LGBTQ rights
- ○ Worker's rights
- ○ Veterans' rights
- ○ Voting rights
- ○ Animal rights
- ○ Environment
- ○ Climate change
- ○ Clean energy
- ○ Health care
- ○ Campaign finance reform
- ○ Public education
- ○ Racial issues
- ○ Immigration reform
- ○ Prison reform
- ○ Foreign policy
- ○ Russia investigation
- ○ 1st amendment rights
- ○ 2nd amendment rights

Where can you give? And how can you give? There are organizations for each of these issues that need your time, talent, and money. One person can make a difference. And you must start with yourself.

296

Scrooge Trump

Marianne Williamson
The only way we will forge a new possibility for America and the world is if we're willing to forge a new possibility within ourselves.
7:07 PM – Sep 8 2017

It starts with your actions!! Or in the immortal words of Nobel Prize recipient Bob Dylan:

> *"Act the way you'd like to be and soon you'll be the way you'd like to act."*
> *-- Bob Dylan*

Yes, I know you want to turn off the news and walk away. I do, too. I know you want to believe that Trump will not interrupt your status quo. I do, too. But the truth is, Donald Trump and his Administration are working hard to deconstruct government as we know it. They are rolling back women's rights and gay rights and human rights. They are giving tax cuts to the rich while cutting services to our most vulnerable. They are pillaging and polluting our parks. They are working to suppress the vote. Everyone and everything is for sale.

If these things bother you—good!

Don't let Trump be your excuse; make Donald Trump your reason!

And for everyone's sake. And as Hillary Clinton would say, do it with "love and kindness." In other words, my words, stop being such a douche!

As Tiny Tim said at the end of A Christmas Carol, "God bless us, everyone!"

What Can You Do?

1. Watch Sir Patrick Stewart in the 1999 TNT original adaptation of Charles Dickens' A Christmas Carol. Watch Sir Patrick Stewart in anything!

2. Watch Bill Murray in Scrooged. See if that doesn't just send a trickle of hope running through your mind and heart. If Bill Murray can awake from his money induced nastiness and start helping others, Trump can too. It's up to us to help him see his options. We are his ghosts: past, present and future. While you're at it, watch Groundhog Day

3. Spare a buck for the guy/gal on the side of the road with the sign: God bless

4. Join an organization and the conversation--in-person and online

5. Volunteer. Donate

6. Promote economic fairness and community with People's Action

7. Support the International Refugee Assistance Project

8. Give to Doctors without Borders

9. Pay it forward

you can, you should,
and **IF** you are
brave enough to start,
you will
Stephen King

Scrooge Trump

Scrooge Trump

An Eclectic Playlist for Coping with Trump

Climb to Safety, Widespread Panic

End of the World as We Know It, R.E.M.

Another Brick in the Wall, Pink Floyd

Burning Down the House, Talking Heads

For What It's Worth, Buffalo Springfield

Le Freak, Chic

Rebel Yell, Billy Idol

Will It Go Round in Circles, Billy Preston

You Get What You Give, New Radicals

I Believe In the Good Things Coming, Nanko and Medicine for the People

Let Your Love Flow, Bellamy Brothers

Lovely Day, Bill Withers

Everlasting Love, The Love Affair

What I Got, Sublime

Best Day of My Life, American Authors

If You Wanna Sing Out, Sing Out, Cat Stevens

Send Me On My Way, Rusted Root

Just the Same Way, Journey

I'm A Believer, Monkees

Top of the World, Carpenters

Joy to the World, Three Dog Night

Standing on Higher Ground, Alan Parsons Project

All-Star, Smash Mouth

Free Bird, Lynyrd Skynyrd

Roll with the Changes, REO Speedwagon

Takin' Care of Business, Bachman Turner Overdrive

Rockin' Into the Night, 38 Special

When It All Gets Too Much

Do yoga
Snuggle your kids
Hug your dog
Pet your cat
Make art
Make love
Go dancing
Sing
Take a walk
Write it out
Talk to a friend
Send a letter to grandma/grandpa
Call your mom
Work out
Take a bath
Read to your kids
Bake some cookies
Donate your time
Donate your money
Go for a drive
Go shopping
Eat ice cream
Watch a movie
Make a sign
Call your congressman/woman
Make a new friend
March
Bake a cake
Listen to Cake
Dress like a cake
Swim in the ocean
Launch a new business
Throw a party
Have a campfire
Take a drive
Adopt a pet

Take a class
Give a class
Learn a new skill
Mow your lawn
Read a cookbook
Try a new recipe
Watch a game
Play a game
Count your blessings
Work in your garden
Bake pie for your neighbors
Go fishing, hunting, hiking
Snuggle your kids
Kiss your sweetheart
Do the laundry
Clean a closet
Clean your car
Read the news
Share your viewpoint
Buy coffee for the office
Remember the donuts
Say your prayers
Read someone a story
Listen w/out judgement
Sing in the shower
Write your biography
Send a thank you note
Eat chocolate
Let yourself cry
Use your anger as fuel
Do something; anything
VOTE
Believe
Have faith
Persist
Resist

Thank Yous

This list is really, really long and full of comedians, actors, activists, and journalists. Without you all, I would have never made it through these first 260+ days. Thank you for the on-air freak-outs and tirades--especially you, Stephen Colbert! The night you told President Trump exactly what we all thought of his transgender military ban made me and the nation proud! These are terrifying times and your commentary has helped us all. And True Confession: when I'm stressed, I eat frosting straight out of the can. I know I am not alone.

Thank you, Rachel Maddow, Lawrence O'Donnell and Joy Reid, for reporting it all--and especially for connecting the dots. Rachel, I especially appreciate your in-depth exposés. Keep that info coming. The American people demand answers; we have the right to know. And regardless of what President DoucheWad says, I know reporters are people with the highest integrity who love this country enough to tell the truth. Thank you Ali Velshi and Stephanie Ruhle, For Facts Sake!

And then there's Keith Olbermann and #theresistance, and Trevor Noah and Samantha B. Special thanks to John Oliver for using Donald Trump and fuckery in the same sentence. And to Bill Maher who originally matched Trump to the Institute for Incorrigible Douchebaggery. Friday night is for getting real. I hope this book does you proud. And you, too, Michael Moore who is fighting Trump with comedy and a Broadway hit!

Thanks *Saturday Night Live* writers and of course Alec Baldwin for his fine Trump impersonation! Kate McKinnon deserves a lifetime achievement award for portrayals of Hillary, Propaganda Barbie, and Jeff Sessions. A special thank you to Melissa "Spicy" McCarthy and fellow Hollywood actors speaking up, i.e. Meryl Streep and Rob Reiner and Tom Hanks and so many others: Rosie, Cher, and Bette. Special shout-out to Mark Ruffalo for your time with the Standing Rock Sioux. I trust Hollywood to tell the true story!

Thank you to the politicians! Maxine Waters, Nancy Pelosi, Kamala Harris, Elizabeth Warren, John McCain, to name a few. Don't miss my very last story, a dedication to Hillary Clinton. May I inspire her as much as she's inspired me. LOVED her book, *What Happened*. I bawled at the end. Love you, Hill!

Seriously, there are sooo many more to thank: Marianne Williamson, my spiritual mentor and the woman who taught me how to pray for the world.

AND GEORGE TAKEI whose wit and courage are informing and inspiring all lifeforms throughout the galaxies. Keep it up George, you are spreading the light.

Douchebag Wisdom

To my band, Widespread Panic, thank you for playing the music of my soul and setting my feet upon the path. You are my inspiration and motivation. You help me drive, dance, and walk on.

Thank you Cambio Yoga Yogis for holding a space and the light. Special thanks to Morgen for warm conversations and hearty hot classes.

For my angel-friend, Staci Bunton, who told me I had to write this book. Staci was my one degree of separation from President Obama. She met him in Chicago when she was a beat reporter and he was running for Senate. He stopped on his way out after a campaign speech and gave her a one-on-one interview because she'd arrived late, and he knew she needed a story. I loved President Obama before, but that story just confirmed what a fine, compassionate man he is. When I asked angel Staci if she would help with my book she said she was working on a book with Katy Tur. Sure enough, Katy Tur's book, *Unbelieveable*, made the bestseller list, right behind HRC's book, *What Happened*. Can't wait to read it Katy Bear. The dedication page alone made me laugh out loud.

Thank you, Lisa Ann Landry, for the pick-me-up November 9th. Without jumbo margaritas, a pitcher of sangria, and your company, I'm not sure how I would have handled the shock. Here's to a new chapter for both of us. Cheers! #bringiton

Thanks to my A-Team: Glo (the first to encourage the passion and the project), Beth (for fanning the flames with an open ear and mind), Gordy (for much needed 8-ball respites), and MC (where in the world is MC?!). I count on each of you for your unique perspectives. Thank you for talking me up and talking me through.

Thank you to my bestie, Marie, who witnessed the Douchebag effect first hand. Again, and again. Thanks, Kook, for keeping me fed and watered and reasonably sane. Sorry about all the freak-outs and fits. Need two tickets... #wsmfp #driving>disco

Thank you to my sweetheart for doing the cooking and laundry and keeping quiet, mostly. Thank you for letting me vent and for saying just the right thing at just the right time. Thank goodness, we think alike. You're so funny. Love you, Grizzle Bear.

Thanks to my kiddos for being my reason why. This book is for your babies, my grandbabies. I write and fight for you and them and the planet. Each of you makes me proud. Pep talks from you kids are the best!

Special thanks to Kilo Bravo...your sense of humor, your perspective, the time you took to really understand...and to help me to understand #mahalo my beach bear. Thank you for introducing me to the ocean ;) We've so much to look forward to.

Thanks to the best parents ever for giving me roots and wings. For fifty-five years you have nurtured and supported me and never let me down. Not once. I won the parent lottery. I hope this book makes you proud.

To Barack Obama...well, read the letter...

And finally, to Hillary Clinton, NOT the lesser of two evils but the best woman for the job. You don't need to be President to positively influence the world. You already have. And I pledge to you, I will 'Do all the good I can. By all the means I can. In all the ways I can. In all the places I can. At all the times I can. To all the people I can. As long as ever I can.' Thank you for that life lesson, as paraphrased from John Wesley.

A love letter to 44 ♥

Dear Barack Obama,

You changed my world the first time I heard you speak. It was 2007 and you had declared your candidacy for president.

Thanks to the collapsing economy, I was losing my job and my house. I ended up moving in with a friend. I'd given up thinking that I had any control over my own economic future. After a college degree and 22 years of hard work, I had nothing to show for it. No home; no retirement account. I was disillusioned, cynical and beyond believing that I could help myself let alone make a difference in the world.

Both government and corporate greed were running amok. I didn't believe; I had no faith. I didn't know what the future held but I didn't trust it would be good.

And then came you. I was awestruck by your demeanor and authenticity and captivated by your message and vision. You helped me understand "Democracy," what it means to be an American, and the importance of adding my voice to the conversation.

I was inspired by your optimism and love for people and this country. You and Michelle were a solid team--loving and real. Everything you said made sense-- for people and the planet. You helped me realize that I can and do make a difference and that the world needs my perspective and my voice. You made me feel like I belonged to something bigger, a collective of like-minded people who simply needed a nudge to bring out the best in them.

"Oh yes we can" inspired a nation to believe and get involved. And even though you've left the White House, your message still resonates. We, I, will continue to support and pursue your and Michelle's agenda of lifting and empowering others knowing that we truly are stronger together.

Thank you, Barack and Michelle, for being a beacon of hope and light for so many. And thank you for your continued service to our great country.

I am fired up and ready to go!

With love as big as the Hawaiian ocean, I remain one of your biggest fans.

Lima Bravo

And Now, a Special Story for Hillary

My dear Aunt Dixie gave me the best advice I've received in my life. I think it's a fitting tribute to HRC, a former New York Senator, First Lady of Arkansas, First Lady of the United States, Secretary of State and winner of the popular vote for President of the United States 2016. She embodies this story.

My Aunt Dixie was the most beautiful woman I've known. I admired her from a very young age. She was flashy and glamorous, Marilyn Monroe/Bettie Page style. She called everyone "sweetie" and "honey," she had a voice that was smooth as silk. She and Mom were close. They lived that sacred bond of sisterhood and my sis and I took notice.

She wore lush, fur coats and big, sparkly diamond rings which she called her "summer" diamonds. You know, some are real, some are not. She said it was nobody's business which were which and it was tacky to ask.

Aunt Dixie owned a lingerie shop in a small town in Iowa. This was waaaay before Victoria's Secret; it was the 1970s. She was a bit scandalous, oh my. Her shop was called Venus Lingerie. Aunt Dixie had the audacity to drive a Cadillac with the license plate VENUS1. She was confident and classy, and I absolutely adored her.

I hadn't seen Dixie in ten or more years. I'd gone off to college and she'd moved down to Texas, but I looked her up when I was sent to San Antonio on business. I was in the middle of a divorce and life had gotten pretty rough. I filled her in on the details over dinner and drinks. Aunt Dixie sat quietly and listened intently.

She nodded and smiled knowingly and gave me the best advice I've ever received. "Sweetie," she said, "when things get tough, just remember these four words:

"Shoulders back; knockers up."

Hillary, you have shown fortitude and chutzpah your entire political career and most especially when dealing with the foul-mouthed, small-minded Donald Trump.

On behalf of the women and men who voted for you, Hillary, I thank you for your efforts to help women, children and families around the world. I look forward to the next chapter in your life. #stillwithher OnwardTogether.org

Shoulders Back; Knockers Up.

About Lima Bravo

The loquacious and sagacious Lima Bravo, aka Lindee Brauer, is a motivational speaker and corporate trainer by day and empowered, raving activist by night. She is channeling disbelief over the election of Donald Trump and anger over the implementation of his policies by writing and resisting, empowering and enlisting, and hopefully helping others take a stand...or take a knee!

Lima is an accomplished speaker who blends just the right amount of "can do" and "how to." She connects with her audience on a personal and genuine way. Lima focuses on perspectives and actions that help wo/men deal with everyday trials so they can live their best possible life.

Lima specializes in communication, marketing, writing, and now politics thanks to the state of the world. Her perspectives are fresh, her ideas smart, and her teaching style "full immersion." Lima Bravo is a student of psychology, sociology, theology, and quantum physics. She's a self-professed cosmic cheerleader that will win your heart and tickle your mind.

Lima is available for customized keynotes and workshops tailored for your specific audience and event. Contact her at lindeebrauer@msn.com or 719 749-6101.

Other books by Lima Bravo include:

Barf Bag Wisdom: When What's Inside Must Come Out

Grab Bag Wisdom: The Surprise is Inside

Available at lindeebrauer.com

Made in the USA
San Bernardino, CA
24 November 2017